Generation INC.

Generation *INC.*

THE 100 BEST BUSINESSES FOR YOUNG ENTREPRENEURS

ELINA AND LEAH FURMAN

BERKLEY BOOKS, NEW YORK

GENERATION INC.

A Berkley Book / published by arrangement with
the authors

PRINTING HISTORY
Berkley trade paperback edition / March 2000

The Penguin Putnam Inc. World Wide Web site address is
http://www.penguinputnam.com

ISBN: 0-425-17229-5

BERKLEY®
Berkley Books are published by The Berkley Publishing Group,
a division of Penguin Putnam Inc.,
375 Hudson Street, New York, New York 10014.
BERKLEY and the "B" design
are trademarks belonging to Penguin Putnam Inc.

PRINTED IN THE UNITED STATES OF AMERICA

10 9 8 7 6 5 4 3 2 1

Contents

PART III
Think Big: It Takes Money to Make Money

229

THAT'S THE SPIRIT!

Up to now, you've only dreamed of the day when you can finally say, "I'm my own boss," with some semblance of conviction. But that's all about to change, isn't it? Yes, you're finally ready to break away from the mold, to take your first steps toward the Great American Dream of financial independence! Since you can't start a business on the spur of the moment, it's a good thing that you picked up this book. Taking the reins of your own destiny requires planning, commitment, an ironclad will, and nerves of steel. In short, it's a tough job. If it were easy, we'd all be doing it.

Yet more and more of our peers are busting loose. In 1996, 11 percent of all businesses were started by people under 25. "The Do-It-Yourself trend is getting bigger and bigger among young people," says Janine Lopiano-Misdom of Sputnik Inc., a trend analysis firm. "Twentysomethings are doing every-thing from producing their own zines to running successful companies." People everywhere are taking the less traveled road of self-employment, and making a great go of it at that. Some 1.3 million business were started in 1997 alone.

So what's been stopping you? Is unscrambling the step-by-step process of business start up all that stands between you and your vision, or are you simply at a loss for the right business idea? This book is our way of making your job easier. We've included a hundred fun and lucrative business picks, as well as several chapters on just what needs to be done to get any company off the ground. Mind you, this book is not your one-stop guide to starting and run-ning your business. It won't show you how to balance the books or deal with irate customers, but it *will* give you a comprehensive overview of your options as well as what it takes to run your own business.

Of course, nothing we can say will be of assistance if you are laboring under the mistaken impression that you're too young and inexperienced to blaze your own trail. Who knows, you could very well be right. But consider that most successful entrepreneurs stepped onto the road to success when they were just about your age. Jerry Yang, cofounder and head of Yahoo!, was only twenty-four when he left Stanford University to create the leading Internet search engine. Dineh Mohajer of the wildly successful Hard Candy Cosmetics was but twenty-two years old when she started what is now a $10 million business. The fact that you are stepping out on your own so early on in the game of life can work to your considerable advantage. Failure is never easy to deal with, but fail now and you can chalk it up to a learning experience. Fall short in your fifties and the disappointment may be overwhelming. The world is replete with role models who proved that youth is not so much a stumbling block as it is a stepping-stone. So, if you loathe the daily grind, there's absolutely no reason to glue your nose to the company grindstone.

Whether you're set on starting your own business, or just giving it some serious consideration, it's no wonder you're looking to strike out on your own. The corporate world is not what it used to be. Security and stability are things of the past. You've got the right idea—why take a chance on your job, when you can bet on yourself?

What's more, the business world is fast becoming a maze of specializations. Companies can no longer afford to take care of all the details on their own. This goes double for individuals. Here is where you step in. Whether it be brewing a mean cup of Java, or organizing a stellar soiree, your talents are marketable. Somehow, the more convenience-oriented we become, the less time we have to fend for ourselves. And that's where you can cash in.

Fortunately, not everyone has your confidence and courage. Many would rather stick with the same old, same old. So we applaud your entrepreneurial spirit. This is the best of times in which to start your own business. Not only will the world welcome you with open arms, but since you're young and vital, you'll be able to take maximum advantage of the warm reception.

All the money in the world couldn't buy your youthful energy! And when it comes to pioneering your own enterprise, energy is the one resource you can't afford to go without. If yesterday's goals are no longer challenges, and you're looking for the next big thing, chances are that you're entrepreneur material just waiting to supernova.

Acknowledgments

Thank you to all the people at Berkley, including Christine Zika, Grace Peck, and Barry Neville, for understanding the importance of encouraging young entrepreneurs. We'd like to thank the people at Tripod, especially our editor, Randy Williams, for taking a chance on the Small Business Brainstorms column. John Nikkah's enthusiasm was as great an inspiration as ever. And finally, for supporting us and making everything worthwhile, thanks, Mom.

Part One

BUSINESS BASICS

Chapter One

ON YOUR OWN AT LAST!
HAVE YOU GOT WHAT IT TAKES?

Launching a successful money-making venture demands a certain type of personality. But take heart, there is no such thing as a born entrepreneur. The ingredients that make up a successful capitalist are yours for the taking. A little concentrated effort is all you need to land on the road to riches. Before you start a business, an honest self-assessment is in order. Glossing over the truth will only set you back in the end. So, ask yourself: What kind of businessperson will I make? If "outrageously successful" doesn't figure high on your list of answers, then get set to put some serious man hours into boosting your own ego.

CONFIDENCE STRENGTH TRAINING

Since self-esteem is crucial for business success, how do you go about getting it? Simple. You must draw upon your past accomplishments, and begin a regimen of strength training that will serve you well in the future. First law of business: If you're not convinced that your business idea is worthy, no one else will be either.

The first step to accomplishing your objectives is to take stock of your history. How have you succeeded in the past? If failures are all that come to mind, then you may very well have an attitude problem that will take you straight to the Bankruptcy Hotline. For every negative event in your life, there's probably a positive. If you're focusing on the valleys, and ignoring the peaks, it's no wonder your self-esteem is flagging. Aside from boarding the Prozac express, there's a myriad of measures you can take that are guaranteed to put the wind back in your sails. Get your pencil and paper ready; you've got some serious work to do.

1. Sit down and think back to the time when you were forming your first memories.

2. Write down all those memories that involved first experiences. Your first ride on a roller coaster. Your first final exam. Your first date. Your first "non-family" vacation.

3. Qualify all these experiences as successes, failures, or a little bit of both.

4. Recall the preparation, emotional, financial, strategic, or otherwise, that went into making these events happen. Write it down.

5. Take note of how well you handled the planning for all your success. Also note whether the failures in your life have been due to carelessness, or simply a force-majeure situation.

6. Once you've realized the important role that preparation plays in your success you can emerge with a can-do attitude and get ready to conquer your next big hurdle.

RISKY BUSINESS

Whether you're talking stocks, bonds, or movie tickets, any investment involves a certain amount of risk. The more drachmas you put in, the higher your risk. It stands to reason then that starting your own business is also a bit of a gamble, to say the least. It's true that you can improve your odds considerably with thorough prep work (i.e., market research, cash-flow analyses, business plan). Still, try as you might, a start-up business is never a sure bet.

Examining risk tolerance may unearth some unpleasant surprises. After all, no one who fancies himself or herself a "high-roller" wants to hear the truth about his or her "penny-ante" nature. But denial isn't the quality most likely to establish your name in the business community. Running a business involves making many risky decisions on a daily basis. Should I invest in new a business software program? Should I hire new employees? Should I sign the contract? If you're unwilling to take the heat, you may want to steer clear of the entrepreneurial pressure cooker.

A BURNING DESIRE

Just as actors need to know their motivation in order to deliver a solid performance, you need to know the *raison d'être* of your venture to deliver it from shaky ground to sure footing. Why do you want a business? The answer to this query is the basis for all of your success. If you don't understand the impetus propelling your actions, you're likely to fall off track way before you can even laminate that very first dollar bill.

To come out victorious, you have to want your own business more than anything else. Running a business is a serious undertaking, possibly harder than anything you've ever had to do before. A time will come when all you'll want to do is throw in the towel, hang up the "gone fishin' " sign, and proceed to liquidate all inventory. You'll need a rock-solid rationale to keep you from making a beeline for early retirement.

Without a firm grasp on your long-term goals, there's no way your enterprise can become the all-consuming passion you need it to be. People have a variety of reasons for going solo. While you may very well have a jillion unique reasons of your very own, some of the most common causes fueling the entrepreneurial drive are:

1. More control over your life

2. Increased income

3. Creative freedom

4. Lack of job security: cutbacks, layoffs, demotions, and the like

5. Flexibility

6. Job satisfaction

PERSONAL BUSINESS

There is no escape. People are everywhere. And if you're not already an expert, you'd better learn how to deal with people, and fast. Clients and employees are the building blocks of business. You'll have to pick up several interpersonal skills if your venture is to thrive.

- **Networking:** Connections are your keys to success. So forget what you know, it's who you know that matters. If you neglect to master the fine art of schmooze today, you'll pay dearly tomorrow. Russ Klettke, the owner of a Chicago-based PR firm, has based much of his success on this principle, and today boasts a client list that includes companies such as Ameritech and McDonald's.

- **Leadership:** The staff, if you can afford any, should view you as the fearless leader. If you're planning on doing a little hiring, be prepared to invest some time into the study of management theory. It really works!

- **Communication:** In this golden age of communication, it's surprising how many people still don't have the first clue. Don't let a lack of a power vocabulary keep you from the success you so richly deserve. Take Wilson Harrell, for example. When Harrell was just starting out, he took a piece of advice that changed his life. That advice: Load up on speech courses. With his newfound skill, Harrell went on to found a company that employed 450 sales representatives nationwide. So go out and buy yourself a book on the subject, then get on the phone and practice, practice, practice!

- **Customer Service:** You've heard it before and you'll hear it again: The customer is always right. That's the attitude that keeps a business above water. Co-founder and CEO of Zingerman's Deli, Ari Weinzweig, is a firm believer in customer service. "I tell our people that you want the customer to think that they're the best thing that has happened to you all day." Learn it, love it, live by it.

- **Negotiating:** Suppliers, distributors, advertisers, and, yes, even clients will try to haggle with you. Don't take the "I'm not running a rug stand in Bombay" attitude; this bargaining thing can work for you—if you learn how to play ball.

PERSEVERANCE

When it comes to entrepreneurship, the attention-deficient need not apply. "If at first you don't succeed, try, try again" is one adage that will take you a long way toward meeting your business goals.

Reality check: The life of a business proprietor bears no resemblance to what is commonly referred to as smooth sailing. One day may see you in the doldrums, while the next may have you smack dab in the middle of a monsoon. This is where the role of perseverance, or "stick-to-it-iveness," becomes a crucial factor. The new-business failure rate wouldn't be anywhere close to the estimated 10 percent it is today if more entrepreneurs knew the meaning of commitment.

If you dedicate your life to seeing your venture through, no doubt about it, success will surely follow. But if good times are all that's on your agenda, then you may want to reconsider. Our hunch is that you may be confusing business with a day at the beach.

RESILIENCE

No, they weren't kidding. It truly is a jungle out there! Only the strong will survive. Tom Scott, founder of Nantucket Nectars, first tested his resilience by starting another company and working 17 hours a day, seven days a week. So, how's your stamina doing? Think you can handle life in the fast lane? If you're hot for an undertaking, but have misgivings about your endurance, it's best to start pushing yourself right now. Begin to test your resilience. Overtime pay or no, if you're working 9–5, arrive at the office an hour early every day. And while you're at it, don't forget to stay about an hour later than everybody else. Weekends are also fair game. Coworkers may roll their weary eyes, but keep this up for months on end, and come quitting time, you'll be ready.

THE BOTTOM LINES

- **Enhance your self-esteem and self-discipline:** To run a successful operation, the first thing you'll need is confidence. You'll need it to make the important decisions that will affect you and your future staff.

- **Evaluate your business's risk factor:** If your risk tolerance doesn't measure up to the amount of risk involved in your business, the American Dream just might end up giving you nightmares.

- **Keep a firm grasp on your long-term goals:** Why you want a business is just as important as what business you want. It's the "why" that will keep you coming back day in and day out. You may not get the stability, big money, or increased sense of control right off the bat. In fact, at first you may find yourself struggling in areas that seemed just fine before. But if you keep your eye on the future, you'll surely stick it out to receive the handsome reward.

- **Hone your people skills:** Unknown sources have it that life would be easy were it not for the people. Of course, they're right, people can be a querulous and meddlesome lot. But you need not let that keep you from making connections all around. Use every opportunity to learn a little something about what makes people happy, mad, or sad. Check out some books on the subject, become an expert. After all, how else are you going to be a great boss to your employees and a model service provider to your customers?

- **Master the art of bouncing back again and again:** Setbacks are daily fare in the world of self-employment. Accept this fact, and keep moving forward no matter what circumstances may seem to conspire against you. Once you realize that running a business is ten times as arduous as your former, cushy desk job, you'll also grasp the importance of self-discipline. So get a grip on yourself now, because after you're in business, it might just be too late.

This entire chapter has been about priming yourself for the life of an entrepreneur. Only after you're mentally and emotionally ready should you begin to investigate the possibility of running a business in further detail. Since your first great idea isn't always your best, the next chapter will answer the much-mulled question "Just what is it that goes into an inspired business concept?"

Chapter Two

AND THE NOMINEES ARE . . .
WHICH BUSINESS IS RIGHT FOR YOU?

Any old business will do—provided, of course, all you really want is an Excedrin-sized headache. Believe it or not, there are obscenely silly ways to choose a business. But we strongly caution against trying any of these at home. Picking a business at random, for example, will come complete with a set of decidedly inauspicious circumstances. The same can be said about focusing chiefly on an industry's "glam factor." Neither should the earnings potential be the primary determinant of your undertaking. In fact, no one reason is enough to get you hunting for office space. The business you decide upon must have a combination of factors working in its favor.

AVAILABLE RESOURCES

Take a good, hard look around. Can you parlay anything—be it talents, possessions, or experiences—into a business brainstorm? If you're deliberating between start-up ideas, resources (or a lack thereof) can cast the deciding vote. What exactly are these potential resources? We call them the A-B-C's of business start-up.

- **Acumen:** Otherwise known as your understanding. If you are versed in the ways of any particular industry, you may just have something there. Why, if you spent three years in the public relations racket, would you go on to pitch your tent in retail? Do what you know. With your connections, reputation, and know-how, a PR firm can net you a bundle, whereas opening a fashion emporium would land you back at square one.

- **Brilliance:** While Mother Nature may not have blessed you with Kathie Lee's vocal chords, or your anatomy with classical features for that matter, this is no time to gripe about what could have been. Bill Gates is a fine example of putting your unique skills to work for you. Back in 1968, while still in high school, Bill Gates was already designing computer programs. But who knows, maybe he flunked P.E.? The point is, you probably didn't get stiffed in every department either. We all have at least one unique gift. What's yours? Are you a creative genius, a culinary expert, a prima ballerina? Can you charm the pants off anybody, perform long division in your head, or leap tall buildings in a single bound? Whatever your strength, one thing is for certain—it's someone else's weakness. Be it ever so humble, your little knack can spell J-A-C-K-P-O-T if you put it to good use.

- **Capital:** Never underestimate the value of material wealth. If you decide to go into business for yourself, and dear old Dad just happens to own three restaurants, what's to say you can't pick up and learn the food biz? A business that's just lying in wait for a return of the prodigal son is quite a resource. As is a hefty trust fund, that property in the Himalayas, and the video equipment you purchased when studying Cinema Verité 101. Michele Hoskins, founder of Michele Foods, launched a thriving business by using an old family recipe for maple syrup her family had been using for years. Just about anything of value can be put to good use, in one business by or another.

PLAY "MATCH THE RESOURCE"

Each resource on the right is best suited to a business on the left. See if you can make the connection.

Granny's famous stuffing recipe	Bed & breakfast
Artistic talent	Direct marketing firm
5 years in advertising	Food manufacturing
Family farm in Iowa	Arts & crafts day camp

THE NICHE FACTOR

Much of a species' survival depends upon how it stacks up against the competition; the survival of your business will be no different. If you want to make it on your own, you'll need to pick a business that satisfies some consumer need. The goal is to rise above the crowd and get noticed. Look at it this way. If you score a seat on the subway, you're sitting pretty. But should the coveted seat elude you, you're pushed, jostled, maybe even trampled, all the way home. So remember, the enterprise that fills a void has a smoother run than one that attempts to infiltrate a saturated market.

Location is a niche all its own. If you find an opportune spot for your parking garage, grocery store, or laundromat, you'll see returns on your investment in no time flat. Should you, on the other hand, decide to set up shop in a locale teeming with similar businesses, you'll have to wait some time before turning a profit.

Another way to meet a need is through invention. If you provide an innovative product or service, you will monopolize a market of your own creation. That is, of course, until the knockoffs start breathing down your neck. Nevertheless, being the first to come up with a viable product or service is always a boon. The reputation alone will have clients beating a path to your door for years on end. The ubiquitous Kinko's was founded in 1970 by Paul Orfalea, a student at University of Southern California. The company began with a unique and simple premise: to provide university students and professors with easy access to duplication services. It is now the world's largest chain of copy centers.

Often a niche may be present without being obvious. A preexisting business may have the corner on a certain market, but don't let this discourage you. If there is only one business supplying a captive audience, check their product or service for flaws and their audience for discontent. If you find that both are present, you've found a need that only your enterprise can satisfy.

If any of your business picks occupy a clear niche, the debate is over. Fledgling moguls, fear no more. This is a full-systems-go situation.

THE RULE OF ATTRACTION

Sometimes, even though all the elements of a good commercial scheme are present and accounted for, you're simply not "into" the whole idea. There's no passion, no heat, in short, no attraction. If you're not the type to enter into a marriage of convenience, then neither should you saunter blithely into a labor that's completely devoid of love. The love of money alone won't get you through the day-to-day operations of running a business. To quote a popular career book title, "Do what you love and the money will follow."

The best caterers, personal shoppers, and decorators have answered a calling. If they weren't cooking, shopping, or coordinating during business hours, they'd probably be typing all day—and cooking, shopping and coordinating all night. Consider your own proclivities and pastimes; one of these may just be a natural. If Martha Stewart could morph her hobbies into a full-scale empire, why can't you?

THE BOTTOM LINES

- **Consider your available resources:** When time comes to pick a business, where are you going to start? The A-B-C's of business start-up are your available resources. A is for acumen, what you've learned about any particular business to date. B is for brilliance, your innate knack for performing a certain job. Finally, C is for capital, your material possessions that are helpful in running a business.

- **Fill a niche:** Presently, needs are going unmet in a variety of markets. There is the consumer market, which includes people like yourself, and then there are the industries. Convenient location and superior service can be your tickets to a niche business. But if you can make any job in any industry, be it manufacturing or food service, any easier or any more efficient, chances are you won't have any problems making your mortgage/rent payments any time soon.

- **Do what you love:** That there, folks, is the real bottom line. Unless you want drive yourself to drink, the business you stake out had better be to your liking. If your heart is not in the venture, you're better off keeping your day job.

Taking all the considerations into account is crucial to succeeding in business. Much like marriage, entrepreneurship is not to be entered into lightly. Bad matches have been known to happen with financially disastrous consequences. Business can be a pleasure, provided you choose your enterprise wisely. Once that's done, you can begin to formulate your strategy. "Strategy?" you ask. Just sit tight. The next chapter will explain how to strategize right.

Chapter Three

PLAN YOUR ATTACK
WINNING BUSINESS PLANS

This chapter will walk you through the various parts that combine to make a successful business plan. Whether you want to clarify your business goals, convince investors to come aboard, or just prevent any unpleasant surprises, having a solid business plan on your side can only further your cause. Without one, you're just a stray itching for a quick fix. It is verifiable fact: Most failed businesses suffer from poor-planning syndrome. So take this time to learn all you can about the financial prospects of your business. Whether you're pleasantly surprised or wholly discouraged by your findings, preliminary research will either help you make big bucks in the years to come, or save you the trouble of shopping for a new shirt after you've lost the one you had.

WHAT'S IN A NAME?

While a rose by any other name may still smell as sweet, you'll not score any points with the public if your company name doesn't outshine the competition. A name can communicate scads of valuable information. The name you choose should reinforce your venture's main selling points, as it will create your business image. A good name can say it all: authenticity, quality, fun, convenience, novelty, creativity, you name it.

Go to the phone book and see for yourself. Run a hypothetical search, be it for a plumbing service or a flower shop. Chances are your first concern is proximity, or you could be the type who calls on only the biggest, boldest, and baddest ads. But, just for the sake of argument, discount these two factors. What do you end up with? The name—no more, no less. Don't ever underestimate the value of a name. Brainstorm until you strike pay dirt, it's worth it!

FIRST THINGS FIRST

Once you've dubbed your enterprise, you are ready to start work on the business plan. The first parts of this document are relatively easy:

- A cover page with the business name emblazoned proudly in the center;
- a statement of business purpose (i.e., a consulting firm devoted to helping corporations reach young consumers);
- a table of contents for your plan.

BUSINESS DESCRIPTION

Chances are that you've already done a lion's share of talking about your business idea. In fact, you may have bent so many ears that your friends have finally begun avoiding you. Writing a thorough business description may be all you need to get this entrepreneurial ranting out of your system. Before you babble away even more energy and become a total pariah, get out your pen and paper, and put your thoughts in writing.

The business description is your idea's opportunity to shine. Every aspect of the venture (aside from the financials) must be described in this section. It can be as short as a 10-page term paper, or as long as a 120-page dissertation—whatever it takes to cover the ins and outs of your business. Your goal: to make your enterprise look irresistible and leave no stone unturned. No business description is complete without the following:

- Description of your service or product
- Proposed business structure (i.e. partnership, corporation, sole proprietorship, etc.)
- Explanation of your target market(s)
- Plans for location
- Description of the competition
- Prospective employees

DOLLARS AND CENTS

Whether you're looking to fulfill your life's purpose or help mankind, the bottom line is still spelled MONEY. Capital is the name of the game. The type of business you decide to start will, in most cases, depend on how much money you have to work with. A great product or idea is all well and good, but coughing up the cake to cover costs is an altogether different brand of bagel. As business start-up costs will determine whether you dip into your savings, fill out loan applications, or tool your idea around town tycoons' offices, it pays to know how much cash you'll have to part with to give your operation a fighting chance.

Cash-Flow Report

A preliminary cash-flow report is a key component in getting a handle on operation costs. A well-thought-out cash-flow analysis is the mark of most successful entrepreneurs. **Cash flow** is the difference between the money flowing in and the money flowing out over a given period of time — it's that simple!

You should begin prognosticating your organization's first few months of cash flow well in advance of the big ribbon-cutting ceremony. This will allow you to zero in on how much financing you'll need and will provide lenders with sufficient info to evaluate your application. Think of the cash-flow projection as your very own Psychic Friends Network, a prediction of the future based on hopes, fears, and certain given facts.

Insufficient sales volumes turn many a business into just another open-and-shut case. You know your business is in jeopardy when necessary expenditures outweigh the available funds. But if you deliberate over your cash-flow forecast and heed its warnings early on, you may be able to avoid the common pitfalls of business start-up. An accurate cash-flow report can be yours in a flash; you need only take the time to learn what its ingredients are.

1. **Starting Balance** — Otherwise known as the baseline, this is the amount of money you've got burning a hole in your pocket at the beginning of each month. If your calculations are correct, your previous month's ending balance and the starting cash should be the same amount.

2. **Cash In** — Cha-ching! This term refers to all cash received throughout the month. Several sources will contribute to your monthly "cash in" figure.

A. *Cash Sales*: All money received from cash sales falls under this category. Should any portion of the sales have been processed by invoice, omit this amount until payment has been collected.

B. *Collected Receivables*: This amount can be tallied once payment is made on invoices. Only then can you include invoiced sales into your projection. Even if the check is in the mail, refrain from including it in the "cash in" section until it's passed into your mailbox. As the saying goes, don't count your chickens before they hatch. If the waiting game has got you down, tighten that credit policy by setting a firm deadline.

C. *Miscellaneous*: This category will house all revenues derived from sources other than sales. Is any of your money invested? If so, count up all the interest that you've earned. Funds from bank loans or freelance or part-time work will also call the "miscellaneous" classification home. You'll have to keep track of all income if you want to keep your cash flow forecast on the money.

3. **Cash Out**—Although this portion of your cash-flow projection is the most odious of all, there is a bright side. Keep your stomach from turning as you log in the various amounts of cash wafting out of your enterprise by recalling the most basic of business rules—thou shalt spend money to make money. Thinking of your expenses as investments in your future will help the proverbial medicine go down. You'll find that most costs fall into one of the two ensuing categories.

A. *Fixed Expenses*: This refers to that variety of spending that remains constant from one month to the next. Try as you might, there's no weaseling out of such basics as

- Rent for premises and equipment
- Insurance
- Taxes
- Payroll
- Interest on loans

B. *Variable Expenses*: This pill is a little easier to swallow. Entrepreneurs wield much more control over variable expenses. Still, there are bound to be ups and downs. The unpredictable nature of variable expenses will see some months weigh in at minimal cost, and others chockablock with unexpected outflows of cash. Stay in the black by keeping a reserve of funds at your disposal, overestimating your expenses, and beefing up your monthly starting balance (calculating the exact amount of capital necessary to perform these precautionary measures is "the magic number" we'll discuss later on). Variable expenses can include any or all of the following:

- Equipment repairs
- Telephone
- Postage
- Office supplies
- Advertising and promotion
- Business-related travel
- Utilities
- Commissions
- Raw Materials

4. **Ending Cash** — A.k.a. the bottom line. No long division necessary; simple addition and subtraction are your tickets to this figure. Just add your starting cash to the total of cash in, and then subtract the total of cash out. The amount you're left with as "ending cash" also doubles as the starting balance for your next month's operations.

5. **Cash Flow** — This is the moment you have been waiting for. The time to determine how much money has been flowing through your business for the past month is upon you. You need only subtract the total cash out from the total cash in. The change (be it negative or positive) is designated as cash flow. Why is this data so important, you may wonder. Well, by getting a grip on your venture's cash flow, you are actually zooming in on your business funds' activity levels. This process will have you spotting potential problems well before they escalate into grand-scale business-busting disasters.

The Magic Number

Now is the time to calculate your minimum start-up balance. Make yourself comfortable, and begin filling in your cash-flow charts. Start your first month off with a balance of zero. That's right, pretend you're going in without reinforcements. Now start inputting projected sales, other sources of income, and all expenses. Don't forget to begin every new month with the ending balance.

If you've been careful about your calculations and estimations, you will most likely be reading negative numbers for the first few months. But this is to be expected. Now do you see where the start-up cost fits in? Your lowest ending balance is the amount you'll need to finance your venture. The funds required to launch your business cannot be lower than your lowest ending balance. So keep this magic number in mind when appraising your financial situation and/or applying for a loan.

Guardian Angels

Consultants and accountants may not come cheap, but after all is said and done, these helping hands can take a lot of the guesswork out of calculating your start-up cash needs. Like-minded business owners have been down your road before. These guys have the inside track on information no schooling can provide. They may have discovered a revolutionary way of cutting start-up costs, or possibly point you in the direction of fairly priced vendors — no small favors to a fledgling entrepreneur. Accountants, on the other hand, will show you tax loopholes invisible to the naked eye, and can also forecast your cash flow months, even years, in advance.

PENNY-PINCHING: WORDS TO THRIVE BY

Playing it safe during the first phase of your business will mean cutting all possible cost corners. While we've already pinpointed several expense slashing strategies, we encourage you to let your thriftiness go freestyle. Go ahead, get creative, work that right brain. Still stumped? Well, what are you sitting around for? Scratching your head isn't going to make your business a done deal! There's research aplenty to be done. Take a month to sift through all available money-saving options. Rest not until you have found the absolute lowest bottom dollar. Begin by getting estimates from dealers nationwide, visiting discount outlets, and attending business closeout sales. And just because you're in business doesn't mean you're above working part-time — many established entrepreneurs proudly admit to having taken this hard-knocks route. Let's face it, ambition doesn't always come on its own sterling platter, and if you weren't born with a silver spoon in your mouth, discounting any potential source of income is ill-advised, to say the least.

Control over your business's cash-out flow is of paramount concern. Many young tycoons incur astronomical start-up costs by going all out to establish a high-profile image. Hotshots take note: Unnecessarily pricey supplies won't impress anyone but the bargain hunters at your going-out-of-business sale.

The formative stages of a well-thought-out enterprise should be characterized by frugality and moderation wherever possible. There are hundreds upon thousands of ways to cut expenses, so why not take advantage? You're a capitalist now; it's time to cozy up to the concept of resource exploitation.

1. **Decrease Your Overhead**—Your mind's eye may have had you sitting pretty in a plush armchair of the vibrating-massage variety, and as good things come to those who wait, there is no reason why such a comfy little goal should not come to fruition. But spectacular offices need not carry spectacular price tags. Unless you're catering to a certain clientele or relying on a steady stream of foot traffic to increase your sales volume, the importance of location will be eclipsed by price considerations.

   Scout for the lowest-rent quarters you can find, and don't rush head-long into signing a lease agreement until you've checked out all of the alternatives. Listen to the demands of your business to determine the amount of rent expenses to tolerate. Depending on the nature of your venture, an out-of-the-way office can turn a profit equal to if not greater than that of a centrally located one.

   Always keep a sharp lookout for a good deal on office supplies and equipment. The purchase of brand-new equipment has been known to dwindle more start-up funds than you'd care to imagine. If you want your dollar to go a long way, check out the business equipment auctions to stock up on high-end merchandise at low-end prices. Suppliers' rates also come in all shapes and sizes, so call several before signing on the dotted line. Finally, if worse comes to worst, you've pared down every conceivable cost, but are still having trouble making those raggedy old ends meet, go ahead and cut down your staff's hours—get your own hands dirty for a while; a little hard work never hurt anybody.

2. **Strike a Deal**—Rarely does one ever stumble across a truly final offer. Any price you are quoted, whether it be for the monthly rent or a computer system, can be scaled down. Within every successful business person lies a great negotiator. Don't be afraid to plead your case to anyone who'll listen. If the price quoted is $200, what's the harm in trying to bring it down to $150? If it works, that's 50 bucks for just asking a question! If the vendor is hesitant, try explaining that you're just starting out and have a limited budget with which to maneuver. Many salesmen will help you out, if only to gain your business in the future. It never hurts to ask—all they can do is say no.

3. **Collecting the Booty**—It's easy to get caught up in the thrill of initial sales, and extend credit to every Tom, Dick, or Sally that comes along. You won't know which customers are poor credit risks until you've established a working relationship with them. Until that time you should always demand that they cough up at least half of the payment up front. If your customer refuses to meet you halfway, be ready to give them the old heave-ho, as the chances of you ever getting your due are slim to none.

    Outstanding invoices are a fact of business life. When following up on such debts, be polite but firm. Either inform the freeloaders that you'll be charging 2–3 percent interest each month the payment is overdue, or calmly threaten to sic the collection agency hounds on their parasitic heinies. Let everyone know you mean business, and you shouldn't have any problems.

4. **The Price Is Right**—You may have noticed the need for comparison shopping when booting up your business? Well this practice works both ways. Consumers are no dummies—they know when they're being taken for a ride. Setting realistic prices on your services or merchandise can be tricky. While you don't want to alienate prospective customers with exorbitant rates and prices, you may very well end up losing money if you sell your wares too cheaply. Investigate the competition's pricing policies to get an idea of what to charge your clientele. Make sure to fairly remunerate your company's labor by keeping the hours devoted to each project in mind when establishing fees. Never forget that time is money.

DOCUMENTARY EVIDENCE

Let's get back to one of the main reasons for your business plan—financial aid. Even if every one of your schemes and dreams for the future holds water, the past is still a powerful presence. Anything and everything that may go to show that you are none other than a responsible, law-abiding, regular pillar-of-the-community citizen will strengthen your case. You and your partners should be prepared to fork over the following:

1. employment histories;

2. credit reports;

3. letters of reference/recommendation.

THE BOTTOM LINES

- **Give it a name:** The first page of your business will display the proposed name of your business. Many business owners like to start their business name with the letter A, in order to appear first in the phone book. But whatever name you decide on, make sure it says something important about your venture.

- **Write a quick overview:** A short description of your business should be found on the second page of your business plan. The third page will house the table of contents. Easy.

- **Write a thorough business description:** Here is where the real work begins. You must describe your business inside out. This section can take up anywhere from 1 to 100 pages, depending on the complexity of your venture.

- **Calculate a preliminary cash-flow report:** How much will it cost to begin operations? How soon do you expect to turn a profit? The cash-flow report can help project your income with some semblance of certainty. If bookkeeping isn't your bag, get ready to part with a chunk of change to pay an accountant or a consultant to do the number-crunching for you.

- **Decrease projected overhead by cutting expenses:** Don't count on top-of-the-line anything when estimating your start-up costs. Slash start-up costs by considering money-saving alternatives such as used equipment, cheap office space, and part-time help.

- **Build your case with background information:** Your business plan is not complete without corroborating evidence. At the very end, tack on your credit report, employment history, and any letters of reference.

Now that the days of laboring over your business plan are behind you, and you're staring at the substantial document lying square on your desk, what next? Footwork, that's what. The business plan will do you no good unless it's making the rounds of prospective investors and lenders. The next chapter will explain how to go about getting that plan off your nightstand and into the right hands.

Chapter Four

FORAGING FOR FUNDS

Any and all attempts to take the world of self-employment by storm can be undermined by a botched financing strategy. Getting your hooks into the loot is an endeavor fraught with many obstacles. But fear is for the weak, and in the immortal words of Napoleon himself, the strong shall prevail in battle. While Americans have a history of preening capitalism into the image of gentility, the Japanese have long acknowledged that business is war. Once you realize that your enterprise can be your one-way ticket to the top, you too will be won over to our Far Eastern friends' philosophy.

Mastering the art of cash acquisition is no easy proposition, and can take some time. But what did you expect? Most overnight sensations are at least a year in the making. Of course, this is not to say that it couldn't happen; illusions of grandeur are the stuff our mercantile society is built on. Let's just say that some businesses are slower to go airborne than others. But you're young yet, and if there's one thing working for you, it's time. So use your most abundant resource wisely and prepare to learn everything there is to know about financing your business.

Once the start-up costs have been tabulated, you may be lulled into a false sense of relief. If you thought the hard part was over, you'd better think again. If your personal cash stash is limited, this is just the beginning of the scramble for dollars. This isn't to say you should grow gray with worry. You're not the first person to lack a start-up bankroll. There's a whole slew of prosperous business owners out there who wouldn't look down their noses at answering your questions. Ask them where they managed to find funding, and you'll be surprised at how few actually used institutionalized methods of financing, such as bank loans or venture capital firms. A few key investors such as friends and family could suffice to see your business through the initial financing stages. And that's your main goal, to weather the first storm and turn a profit, any profit, be it ever so humble. Recall that financing is an ongoing process. Once you get a solid track record, the big guys will deem you a safer bet and may help to expand your operation. You'll need help every step of the way, so settle in for the long haul and leave no financial stone unturned.

PERSONAL FUNDS

Ideally, the more money you have to contribute the better. If you are the only investor, you answer to no one but yourself. It stands to reason that such a sole proprietorship considerably simplifies the politics and hierarchies of free enterprise. In fact, this is the reason many of you chose to blaze your own trail in the first place. If you or your parents have a tidy little bundle of investments tied up in your name, there's nothing wrong with reinvesting that equity in your venture's favor. And since most of you will probably find your-self climbing out on that limb, and sinking a considerable chunk of change into your own businesses, it may be a good plan to ask your parents whether your financial position is brighter than previously suspected. If resounding laughter is your only response, well, at least you gave it the good old college try, and brought joy to your loved ones while you were at it.

While the self-starter talk is all fine and dandy, looking before you leap is never a bad idea. There is a downside to investing your life savings—a little thing known as the risk factor. The thought of watching years of hard work go up in smoke has been known to scare more than a few budding industry giants into tapping other people's money. But while the idea of foolproofing your venture by keeping your coin under lock and key may sound appealing, the various drawbacks associated with this stratagem are sufficient to dissuade many first-time business owners from following through.

PERSONAL LOANS

Let's hope that you know you're worth more than the number of zeros in your bank account. The concept of credit alone is enough to prove that your potential goes much further than your dollar. Let's take the everyday, standard-variety credit card. You may have zilch when it comes to money, but apply for several credit cards, and suddenly you can buy anything your greedy little heart desires. Provided, of course, that your credit history is up to snuff, you can easily apply to banks or vendors to score yourself a credit line of anywhere from $10,000 to $50,000. Not too shabby. The catch? Staggering 18.5% interest rates are far from nickel-and-dime considerations. Your business will have to fly high if you expect to make good on such loans. If the cash-flow charts indicate that your business will take some time to get up and about, other financing options may prove more apropos.

While many a bank loan applicant has a horror story to unfold, avoiding it simply on the basis of others' bad experiences is just plain silly. It's not as if you're going to have to swallow your pride, beg, grovel, or fawn. The S&L is one place where numbers speak louder than words, and flattery gets you absolutely nowhere. Make sure to provide an accurate and precise breakdown of start-up and operational expenses and anticipated profit margins. The bank can issue a loan to you as an individual if you put up collateral or have a cosigner to back you up. Hitting a bank up for a loan as an individual rather than a commercial undertaking is the most common method employed by small-business operators. The amount of processing time is considerably longer for corporate loans, so if you're antsy to start transacting business, you'd do best to follow suit. What's more, the risk of a corporate loan application being denied is much higher than that of a personal loan. Still, a significant percentage of entrepreneurs, almost 25 percent, apply for and receive small-business loans every year.

MILKING THE FAMILY CASH COW

There's something to be said for keeping your enterprise all in the family. Your immediate relatives are an invaluable source of funding. In fact, if any kinfolk do have the cash to back you, approaching them should be top priority. Trust us, your family has a lot more riding on your success than the average brass-tacks banker. Designer Cynthia Steffe and partner Rick Roberts started their line of clothing with $500,000 collected from family and friends. Just don't make the mistake of expecting to make off with the family jewels without putting forth the requisite effort. While no close relatives want to see you fail, neither do they want the double whammy of watching their loot go down the drain along with you.

Approach the relative as you would any other potential investor. Meaning, you should call and set up the appointment in person. That's right, no running Mom ragged as a go-between. Make sure to bring your cash-flow projections, business plans, and professional manner to the appointment. Discuss how much money you'll need, mention how much of your own you'll be putting up, and detail the reasons you expect the enterprise to grow.

Most business consultants agree that resources close to home should be tapped before any others are even considered. Still, if your sugar daddies claim to be running low on funds or are hesitant about the viability of your concept, do not try to twist their arms or attempt to force-feed them any more "happily ever after" business scenarios. Simply thank them for having taken the time to hear you out. Take a cue from America's department stores and never alienate a potential source of income. Do you think Neiman Marcus would be where it's at today if the salespeople insulted and belittled every customer trying to make a return? Highly doubtful. Conduct yourself with the utmost dignity and you may still be able to smile at each other over Thanksgiving dinner.

FRIENDS IN NEED

If your pals are willing, financially able, as well as of sound mind and body, they can go a long way towards alleviating your monetary woes. Approaching the bosomest of your buddies for loans or as investors can be the beginning of an even more beautiful friendship. But be forewarned. If your mates are the only ones who'll go down with the sinking ship of your venture, your friendship can be on the rocks faster than you can say "Laverne and Shirley." Sob stories of good relationships gone sour are not uncommon, so make sure to enlighten your nearest and dearest about all the risks before you cash in their chips. The better informed your friendly benefactors are, the less prone they will be to adorn your weary shoulders with the blame for their losses. So forget about what you've heard about leaving out the gory details, and endeavor to deserve the title of friend by voicing the drawbacks associated with your idea.

PRIVATE INVESTORS

Believe it or not, there are people who are willing to take a chance on a young rookie with a dream. Independent investors, usually wealthy entrepreneurs or executives, have an ongoing flirtation with investing in early-stage companies. Call it a hobby or the all-consuming desire to see their dollars multiply, but these bigwigs rarely shy away from a profitable venture. Finding private investors to hear out your proposal is another matter altogether; to say nothing of ironing out a fair deal, which is often even more difficult. Many entrepreneurs have a misguided notion of the motivation driving individual investors. These guys are not in the charity business. No, you'll find that most investors sing the same popular ballad that goes something like "What's in it for me?" Unless you can demonstrate how they will profit from your undertaking, be prepared to leave their offices empty-handed.

Some first-time businesspeople have a disproportionate fear of such partnerships. True, if you get yourself in cahoots with a private investor, you'll have to give up some breathing room. The practice of sharing will begin to figure more prominently into your life. Sole creative control and capitalistic integrity may become ideas of the past. But stop and consider. Is partnership really such a sticky issue? After all, your accomplices do have the same goal in mind. Everyone is looking to make off with a tidy profit, and if you learn to play ball, the chances of this happening will skyrocket.

The Internet is turning out to be a great meeting place for entrepreneurs and investors. For a mere $150 per year, Pricap (www.pricap.com) offers entrepreneurs the opportunity to network with investors. You can either exchange ideas or secure venture capital, depending on the response your posted business plan receives.

The Search Is On

Once you've reconciled the do-it-yourself-er within to your need for outside help, the next step is to learn how to approach and deal with Mr(s). Moneybags effectively. "Give me all your money!" is a strategy best left to the ski-mask-inclined. Investors must be handled with care, so put on your most suave demeanor and make the smoothest moves. And remember, in business there's no shame in asking strangers for money. Here's how it's done:

1. **Investigate your private investor:** Getting the goods on the potential investors will not only clue you into the types of businesses they're interested in funding and how successful they have been in the past, but by chatting up past beneficiaries, you'll also find out about your prospect's modus operandi. If the person you're applying to has a history of making unfair demands, you'll know to steer clear. Or if your target is only interested in telecommunications, you and your pet-grooming business will waste no time barking up the wrong tree. And if everything you discover is to your liking, you'll get an invaluable edge by knowing who you're dealing with.

2. **The perfect pitch:** Never underestimate the importance of a first impression. Your presentation must be composed with extreme care and foresight. This is no time to wing it. Your business hangs in the balance. A few precious minutes is all you'll have to convince the investor that you and your venture are rock-solid. Don't forget the main points of any business proposition: start-up costs, market analysis, and distribution of equity. Be ready to field all possible questions and counter any objections by rehearsing before the big day. You and your business plan will be on trial. If you appear incompetent at the meeting, a dark shadow of doubt will be cast over your ability to run a successful business.

3. **A winning pair:** Once you've passed the presentation exam with flying colors and have received the thumbs-up from an investor, you may be ready to do cartwheels and praise the powers that be. Slow down. No deals have been made. You will still have to spend countless hours hammering out the final agreement. An effective negotiation strategy begins with an outline of your terms and objectives. Making your position clear at the outset of the negotiations will help to stave off problems in the long run. You won't discover how compatible you and your backer are by playing the role of a yes man. If the investor agrees to finance your enterprise, request a second meeting where both of you will have a chance to discuss your goals and expectations. The moment of truth will soon be upon you. You'll know once and for all whether this is a match made in heaven, or a recipe for disaster.

LOOKING TO THE PROS

Ever since the early 1990's, things ain't what they used to be. No longer are banks and venture capital firms the first stops on an enterprising neophyte's search for start-up change. The big boys have been relegated to the financing wagon's backseat. More and more people are relying on their calling circles to provide them with the necessary dollars. Could the Family Values crusaders be behind this retreat to yesteryear? Hardly. A few too many wildly optimistic deals in the 1980's have finally forced the pros to consolidate and retrench their assets. But while the professional players may be down, they're certainly not out.

What, then, is a tenderfoot like yourself to do? Keep hope alive for all is not lost. You could still appeal to the establishment, just don't go banking on the bank. Your first order of business is to stop asking what the lender

SPOTTING A CROOKED INVESTOR

Shady shysters don't always present themselves in the form of used-car salesmen. Some come in the guise of independent investors with one goal, to make a run for the border with your money. In separating the legitimate investors from the flakes, you've got your work cut out for you. But we've come up with a system that should eradicate much of the confusion encountered by first-time entrepreneurs. Study your prospective investor to see what heading (s)he falls under.

Profile #1: The Real-Deal Investor

1. Acts quickly: People who are serious about the business of making money don't have a lot of time to waste. Most will set up an appointment within a week of your initial consultation, ask to see a business plan, and request a list of terms. You should receive word of their decision within a two week period.

2. Is detail-oriented: Will point out the specific problem areas of your proposal and make suggestions, instead of throwing a lot of meaningless generalizations your way.

3. Is curious: You'll be grilled about your market, product, and team. If your replies are less than speedy, you'll be asked to come back when the data is collected.

Profile #2: The Poser Investor

1. Wants the money up front: Anyone who asks you for a down payment or any sum of money up front has to be discounted as a viable source of financing immediately. Save yourself the heartache and let our advice be your only lesson. Demanding to get hold of your cash is the most obvious clue that your investor has evildoing on the mind.

2. Disparages the proposed investment: An investor who goes on at length about the ineptitude of your proposal is not only a big meanie, but is also not a serious prospect. If after this lecture, they insist that you take notes and incorporate their ideas, cut your losses and hightail yourself right outta there.

3. Is mysterious about his/her money: Crooked investors will often skirt the issue of finances. If your prospect refuses to divulge his/her sources of income, or strikes you as a sketchy character, plead a full bladder and head straight for the back exit.

could do for you, and go on a soapbox rant about what you could do for your lender. While a recent trend of fiscal belly flops have caused the mighty investors to get tightfisted with small businesses, you can pry those pudgy fingers loose by showing them that you're worth it.

The Loan Officer

If you thought the combination lock on your high school nemesis's locker was tough to crack, wait till you get a shot at the banker. The loan officer's main interest lies not in the expansion and eventual world domination to be enjoyed by your organization, but simply in getting the bank's money back. This is no partnership. For all your loan officer cares, your business can go the route of the pogo stick, just so long as you make good on your loan.

The loan worthy will have to nod an affirmative to two fundamental questions: First, will the venture generate sufficient cash flow to repay the loan (with interest)? Second, will the collateral of the business or the petitioner compensate for any cash-flow deficiencies? Shake your head to both, and you'll be on the tenure track in the reject-file department. So act fast, and be ready to flaunt those auspicious cash-flow projections at the loan interview.

Apply Yourself

Any bank worth its neon sign will require that you fill out an application before lending an ear to your proposition. This is not the time to embellish. Follow the directions carefully and forget about exaggerating or falsifying any data. Make no mistake, you will be discovered and dealt with accordingly. You'll be asked to provide personal and business references, the names of all partners and stockholders, the amount of debt you've piled up to other banks or lending institutions, the organization of your business (partnership, corporation, sole proprietorship, etc.), the principal purpose of the loan, your means of repaying the debt, a balance sheet, and an outline of your business sales and liabilities. So preserve your credibility for future negotiations and do not set foot in the bank until you are equipped with the aforementioned info. Banks are sticklers for the rules and do not look kindly upon unprepared applicants.

Interview Smarts

You don't have to be a modern-day Machiavelli to master the art of getting what you want. A few key points are all it takes to conduct a fluid loan interview with a banker. Since there's a proper way to do just about everything, don't you think requesting large sums of money should be done in good form?

OUACHITA TECHNICAL COLLEGE

Select with care: Get the lowdown on the bank you're hoping to hop before sailing out into banker's waters. Not every bank is as stable as its brick walls and bullet-proof teller windows. Many banks have a history of poor lending decisions. Some of these ne'er-do-wells have even been known to back themselves so far into the corner as to be forced to demand early repayment from companies in good standing. Getting the 411 on a bank's rep will require that you quiz existing and former patrons. Are they satisfied with the service they received? Have they experienced any problems in dealing with the bank's employees? A troubled bank that's been known to recall loans when market conditions deteriorate ranks right up there with a hole in the head. Talk about a headache!

Get a referral: Hobnob with any business owners lately? If so, by all means probe the very depths of their connections bin. These are the people who may very well help you to get that much-needed loan. Influential entrepreneurs can be a young gun's salvation. They can make all the appropriate intros, and nudge you in the direction of the best loan officers a bank has to offer. Relatives in such lofty positions are a double bonus, willing as they are to go all out for anyone in their gene pool. Your mother's cousin, Chuck, will be magically transformed into Good Old Uncle Charlie just as soon as he introduces you to the senior loan officer (and long-standing golf buddy). Just one such contact is enough to edge out much competition and raise your odds of getting that bank to put out.

On your mark, get set, schmooze: Even if you don't subscribe to the majority opinion—that the best way to get to the top is not to work hard, but to kiss butt—a little well-rehearsed flattery couldn't possibly hurt your cause. The number-crunchers heading up the loan interviews are still human, and will appreciate the hours of painstaking research that went into your finding their bank by far the most solid of the lot. Now is no time to act coy. Go ahead and tell the interviewers that it would be your life's greatest pleasure to deal with a bank such as theirs, a bank that really knows how to support small business, the backbone of America's economy. Once the groundwork has been laid, you can begin to sell the officer on yourself. This strategy may just give you the fair hearing and consideration you need.

Don't sell your soul: Entrepreneurs beware. Many times obtaining a loan is something akin to striking a bargain with Beelzebub himself. Imagine losing your house should your business not see the light of profits. A less than inviting prospect, isn't it? Never be so psyched about a loan approval as to zone out what is actually at stake. The monastery is a nice place to visit, but don't ever consider pledging all of your worldly possessions unless you want to make it your permanent address.

The cherry on the cake of your argument: After blitzing the banker with cash-flow analyses, business plans, etc., up your chances of approval by throwing in the following points:

1. Your reliability and history of making timely payments on items such as credit cards, utilities, and student loans.

2. Your and your staff's business experience and competence.

3. The favorable market conditions.

4. Any and all unfulfilled orders and business prospects.

Venture Capital Firms

Venture capital firms are worth a look-see. Provided you're confident that your business will be a high-growth enterprise and you're willing to part with a megadose of equity — in some cases over 60 percent (talk about an indecent proposal) — these firms are hotels well worth checking into. After all is said and done, their participation and financial assistance can fund your bed-and-breakfast from here to eternity. But while you may be ready for a mutually profitable liaison, venture capitalists may not be ready to commit. More and more such firms have been contracting a bad case of cold feet when it comes to young operators, looking instead to the lower profit margins but higher security ratings provided by the stodgier companies.

So, the question remains. How do you get one of these reluctant venture capital firms to shed their inhibitions and hook up with your rising star? For starters, let's clarify the term "venture capital firm." This breed of company is responsible for raising money from a variety of sources — corporations, insurance companies, pension funds — to invest in a money-making deal. The funds raised for investment can run anywhere from a cool ten mill to a $100-million powerball. The venture capitalists' M.O. is to invest the funds in your company for a period of two to four years, at which point they will proceed to pull up stakes and make off with their earnings. But if the profits are still on the upswing, you may very well be able to negotiate a new deal once the initial one comes to its conclusion.

Before you lament the loss of control in your company, and refuse to consider anyone who expects a larger-than-life portion of your company's equity, stop and ponder that a venture capital firm's involvement may make your business go boom. So much so, in fact, that even a small share will tower head and shoulders over what you would have had without the help of organized investors. While still in college, Bo Peabody began Tripod Inc., an on-line magazine/community for young people, by looking for key investors. Today, Tripod Inc. is consistently ranked as one of the top ten most trafficked Web sites. And while you may view the remittal of majority interest in your company as a great, big favor to the recipient, remember that acquiring the backing of a venture capital firm is still as tough as boot camp. The competition is indeed stiff, but if you keep certain points in mind, you may just be able to get a venture capitalist to warm up to your schemes and dreams.

Great expectations: If you're not planning to be a prime candidate for *Lifestyles of the Rich and Famous* by the time the big three-oh rolls around, your romance with venture capitalists will end before it's even begun. This brand of investor is looking for the pie-in-the-sky, big-bang-for-the-buck-payoff opportunity. Now ask yourself, are you entrepreneur enough to deliver?

The players: A strong management team is by far the most important consideration for venture capitalists. Now is the time to assure these investors that their pet project will not be riddled with ineptitude. Play up the credentials of your team, provided, that is, that they have some. If the management is lacking experience, commitment, or skill, you'll get nothing but the big kiss-off.

Bring in a middleman: Before revealing your intentions to the prospective investing firm, see if you can't rustle up an intermediary to speak on your behalf. Preferably, this third party would be someone who has previously worked with the firm you're trying to impress. Give this potential master of ceremonies your best possible effort in terms of business plan and sales forecast. His or her past experience with the firm will either finagle you a meeting or special consideration, neither of which is easy to come by on your own.

Hitting Up Uncle Sam

What?! Will the government come to your rescue and will wonders never cease?! Well, truth is stranger than fiction, so believe it—the government does provide several types of assistance programs for business owners. As a matter of fact, scamming a loan from Capitol Hill is a very popular method of financing newborn enterprises. You've got a variety to choose from, the SBIC's, MESBIC's, and of course, the SBA. Heck, if your business is a demo of positive social ramifications, you may even be eligible for a grant!

The U.S. Small Business Administration prides itself on a standing tradition of boosting Small Business U.S.A. by stepping in where institutionalized financing steps out. The SBA gives banks a guaranteed repayment on all SBA-sponsored loans. While you can't argue with that type of promissory note, the SBA's strict regulations on interest rates have discouraged some banks from cooperating. But as of late, the Administration has been allowing the banks to charge higher rates on loans to promote broader participation. Pumped-up interest rates may seem like bad news, but once your business is off and running, you'll be only too glad to make good on your part of the bargain.

THE BOTTOM LINES

- **Hone your professional image.** Always conduct yourself in a professional manner, whether it be at a loan interview, a meeting with a private investor, or just a tête-à-tête with dear old Maw and Paw. Be direct and straightforward when discussing your financial needs and prospects. What's more, if you don't know your stuff better than the targeted investor, you'll not impress, no matter how well you dress. So by all means, investigate the latest in industry news prior to going off on a rant about some Draconian mergers and acquisitions.

- **Start with private financing:** Any tender you can scrounge up on your own — be it a personal bank loan, borrowing from family and friends, or digging into your own stock portfolio — should be used as the initial source of funding. Once your company is off thin ice, it will become easier to secure institutional financing.

- **Approach private investors:** Behind many a great entrepreneur is a great private investor — the silent partner who made everything possible. In order to win over one or two such beneficiaries, you'll have to do some research. Look into your potential investor's background to make sure he or she is on the up-and-up. Perfect your pitch, and get ready to negotiate the terms of agreement if you're lucky enough to get the green light.

- **Apply to banks for a business loan:** Walk into a reputable bank and ask for an application. Fill it out, submit it, and prepare for your interview. Don't sit by idly as the minions of the commercial loan division process your paperwork. Use this time to find out whether you have any connections at the bank and to collect loan-friendly information, such as additional favorable market research, an outstanding credit history, proof of business experience, and so on.

- **Sweeten the deal for venture capitalists:** These organized, professional investors don't go into business for small stakes. But if you see megabuck, NASDAQ-listing potential for your enterprise, these are the people to see. If you can get a middleman—someone who has already worked with the venture capital firm in question—to present your case and talk up your managerial competence, so much the better.

- **Get your taxes' worth:** Nascent business owners can apply for government assistance. There is no shortage of programs to get you started. You are also eligible for governmental grants if your business performs any not-for-profit functions, such as a drama camp that sometimes gives workshops for inner-city kids.

- **Patience is a virtue:** As anything worth doing is worth waiting for, reconcile yourself to a long and often arduous struggle to pull in financial support. There's still research to be conducted, applications to be processed, arguments to be crafted, and minds to be swayed. Even for you self-proclaimed masters of manipulation, this is the big time, and you'll have to go the full nine yards to get the goods. So settle in for the waiting period, pop a Dramamine, and enjoy the ride.

With enough determination, you'll eventually find the funds necessary to start or grow your business. But to make sure that your business is legitimate, you may decide to retain the services of a corporate lawyer or an accountant. The next chapter will discuss how to find good legal help, or how to do it all yourself.

Chapter Five

GOING LEGIT

Pesky details—that's what you'll find in this chapter. There's no getting around the technicalities, no loopholes to slip through, no back exits, and above all else no get-out-of-jail-free cards. In fact, jail, or at least court, is where you will most likely end up if you don't learn to run your business strictly by the books.

Doing business with a handshake is a nice notion, to be sure, but you leave that to the copywriters of those folksy television commercials. You're dealing with hard facts—the kind that fill up entire law libraries. Depending on the nature of your operation, you'll need to register with the state, acquire a list of licenses, obtain a federal tax identification number, prepare a slew of unfamiliar tax documents, as well as fulfill a host of other legal and financial requirements.

To keep you out of dire straits—and in the penthouse apartment that is the natural habitat of all young enterprisers—is the job of an army of lawyers and accountants. Sometimes, these brave troops are your only defense against the insidious I.R.S., or the all-too-popular "slip and fall" claimant. True, they demand a lot for their services, but who ever said that the pursuit of happiness is free? If your wallet is just sturdy enough to withstand the kick, spare your eyes the agony of reading fine print, and start looking for a lawyer and an accountant. If, on the other hand, your balance reads like that of a church mouse, roll up your sleeves and prepare to dive head long into the dirty work.

IS THERE A LAWYER IN THE HOUSE?

With the number of accountants and attorneys crowding commuter trains today, it's hard to believe that everyone doesn't know one personally. But, should you find yourself in such a bind, don't despair—good legal help is not hard to find.

- **Referrals**—Chances are you know someone, or at least know someone who knows someone, who's had a stellar lawyer experience. And we're not talking personal injury here; you need a good corporate lawyer to set you in the right direction.

- **Let your fingers do the walking**—Yes, the old directory. However did you guess it? If you choose to use this method, make sure to interview several lawyers. A swanky office could just be an indicator of exorbitant rates. Also, ask for references—and follow up.

Your Shopping List

When you first walk into a lawyer's office, you're not fooling anybody. Everybody knows you're shopping around. And while you don't have to bring a list, it does pay to know what to look for. Keep the following factors in mind during the interview:

- **Rapport**—It matters! You had better get on famously, because you'll be seeing a lot of each other in the future. Watch out for seemingly minor differences in work styles. Know thyself. If you're a hands-on client, insistent upon hearing all the details, but your lawyer is of the super-busy-no-time-to-talk persuasion, you're bound to end up at loggerheads.

- **Trust**—The potential advocate may be a natural-born charmer, but before you sign on the dotted line, stop and listen to your intuition. Do you have the proverbial funny feeling in the pit of your stomach? Heed the warning.

- **Experience**—The area of expertise is very important. As is the amount of time that the attorney has been practicing. While a younger attorney may be a bargain, do try to stay away from anyone just off the bar exam stool. Whereas a young attorney, working at building up a reputation, may be a bargain, one that's fresh out of law school may mean the end of your career.

- **Clientele**—Ask about the type of businesspeople the lawyer represents. Is it mostly large companies, Mom & Pop operations, or mid-sized firms? This is important, because the size of the business often affects the legalities involved. Furthermore, find out whether the attorney has ever dealt with businesses in your field. If they have, chances are they know what they're talking about, and can provide you with a host of valuable tips.

- **Fees**—No doubt about it, when it comes to parting with legal tender, less is more. But even the cheapest lawyer costs a money-clip-full, so don't make money your top priority. If you do stumble upon a "discount attorney," make sure he/she fits your profile. If not, take your show on the road.

ACCOUNTANTS AND CPAs

Unless you majored in accounting or business, you are no match for the mighty I.R.S. No one's doubting your grasp of basic math skills; it's your tax knowledge that's got us in a panic. All the algebra in the world won't be able to help you when it comes to grappling with the tax man. Remember, the decisions you make today will affect you for the rest of the year, and come April 15th, the day of reckoning, no amount of atonement will suffice. So even if you are the staunchest of do-it-yourself-ers, there's no shame in calling for reinforcements.

You can easily find an accountant by implementing the lawyer search method outlined earlier. Or you can take an altogether different direction. There are scores of good accountants who are readily available for consultation—you'll be surprised at the wonders that simply asking around can do. Call on some of your friendly neighborhood business owners, and see if you can't finagle a few names out of them.

STRUCTURE YOUR ENTERPRISE

Since so much of business start-up involves paperwork, it's best to figure out what forms you'll need to complete before taking pen to paper. To do this, you must first decide what shape your business will take. Easy, right? If you're thinking an L-shaped office suite or a rectangular storefront, don't look now, but you've got another think coming. The following are descriptions of the three most popular business structures—the sole proprietorship, the partnership, and the corporation.

- **Sole Proprietorship**—No two ways about it, you alone own the business. This means that your business income is filed only in your name. But the same goes with losses and lawsuits. The advantage is that the sole proprietorship is the cheapest and most hassle-free way to begin an enterprise. All it takes is a phone call to your state business services department. Request a business registration kit, and you're on your way.

- **Partnership**—Whatever your reasons, you are going into business with a copilot. In other words, you divvy up the take, the costs, and the responsibilities. To make sure no toes get trampled in the scurry for financial rewards, draw up a contract outlining each partner's business obligations prior to opening your doors to customers.

- **Corporation**—Think of a corporation as a separate entity. Something with a life all its own. If anything should go amiss, you are not so much responsible as is your corporation. There are a variety of fees, but unless you use an attorney, these do not have to exceed $150. The real rub is in the additional forms and tax documents that you will have to fill out. But if a corporation makes sense for your business needs, follow our quick steps to incorporating. Additional resources are also readily available at your local bookstore and/or library.

After you're done sifting through the documents, congratulations are in order—you have just cleared the greatest hurdle. And if you did this without enlisting the aid of an attorney, you also saved yourself quite a powerful pile of pesos. This calls for a celebration—nothing outrageous, perhaps a dinner and a night on the town. Do this now, while you still have the chance. Remember: All work and no play makes for one dull entrepreneur.

THE BOTTOM LINES

- **Use referrals to find an attorney and an accountant:** Despite what you may have heard, all lawyers and accountants are not created equal. If you don't know any such professionals firsthand, ask around. A good reference is as good a measure of competency as you're likely to find.

THE CORPORATE QUICKIE

1. Call your Secretary of State's corporate-name-availability phone number. This will let you know whether you can use your company's name, or whether another corporation with the same name already exists, in which case you will have to think again.

2. Obtain an Articles of Incorporation form. Complete it and send it to back to the Secretary of State with the required fee.

3. After waiting for 2–4 weeks, you should receive stamped articles of incorporation, formally welcoming your corporation to Earth.

4. Take this to your county recorder's office to record your corporation. You may have to pay a nominal fee for the privilege.

5. Fill out an SS 4 form in order to obtain your Federal Employment Identification Number (a.k.a. tax I.D. number).

6. Decide whether you want to be a C or S corporation. In a nutshell, if your corporation qualifies for S status, you only have to pay one set of taxes on your corporation's income. If it doesn't, you will have to pay taxes twice, once for the corporation's income (like we said, it's a separate entity) and another time for the income you gain from it. For more information, consult the resources listed at the end of this section.

7. Register with the state just as you would with a partnership or a sole proprietorship.

- **Make sure you're comfortable with your professional services providers:** Meet with several attorneys and accountants before making your decision. Factors to consider when interviewing would-be legal and financial advisors include their trustworthiness, area of expertise, client-base characteristics, fees, and the type of chemistry that exists between the two of you. Most importantly, be careful not to get taken in by an unscrupulous charmer.

- **Decide on how to structure your business:** Whether you're getting professional help, or are going at it alone, you'll first have to decide how to structure your business in legal entity terms. Sole proprietorships, partnerships, and corporations are the three most popular ways of structuring a business.

- **Do-it-yourself corporate law:** If your business transactions fall into the "rather basic" category, you may decide to forgo the help and expense of an attorney. "The Corporate Quickie" sidebar and the references listed at the end of this chapter can save you hundreds of dollars.

Remember that business plan you worked so hard to compile? Where is it now? Get it out and reread it; bond with it. Because once your startup is of sound financial and legal status, the time has come for a new brand of struggle. No longer are you looking to succeed at starting a business. You are now charged with the weighty task of succeeding as an entrepreneur. The next chapter will attempt to sharpen your marketing sensibilities to a razor's edge. Armed with an understanding of your audience, you'll become the maestro of foolproof business strategy. Hey, if it worked for Madonna, it can work for you.

Chapter Six

MARKETING SAVVY

Let's say that you successfully navigated your way through the labyrinth of business start-up—the financial strategy, the legalities, all those hassles are behind you. Now what? Do you kick back in your swivel rocker and pat yourself on the back? Probably not. Chances are you're racking your brain for "the next step."

Not so fast. Take a little time to think about the big picture. What have you been scrambling for all this while? Were the tax identification number, the bank loan, and the business license ends in themselves? No, they were all steps that enabled you to do something, and that "something" is to provide a product or a service—in other words to create a supply.

Think back to economics class and the supply/demand curve. By starting a business and jumping through all those technical hoops laid out in the previous chapters, you've pretty much taken care of the supply end. So what's next? You got it, the demand—or your customers.

No longer do you question where, why, and how you can start a business, and with what, but how will you draw attention to your product or service? Will customers just magically flock to the doors of your enterprise? Do you find yourself saying, "If I build it, they will come"? It may have worked for Kevin Costner, but you're not building on a field of dreams; you're building a business that will only survive if nurtured with seasoned success strategies.

Marketing is a serious business concern—equally as important as your product, if not more so. You'd be surprise to find out just how many great business ideas and products went bust all because of an inadequate marketing plan. Take the case of Irene Viento. She spent almost $70,000 opening GrandKids, a clothing boutique for children. Unfortunately, her attempts at market research were flawed, and she overestimated the number of potential customers. She closed shop after only three years in business. "A few people warned me that this town can't support local merchants. . . . Of course you don't want to hear that when you're all hopped up about the idea," warns Irene.

On the other hand, there's quite a number of inane products and services—think Beanie Babies and pet rocks—with no shortage of consumers clamoring at the gates, due only to powerful marketing campaigns behind them.

The only wonder is, how can something so good for your business be so much fun? That's right, marketing is often the most creative and fun part of running a business. And talk about a simple concept to grasp, marketing has the monopoly on easy. It's just a matter of determining your core customer base and then drawing their attention to your product or service via creative ads, brochures, special offers, and other promotions. You have something your customers want, but to sell them on your idea, you first have to inform them of your existence.

The tough part comes when you find yourself limited in time and funds. But every problem has a solution. As a parvenu in the realm of business, you have to discover how to get the most exposure in the least amount of time and on the smallest budget. The ideas and tactics outlined on the following pages should start you off on the right foot.

MARKET RESEARCH

Before you venture into the exciting world of marketing, you will have to determine one crucial factor—your customer profile. By honing in on your target customer, your marketing campaign will have the direction it needs to get the high sales numbers you want. Since you have probably already identified the target consumer in the planning stages of your business, all you need to do is revisit that initial target customer description. Remember "The Niche Factor." Who needs your product? Executives, homemakers, socialites, parents? Fill in the picture with vital details, such as household income and geographical location.

Selecting your customers is very important to creating an effective campaign as it will influence the marketing techniques you will be utilizing. If your business targets senior citizens living on their own, then a good place

MARKETING RESOURCES

An in-depth look at what makes your customer tick and, most importantly, purchase will serve your business well. Each consumer group has its own spending habits, preferred payment methods, and preferred selling approach. Lucky for you, marketing experts have already done most of the work for you, so it will be up to you to acquire their painstakingly compiled data and make it work for your enterprise. The following is a list of publications that may provide the insider's peek you've been looking for:

- *Advertising Age:* (www.adage.com)
- *Ad Week and Media Week:* 212/536-5336 (www.adweek.com)
- *American Advertising:* 202/898-0089
- *American Demographics:* 800/529-7502
- *Advertising and Marketing Review:* (www.ad-mkt-review.com)

to start would be to advertise your services in special publications geared toward older people, or on radio stations that feature classical music and golden oldies. Once you figure out who exactly you want to sell to, there will be nothing standing between you and a successful business launch.

ADVERTISING KNOW-HOW

You've determined your customers, their buying and spending habits, and the best outlets for your business message. Now is the time to put your money where your mouth is and proclaim your business to the world. And advertising begins where shouting from the rooftop leaves off.

When you're ready to advertise, remember that buying space in a publication or time from a radio station is by no means the only way to reach your customers. But such a costly marketing method may be an effective way to make the most waves in the shortest amount of time. If money is no object and you're looking to make a big splash from the get-go, then advertising may just be what your marketing strategy needs.

Before settling on any particular medium (print, radio, or television), always contact the company's ad sales representative to obtain a rate card. To help you decide whether to invest in advertising space, also request a demographic report to determine the primary audience. Then, if the price is right and the customer fits the bill, go ahead and secure the space.

CHECKLIST FOR DIRECT MAIL SUCCESS

There are certain elements that all successful direct-mail pieces have in common:

1. A detailed description and photos of your service or product

2. Pricing

3. A 1-800 number for orders

4. Acceptable payment methods (credit cards, checks, and /or money orders)

5. Company logo, address, and contact name

6. Return policy (if any)

7. Special offers or discounts

8. Testimonials of satisfied customers (friends and relatives are eligible)

9. Order form

10. A reply envelope

Tips to Thrift By

• Never assume the quoted rate is the final offer. Be ready to haggle if the price seems high.

• Ask about the discount policy for multiple appearances. Most media outlets will echo this sentiment: The more you advertise, the more money you'll save. You may want to look into this option only after tracking the results of your first advertisement.

• Open your own in-house advertising agency. You'll need a business license and company stationery. Most publications offer a 15 percent agency discount. You'd be surprise at how quickly the savings add up.

The Direct Approach

Arousing customer interest via the postmaster has been around for years. Just think about all the marketing material your mailbox is crammed with each day. This marketing strategy involves sending a brochure describing your business, an introductory letter, and an order form with the vital contact information. The best way to determine who the lucky promotion recipients will be is to rent a mailing list from a broker. This strategy will allow you to customize the list to match your customer profile. When you call Rent-A-List, ask to conduct your own sample mailing to measure that list's effectiveness. Most brokers will provide you with a sample of 100 names to gauge results. You can save a bundle by using this popular trial-and-error technique.

Once you've got your list in hand, you must determine the look and content of your mailing. The more professional your material looks and reads, the higher the response rate will be. Use durable paper and eye-catching copy. If your writing and design skills need polishing, hire outside help to carry out this important task. You can often save money by hiring design students and struggling writers to assist you. We're not condoning slave wages, but their rates will be lower and they will probably be more receptive to any feedback you have to offer.

POWER OF THE PRESS KIT

Would you be surprised that the best publicity for your business is also the cheapest? Promoting your business to mass-media outlets in hopes of scoring future coverage is an effective way to land in the public eye. Dineh Mohajer's appearances on *Oprah* and MTV's *House of Style* catapulted her Hard Candy cosmetics line to household-name status. You, too, can follow in her well-pedicured footsteps.

Once you've created business pamphlets and brochures, you're ready to contact the press. Promoting your business with a press release (a description of your business, how it started, its goals and benefits, how it's indicative of a social, cultural, or business trend) is an extremely popular method. Target the editors of publications, as well as television and radio stations that cater to your types of customers—then dispatch your press release either via mail or fax. Send out mass quantities of this announcement to arouse as much interest as possible. Your goal: free public exposure. And if that weren't enough, a PR campaign can also give you the kind of credibility you couldn't get with a paid advertisement. Most people still believe everything they read— just so long as it doesn't come in the form of advertising.

Working an Angle

There isn't a snowball's chance in Hawaii that your business will receive any sort of media attention if there isn't some sort of human interest spin on your story. Your press kit must highlight either the inspirational, the socially responsible, or the innovative and offbeat side of your business.

Reporters will be more likely to feature your business if your press release reads like a real-deal article. One way to write your way into the hearts of your readers is to include a story that emphasizes your personal background and all the trials you've had to endure to start your business. If your business is in some way socially responsible, include a detailed account of how you endeavor to aid certain members of society. An innovative and offbeat angle can be worked by writing about how your idea is indicative of some future trend. Once you play up these aspects of your biz in your feature article, your shameless self-promotion to media contacts will be completely justified—and pretty soon you'll be seeing your name in print.

Another way to get the editorial spotlight is to include a mock interview with yourself. Pretend you're a reporter and think of interesting questions you could ask yourself. Write these down and then prepare your answers. Once your interview is ready, send it off with your promotional materials, a black-and-white photograph of yourself, and most importantly, your contact information. Remember, editors and producers are busy people. Make their job easier and you'll be well rewarded.

Handling the Press

Dealing with the press isn't always easy. There's the constant rejections, the little white promises, the flat-out brusquerie, the abhorrent rudeness, and a bounty of other tales of woe everyone in the promotions racket has experienced at one time or another. All you can do is to keep sending out your material until someone notices. Calling once to follow up is a good way to introduce yourself and your pitch to the editor. But keep in mind that in this business, a firm no means just that. In other words, don't follow up a second and third time unless your contact has led you to believe that your chances for being featured are promising—in which case you should ring back to ensure that your cause is not forgotten.

Sometimes only one out of a hundred recipients will call for an interview or for more detailed information, so whatever you do, don't get discouraged. Keep telling yourself that your fifteen minutes are still out there, and the big time is only a phone call away.

If you're lucky enough to get bombarded by hungry reporters, here are the rules:

- always remain polite, direct, and to the point;
- don't get too excited as spasms don't go over too well with the press;
- always appear well-informed and businesslike;
- and never ever end an interview without requesting a copy of the finished article to use in future press kits.

MEDIA AND PUBLICATIONS DIRECTORIES

Before you can send off your press kit, you'll have to find out where and to whom to ship the goods. Directories listing national magazines, weekly and daily newspapers, as well as radio and television stations, abound, and will make short-work of your labors. For half the price of what you'd pay for one advertisement, you can get disks or ready-to-mail labels listing the addresses and contact names of editors and producers throughout the country. Once you invest, you can use these over and over again to insure a good reception. (Note: You will also be provided with a fax number for each listing. And while faxing your press kit may not be as distinctive an approach as mailing a four-color kit, you can save considerable amounts of time and money by enlisting the aid of communication services that will fax your material to thousands of recipients in an hour or less.)

1. *All-In-One-Directory*
   Gebbie Press
   PO Box 1000
   New Paltz, NY 12561
   914/255-7560 (www.gebbieinc.com)

2. Bacon's Directories and CD-ROM's
   Bacon's Information Inc.
   332 South Michigan Avenue
   Chicago, IL 60604
   312/922-2400

3. *Editor and Publisher International Yearbook* and CD-ROM
   Editor and Publisher, Inc.
   11 West 19th Street
   New York, NY 10011
   212/675-4380

4. *Gale Directory of Publications and Broadcast Media*
   Gale Research
   7625 Empire Drive
   Florence, KY 41042
   800/877-GALE (www.thomson.com)

5. Working Press of the Nation
   121 Chanlon Road
   New Providence, NJ 07974
   908/464-0800

THE BOTTOM LINES

- **Determine your customer profile:** The type of consumer most likely to benefit from your product or service will dictate your marketing strategy. Recall the audience you targeted in your business plan and keep the interests of these people in mind as you map out your marketing plan.

- **Take advantage of available marketing resources:** There's no end to the publications that make it their business to write about the spending habits and trends going on within America's many demographic groups. Instead of wasting your time reinventing sliced bread, get off on the right foot by digging into the archives of appropriate journals.

- **Choose a medium that targets your customers:** Radio, TV, and print ads are common means of getting the word out, often the first steps to buzz-generation. But if you misplace your advertising, you may find your money misspent. Request a demographic report from your would-be advertising medium to see how its audience stacks up against yours. Ask for a rate card while you're at it. If the demographics are a match and the rates are reasonable, it's time to place the ad.

- **Invest in an updated mailing list to begin a direct mail campaign:** If direct mail advertising didn't work, your recycling bin wouldn't runneth over with junk mail. Large corporations know the value of promotion via the U.S.P.S., and once you get your hands on the right mailing list, you will too.

- **Wage a public relations campaign:** There's no mystery to public relations; it's easy, more credible than paid advertising, and a crucial component of buzz-generation. Don't wait until your business is open to write and distribute a press release. Nothing assures a big opening week like advance publicity.

With an established business and a stream of customers to your credit you're well on your way to discovering the formula for success. But to keep your business going strong, you're going to have to remain productive. Management is the key to efficient operations and, as it so happens, that's just what we're about to discuss. After all, someone still has to supervise you and your employees—and since you wanted to be the boss, the job is all yours.

Chapter Seven

BEING YOUR OWN BOSS

As a relatively young person, you may find being in a position of authority somewhat daunting. Still pulling for the little guy in labor-management disputes, you may be more comfortable throwing back a few brewskis with your staff than giving them orders. Whatever you do, resist this urge.

First-time entrepreneurs often make the mistake of being too nice. Think back to high school. Remember the new teachers, whose classes were always so simple their first year in? Recall what happened to these very same teachers their second year—these champions of the blow-off class and the easy "A" would suddenly change into tyrants of the first order. Take a lesson from this past experience, and do not get too buddy-buddy with your new employees. Sure, it's the easy way out now, but buckle to social pressure today, and you'll only have yourself to blame when the inmates start running the asylum tomorrow.

When you decided to go into business for yourself, you probably wanted to call the shots and take responsibility for your own future. Now that you have all the authority, it's up to you to keep both yourself and your employees on the ball. Someplace between Dilbert's cubicle and Ally McBeal's unisex bathroom lies a happy medium—your job is to find it.

But before you venture forth, ask yourself whether you think that it is good to be the king/queen, or whether you're of the opinion that it's lonely at the top? What's more, do you trust yourself to manage your business efficiently, or are you afraid of running it straight in to the ground? Chances are you'll find that being the boss involves all these factors, the good, the bad, and the horrifying.

While on some level, running a business provides a great sense of accomplishment, it is also fraught with disappointments and the painstaking process of trial and error. And while it's fun to call people your employees, and have them call you their boss, it can also be a little lonely to sit on the other side of the fence. This chapter will prepare you for what's in store, since you'll have to come to terms with these facts of a boss's life eventually.

MANAGING YOURSELF

Now you're in charge. You sign the paychecks, you set the hours, yes, you are the head honcho personified. But regardless of this newfound independence, you will still have to follow a set of rules. Because we're all our own worst critics, this set of rules will most likely be more stringent and exacting than anything you've had to deal with heretofore.

Most beginning entrepreneurs believe that working for themselves will be a carefree romp—filled with three-hour lunch breaks, long-winded personal calls, and midday adventures in cyber-erotica. But as any successful entrepreneur learns early on, you've still got a lot of working to do. And because you're going at it alone, you'll probably have more than your fair share in the start-up stage of your business.

Additional responsibilities mean that you'll have to learn to manage your time and organize your life. You'll have to exercise more discipline than when you were working 9 to 5 for someone else. There will be no one to tell you to get back to work or to clean up your act—that will be all up to you.

Many home-office business owners experience this same difficulty: the problem of having to concentrate on work in a domestic and comfortable setting. Reports have shown that many business owners working out of the house even go so far as to dress up in work clothes to keep themselves from straying from their work path. So if you've been dreaming of working in your Lion King slippers and watching television as you complete your bookkeeping, you may have to realign your views of owning a business.

TIME MANAGEMENT

Time is your greatest asset, so the less you squander, the more bucks you will rake in. When you first open shop, you'll probably have to take care of the details yourself. When Gail Sharp and Nancy Bible opened the TallGrass Aveda Day Spa, their twelve-hour work days were a lot more than they bargained for. The amount of work you'll have to do is something that can't be determined until you're well on your way to establishing your business. But making sure that all the bills are paid, taxes filed, and calls returned can turn into hours of aggravation, so there is no time like the present to learn the art of effective organization.

MANAGING YOUR STAFF

As your business develops, the jack-of-all-trades bit may become an abysmal yawn. If you're swamped with work, a pair of helping hands will look like a lifeline. After checking your budget, you may realize that you can finally afford to provide someone with a living. Such an epiphany will call for a celebration—it is the first sign of success.

The difficult part of bringing new people on board is that up to now, you've been handling everything yourself. You should expect a megadose of separation anxiety to set in. But that's only normal. Your business is your baby. It's hard to relegate even a small part of its maintenance to a stranger. But remember: Without extra help, your business cannot grow and flourish. Just keep telling yourself, "It's for the good of the company," and you'll welcome any new assistance with open arms.

Calling All Job Applicants

Determining whom to hire is a very tricky business. Unless you hear of candidates through recommendations from friends, your search for the perfect employee will cost you.

If your friends and business contacts are short on potential applicants, you will have to place an ad in the local paper. Spend some time thinking about what you want from an employee. Is a college education top priority, or does experience rank first on your list? You'll have to lay it all out in print if you don't want to spend hours pouring over unsuitable resumes.

A cheaper alternative to local papers are the Web-based job databanks. Many of these offer free ad space for qualified employers. The only drawback is that Internet job databanks yield a lower response rate.

The Interview

Exemplary credentials are one thing, but what about the chemistry? The rapport you have with your employees is very important to workplace pro-

THE BUSY BUSINESS OWNERS' GUIDE TO SAVING TIME

1. First Things First: An average day in the life of a business owner involves juggling a million little urgencies. To keep up with the constant flow of daily tasks and chores, you will have to learn how to prioritize your activities. The best way to accomplish this is to make a list of ten things you want to complete that day. If you manage to scratch off even five items of your daily "to do" list, then you can honestly call yourself a winning prioritizer.

2. User-Friendly Phones: Depending on how you look at it, phones can be a struggling entrepreneur's best friend or worst nightmare. The constant ringing of the phone may frustrate you no end when you're in the middle of an important task. So what to do if a highly time-sensitive business activity is on the agenda, and you don't want to miss calls from important business contacts? Don't worry, all is not lost.

A multi-option phone provides a simple solution. It allows callers to obtain basic information about your business with the push of a button. This option can actually save your business and, most importantly, your sanity.

3. Cleaning Up House: An orderly workstation can save you many hours of searching for that misplaced invoice or file. Whether you decide to scan all your important documents into a neatly organized computer database, or invest in plenty of file cabinets to house that endless stream of paper, organization is key to your up-and-coming enterprise.

When you're in the middle of simultaneously handling several emergencies, you don't want to be caught empty-handed. Don't be fooled by people with disastrous-looking offices. They'll tell you they know where everything is, and that they have their own unique brand of organization. But after watching many a messy supervisor pop an artery in a vain attempt to uncover the missing goods, we recommend you adopt the one organizational style that works—neatness.

4. Schedule Savvy: A daily planner is another winning factor in your race against time. Scheduling your daily activities can keep your mind on important deadlines, and off the mundane details of every day. But consistent use and accuracy is the key to keeping your schedule on track. If you pencil in activities at random, you'll be less likely to stick to the set game plan. So when using this time-management tool, make sure you allow plenty of time for each activity and schedule breaks when necessary. And by all means, don't quit using your book if a well-intentioned effort goes awry. As the old saying goes, "Try, try again." You'll soon fall into the habit, and will never even think of leaving home without your trusty daily planner.

ductivity. That is why you will want to set up an interview with every candidate that fits your educational and experience requirements.

Once you narrowed the list down to, say, ten or so candidates, you will have to decide what kind of interview to conduct. Since this is probably your first time on the right side of the desk, you may feel odd about the experience. But look at this as a chance to role-play, and in no time you'll become an old hand at all this boss business.

Now, there are as many different types of interviews as there are applicants. But just as most people can be categorized into introvert and extrovert, you can also group interviews into two basic types—the casual and the formal. The former will allow the applicants to ramble on and on about their likes, dislikes, and background, while the latter is a more structured approach. The formal interview is an inquisition of sorts, where you ask direct, pointed questions and evaluate candidates based on their varied responses to similar queries.

Keep in mind that you can customize your interview however you like. For example, the chief of Louis Vuitton S.A. presents 100 neckties for all candidates to inspect. Those who choose tasteless ties are politely dismissed, but not until they're given a second chance by trying their hand at a similar process of scarf selection. Remember, you don't have to settle for less than a reliable and compatible employee, so keep searching until you find just the right person.

Payday: Much More Than Just a Candy Bar

This here's the aggravating part, determining what to pay your new employees. To lure skilled labor your way, be prepared to provide a competitive salary. The best way come up with an enticing figure is to do a little digging. That's right, it's time to scour industry magazines to find out what others in your field are making. Then, depending on whether you're looking to hire an entry-level employee with limited experience or a seasoned player, the compensation you offer should fall a little shorter or a little higher compared to the average salaries.

If you're low on cash, as you may very well be during the start-up phase of your business, there are low-cost alternatives that may suit your needs wonderfully. In the beginning, you may want to secure part-time assistance. This will effectively eliminate the expense that goes along with providing a benefits package. Part-timers are usually paid by the hour, thereby saving you the expense of paying for sick days, personal days, vacations, holidays, and

FIVE POWERFUL QUESTIONS TO ASK YOUR APPLICANTS

1. *Where do you see yourself five years down the road?*
If they are slow to answer or leave out the juicy details, you'll know right away that they aren't the ambitious visionaries you're looking to find.

2. *How well do you take criticism?*
This is pretty much a no-brainer. If he or she tells you they are averse to any negative feedback, move on to the next applicant who can hopefully take a few pointers here and there.

3. *What are your flaws?*
If the applicant responds with "I'm a perfectionist" or "I'm a workaholic," you can be pretty sure that they lack the sincerity and ingenuity you'll want to see in your employee. If, on the other hand, they jokingly claim that they can stand to drop a few pounds or resolve their intimacy issues, hire them on the spot—they're funny.

4. *What was the last book you've read?*
The blank look is something to watch out for. If the candidate looks lost, they are probably trying to think of the last author they heard about on Oprah's book club. A well-read employee is a greater asset to your company. It shows they go beyond the requirements of their educational institution, and pursue knowledge whatever the circumstance. You will always be grateful for having this type of self-motivated worker around.

5. *Why did you leave your last job?*
If the candidate starts complaining about his or her boss, the overtime, or the workload, you can bet that he or she will have the same complaints about you and your company several months down the line. The last thing you need is an employee with a negative attitude and a slacker mentality.

daily lunch breaks, while still providing you with the opportunity to indulge in that much-needed break every once in a while.

You can also create an internship. This involves posting your notice at nearby colleges and in internship bulletins. Many companies today are praising the value of this popular alternative. Here's how it works: College students exchange their time for the experience of working in a field of their interest. There's absolutely no cost to you. It is often the case that the college student of your choice can use the real-world work experience toward completing his or her coursework. So count on having the pick of the student litter. But remember: Interns deserve your respect. The fact that you're not paying them doesn't mean you can treat them like indentured servants. Taking on a qualified intern can be the beginning of a mutually beneficial relationship.

Motivating the Troops

No matter how competent and excited your employees feel during the first few weeks on the job, you can bet that their spirits will flag from time to time. To get the most out of your dollar and keep your business operating at peak levels, you will need to pay close attention to the needs of your employees.

As the boss, your encouragement and support means a lot to your staff. So be sure you always recognize and compliment a job well done. Vice presidents of the ubiquitous food distribution company Nobel/Sysco take the time to personally prepare and serve meals to employees to recognize their performance. And while you don't have to fall all over yourself trying to excite your team, a few words of praise now and then can work wonders where the general morale is concerned.

While kind words are important to your employees, there are other motivating forces that you can use to your advantage. Money talks, and its not for nothing that incentives such as cash bonuses have a considerable impact on job performance.

But there are many different types of bonuses. Giving monetary rewards for meeting a quota is a very popular catalyst of superior performance. You can also offer time off for good attendance. Diane and Steven Warren, owners of Katzinger's Deli, implemented an incentive system to keep food costs down. "You guys reduce food costs down below 35 percent of [total sales], and we'll split the [savings] with you," Diane told her staff. Food costs fell almost immediately, and employees got to go home with extra money in their pockets. You too can get creative when determining the bonus plan—you're bound to come up with a unique system that works for you.

Performance Evaluations

To keep your team on the right track, you will have to conduct in-depth performance evaluations for every employee. None of your staff members should ever be left in the dark until the ax falls. Performance evaluations are a good way to offer constructive criticism to your employees without injuring their feelings.

Many companies are also realizing the benefits of turning the tables, and offering their employees the chance to voice their opinions about the company's policies and practices. When you give workers the chance to express themselves they will, in turn, respond more positively to your feedback. You may also find that you can benefit from the input of your employees.

When creating a performance evaluation, keep the duties of each employee in mind. And remember: Favorable performance evaluations are often followed by requests for a pay increase. Be prepared for this by determining, in advance, how generous you can afford to be.

Handling Problem Employees

Maybe Joe Schmo was the picture of conscientiousness when you first welcomed him into the fold, but as you may soon find out, looks can be deceiving. It is often the case that the employee you hired turns out to be difficult to work with and sometimes even contentious.

As the saying goes, "One bad apple can spoil the bunch." If you find yourself saddled with a problem employee, take measures immediately to insure your other team members aren't negatively influenced. Morale can plummet at the speed of light, so keep your office trouble-free by identifying problem employees before they get out of hand.

Prevention is the name of the game. Watch for things like sleeping—or reading the latest Clancy—on the job, continued tardiness, and sloppy work. If you do happen to notice such behavior, express your concern immediately.

If after repeated warnings and discussions the employee fails to improve his or her performance, it may be time to find a replacement. Firing people, no matter how pesky, is probably the worst part of being the boss. But a swift declaration of your intentions is the best way to go about it. Don't get upset or show emotion. You should also avoid stretching the process out. It will only make it harder for the employee as well as yourself.

THE BOTTOM LINES

- **Learn to manage your time:** Fledgling entrepreneurs can't afford to waste a minute of time. Learn to stay on the ball by making to-do lists, keeping your work space in order, setting fixed work hours, buying a daily planner, and investing in a quality phone-answering system.

- **Hire employees through references and "help wanted" classified and Internet ads:** You'll get the largest response by placing an ad in the daily paper, but Internet ads and personal contacts can also prove effective.

- **Prepare your interview in advance:** Whether your opt for a formal Q&A or a casual chit-chat type of interview, your interviews will prove most informative if you decide what to ask beforehand.

- **Compensate your employees fairly:** Competitve salaries will not only lure solid candidates to your door, but they will keep that door from revolving. Because high turnover is the scourge of workplace productivity nationwide, you'll have to find a way to pay your employees fair wages and provide them with a comprehensive benefits package. If that means hiring only part-time employees at first, so be it.

- **Use motivational strategies to energize your team:** Monetary incentives are just the tip of the iceberg when it comes to getting the most out of your employees. Learn to motivate your employees by checking a couple of books on motivational leadership out of the library.

- **Don't keep your performance reviews a secret:** Schedule a time to meet with staff members out of the office three months into their term of employment. Let them know what you're looking for as regards performance, tell them how they're doing, and set a date for the next performance evaluation.

- **Discharge with confidence:** Resist the temptation to avoid confrontation. Insubordination, chronic tardiness, and excessive absences are all valid reasons to terminate employment. Sit the employee down, present your case, hear what the employee has to say, act understanding, and bid adieu. It's that simple.

Once you hire employees, you'll have a true sense of life in the entrepreneurial lane. Your workload may lighten up, but hiring a staff will come complete with a whole new set of responsibilities. Take some time to get used to your new role of authority; you'll be a natural supervisor soon enough. Eventually, you'll have longtime employees with whom you can pal around. Of course, the same can't be said about your equipment. The longer it works for you, the more likely you are to want to kick it. Our next chapter will discuss ways in which you can keep your office up to date, without draining your corporate checking account.

Chapter Eight

ADVANCE YOUR ENTERPRISE

The frenetic pace of technological progress has spawned two kinds of entrepreneurs: the technophobe and the techno-enthusiast. The entrepreneurs falling into the latter category often believe that an assortment of top-of-the-line equipment is the only way to succeed in business, while the former frequently subscribe to the Unabomber's neo-Luddite Manifesto—that technology is taking over the world and must be stopped.

But there is yet a third form of entrepreneurship—one that embraces the technological advances necessary to meet the demands of a growing marketplace, but does not rely on technology to see a business through. Just consider where the average small business would be without computers, fax machines, photocopiers, and voice mail? Imagine the difficulty of getting in touch with customers, organizing vital data, and bookkeeping without the modern appliances our brave new world has to offer. It's a fact. The right equipment can fulfill the duties of a small support staff—and with competitive salaries well on the rise, that's one benefit that no fledgling enterpriser can afford to ignore.

Due in no small part to technological progress, the number of small business ventures has grown dramatically in recent years. After all, if not for technology, how else would so many be able to run a corporation from the confines of their very own basements? Nowadays, we don't even need to worry about being computer-illiterate or cash-poor, because most of today's technology gets thumbs-up for being user-friendly and affordable.

Neither do the entrepreneurs in this third category put all their faith in high-grade equipment and buy into the notion of techno-induced success. Because while a turbocharged modem may be a nice luxury, the reality is that no machine can ever replace human skill and determination. Sure, some businesses may require high-end products, but the vast majority can be started just as happily with a select sampling of moderately priced or leased equipment. So there's no need to prowl Radio Shack or blow all of your start-up dough on failure-proof gizmos.

So now that you've accepted your mission, to capitalize on the advances in technology, you're almost ready for the techno-shopping spree. But first you'll have to determine which equipment suits your business needs. Consider the primary functions and day-to-day operations of your business. Not all start-ups require the same technical support. We've compiled a list of basic equipment all businesses will require at one point or another. Now whether you decide to invest in the following gadgetry will depend largely on your specific business needs.

PERSONAL COMPUTERS (PCS)

Buying a computer can prove complicated subject matter for small-business owners. There are just so many manufacturers and components to choose from. But once you zoom in on the type of system you'll need and the right brand or model for your business's computing needs, you'll be glad you gave this issue the consideration it deserves.

Clash of the Titans

There are two groups of computer users: those who swear by the Macintosh system and those who believe that IBM-compatible PC's will one day rule the computer industry. While PC's are more popular with large financial corporations, Macs are cited as being user-friendly and ideal for graphics and multimedia applications.

When it comes to pricing, PC's on average run much cheaper than Macs. Software availability also leans toward the PC side. But your best bet to settling the heated PC vs. Mac debate is to call on businesses similar to yours to determine their preference.

Choosing a Processor

A vital element to consider when purchasing a new computer system is the type and speed of the processor. The computer processor is much like the headquarters of a large corporation. It is where all the major decisions are made.

If you've decided on a Mac system, you will have the option of Motorola/IBM's PC chips. These chips provide clock speeds raging from 60 MHz to 300 MHz. This processor is reflected in Mac's higher per-unit cost.

PC users do have a greater processor selection. A very popular processor among PC users is the Intel Pentium Chip. Pentiums come in a variety of clock speeds. These range from 75 MHz to 200 MHz. But Intel also makes a faster and more expensive chip called Pentium II, which is available at 233 and 266 MHz clock speeds. Remember, these figures are subject to change due to the rapid development of newer versions.

Memory and Storage Capacity

If you're planning to run multiple applications, consider investing in a computer with lots of memory or RAM. Most models come with 16 MB of memory, but those who need to keep multiple programs at once could benefit from at least 32 MB of RAM. If you're budget is tight, consider upgrading your computer's memory at a later time. Extra memory can be easily installed once you're ready to upgrade.

A hard drive is the storage space for your applications and documents. The computer you choose should be equipped with at least a 1-GB hard drive. But unless you're planning to create files with sound, graphics, and video, don't bother purchasing the expensive 2–4 GB hard drive–equipped models.

The Price Is Right

The type of processor you choose can dramatically elevate the cost of your computer. To save money, avoid purchasing a computer with a newly introduced processor. If you wait a couple of months, the price will be sure to drop.

Another way to cut costs is to invest in a less-expandable model. Unless you're planning to add on a variety of accessories, you'd be wise to avoid the high costs associated with highly expandable computers.

LASER PRINTERS

The type of printer you purchase depends on the kinds and quantity of documents your business will need to produce. If your plan is to produce a large volume of printed material, then a laser printer may be just what you need. It is by far the fastest and most economic way to reproduce text or images.

Speed

The best way to measure the speed of your printer is to investigate the speed of the printer's processor. These figures are rarely advertised, so you will benefit from determining this vital factor. Printers with RISC technology will be more expensive, but are the fastest on the market.

Resolution

Dots per inch, or dpi, is the measure by which your printer's resolution is determined. If you are planning to make a habit of image reproduction, you would be well served with a printer boasting 600 dpi. But if printing text is your main concern, you can save money by choosing a printer with 300 dpi.

The Price Is Right

The cost of a laser printer can vary dramatically. The smaller, slower versions, used mostly in a home or small office setting, start at around $300. But if you're planning on opening a grand operation, you'll benefit from a network-compatible laser printer that can be accessed by multiple users. That variety of laser printers can cost you anywhere from $1,300 to $4,000. And when you calculate the price of consumables—toner, developer, drums, and corona wires—you can easily exceed your target price. Factor in these necessary expenditures when deciding on the laser printer that's right for you.

COLOR PRINTERS

The two most popular type of color printers are ink-jet and laser. Color laser printers yield higher-quality documents and better resolution than their cheaper ink-jet counterparts. They are also much faster, and as a result, are much more expensive.

If you plan on printing color documents frequently, avoid purchasing an ink-jet printer. While these may cost anywhere from $250 to $1,200, they are very slow, often printing only one to two pages per minute. And while color lasers offer the best results in terms of speed and resolution, at prices starting at $3,500, they are very expensive.

Most businesses requiring a smaller to medium volume of color documents choose to out-source their color materials to outside printing companies. This strategy can actually save you money down the line—considering the significant cost of color printer consumables.

Scanners

Scanners are very useful when it comes to transforming documents and images into computer files. These days, with the aid of additional software, scanners allow the user to edit scanned text, making hours and hours of data entry virtually obsolete. Any image can easily be imported into an existing document using a variety of scanners. Whether you'll need to store important documents, input volumes of vital data, or capture captivating images, there's a scanner out there that's just right for you.

There are three types of scanners to choose from. The handheld variety are most difficult to use, but are good for those seeking a cheaper alternative. Handheld scanners can be operated by pulling the device across a page. This technique is time-consuming and often requires a good deal of concentration. Handheld scanners cost around $100 to $250.

Sheet-fed scanners are much easier to use and are actually very affordable, with a price range of $200 to $400. Using this type of scanner is easy. Just feed the documents through and watch your image magically appear on your computer screen.

Flat-bed scanners are very popular among the graphically inclined. They are the perfect, if not the only, scanner to use for importing graphic images into a computer file. Because current software makes it so easy to alter and manipulate computerized images, most designers prefer working with this type of scanner. Because of the flat surface of these scanners, it is quite easy to grab images from magazines and other forms of print media. Flat-bed scanners can be purchased for as low as $300 or as high as $2,500.

PHOTOCOPIERS

Some business owners say this is one machine they couldn't work without. Copying documents, brochures, order forms, and receipts are all pretty universal office-related tasks. But the type of photocopier you choose to purchase depends on how many copies you currently make and how many you will expect to make in the future.

When you consider the many thrifty features that accompany most photocopiers, you may be hard pressed to resist. But the price may skyrocket if you elect to buy all of them. Take the feeder, for example. This device dramatically cuts the amount of time it takes to copy multi-page documents by automatically feeding the papers into the machine. This function may come in very useful. But the sorter may be an unnecessary feature, since only those who produce many copies of multiple-page documents would find its services necessary.

Copier prices range anywhere from $500 for low-end models to $20,000 for the high-end variety. So you can see why it pays to check out the options before purchasing. Many start-ups opt to rent or lease this often pricey piece of equipment. Consult your local office equipment dealer for rates and length of the contract term.

FAX MACHINES

Faxing documents is an easy, fast, and economic way of relaying data. And you'll probably make good use of this often-affordable piece of office equipment. Many companies actually rely solely on the fax machine for transacting all their business activities. Newsletters, reminder services, and other information-based companies have put this machine to work for them, making a pretty profit in the process. Before purchasing a model, consider that the speed of the model's transmission will determine how much you pay in the long run, since inefficient or cheap fax models can raise your phone bills. A good average speed for fax machines is 9,600 BPS.

As with all products, prices vary. The cheapest fax machine can cost you about $200, but you should probably consider purchasing either an ink-jet fax machine, which typically comes to about $400, or a laser model which starts at $700. If you're shy about investing, these machines can also be leased or rented until your business is up and running full speed ahead.

There is, however, an even better and cheaper way to send data via fax. If you've bought a computer with a modem, then you can start faxing almost immediately without even having to purchase another machine. Just purchase fax software (starting at $75) at a nearby computer store and you're ready to fax. Compared to the regular fax machine speed of 9,600 bpi, computer-generated faxes send and receive information at 14,000 bpi. Your phone bill will thank you. And you can send as well as receive documents directly from your screen without ever having to print them out. This is one option you should definitely look into before buying a traditional fax machine.

E-MAIL

Since we're on the subject of e-mail, allow us to take this opportunity to emphasize the value of e-mail to business owners everywhere. Not only does it decrease your valuable phone dollars, it's an easy way to get in touch with out-of-touch customers. No terminal hold, no painfully prolonged small talk, just you and your target audience.

Certain business owners use e-mail every day. It all depends on your clients and potential customers. For example, when we were first starting out as writers, we e-mailed articles and even book proposals to editors everywhere. It is often very difficult to get in touch with editors, but with e-mail we were able to get the proverbial foot through the door. Just remember, keep your messages short and to the point. No one enjoys having to scroll indefinitely.

COMPUTER MAGAZINES

If you're still confused about what type of computer equipment to purchase, or just want to keep up with the industry's latest developments, consult these informative on-line and print magazines.

- **Shift**
  (www.shift.com)

- **Wired**
  (www.wired.com/wired)

- **Computer Shopper**
  (www5.zdnet.com/cshopper)

- **BYTE**
  (www.byte.com)

DIGGING IN THE VIRTUAL GOLD MINE

By now, you've probably heard much ado about the Internet, and many of you are probably seasoned Web-surfers. But did you ever stop to consider the business benefits of maintaining a Web presence? Surveys say that the number of people currently on-line is 57 million. That number is also predicted to grow to 400 million by the year 2005. And Internet sales were forecasted to reach a whopping $106 billion in 1998. "Everybody's shifting over to the Web," says Harry Wolhandler, director of research at ActivMedia. "People will be learning better and better ways of using it to their advantage." And when you consider the low cost of maintaining your own Web site, you'll understand why so many businesses are making good profits off their savvy Web pages.

Many companies develop their own sites to gain an added promotional advantage. Many others run their entire business by way of an Internet Web site—taking orders, closing sales, the whole nine yards, right there at dot.com headquarters. Unless you're versed in the HTML language of Web page developers, your best bet is to consult a professional Web page designer. But there are many Web sites and Web builder software packages that will provide you with the affordable or free guidance and storage you'll need to get your Web page up and running in no time.

The challenge for all Web-based businesses is to generate enough interest and visits to attract new customers and keep the old ones coming back. Studies have found that interactivity in the form of chat rooms and searchable databases is key to a successful Web site. To become listed with a database directory, you'll have to put your site through the application process. While it may take a little time, once this step is complete you can count on increasing your audience.

Consistent updating of content is also an important factor. It seems that today's Web consumers want to stay and visit a while before purchasing. Make sure the information you provide is dynamic and gives your customers a reason to stick around.

THE BOTTOM LINES

- **Accept technology as your personal time savior:** Forget what you've heard about the Y2K bug and its role in the impending Armageddon. The right technology can help your business to no end. Provided you don't go overboard, a good computer, fax machine, and photocopier can be money well spent.

- **Think through your computer needs:** You'll have to pick a side in the Macintosh vs. IBM-compatible computers controversy. Then there are the printing and scanning functions to consider. Remember, all extra functions require extra dollars. Take your needs into account, because what costs more today can save money down the road.

- **Buy or lease a photocopier:** If you require a highly intelligent copier, even a used machine will run you a bundle. You may decide to rent from a variety of rent-an-office-machine establishments until you can afford to buy. Basic photocopiers come with a less intimidating price tag, but depending on your business needs, these sometimes come up short in the performance department.

- **Purchase a fax machine:** In today's day and age, a fax machine is just as important as a telephone. If you don't have at least two numbers to your business name, potential clients will perceive yours to be a smaller-than-small-time operation.

- **Embrace e-mail and the Internet:** If client contact is your goal, e-mail and the Internet can help you achieve immediate results. Keep in mind that if you want to conjure an image of a well-established company, you'll need your own domain. You can contact your Internet service provider to exchange your aol.com or compuserve.com to yourcompany-name.com anytime.

If some of the equipment in this chapter sounds too rich for your start-up fund, don't worry. While you may not be able to get all the business trappings in place from the word go, a time will come when you'll look around your workplace with some measure of satisfaction. For now, concentrate on scraping together the bare necessities. These are the elements of a successful business, and once they're in place, you're well on your way to a twenty-fifth-anniversary celebration.

Part Two

BUSINESS AND PLEASURE: A WINNING COMBINATION

We've based our choice of business ideas on the premise that taking pleasure in your work is the main ingredient in a flourishing venture and the feeling of pride that comes with it. As someone who is just beginning to entertain the idea of entrepreneurship, you may not be aware of all the opportunity laid out before you. The following 100 business options illustrate the endless possibilities of business start-up. Some you can start for as little as $1000; others will run you one thousand times that figure. We've broken this section into two parts; one discusses businesses which take under $20,000 to start, while the other outlines more costly business alternatives.

As writers of *Tripod's* Small Business Brainstorms column, we had a large volume of young, independent-minded readers respond to our articles. Each had a business idea or two to recommend. First, we used this feedback as a springboard to write new Small Business Brainstorms columns; then we decided to compile the information and conduct additional research to write this book.

The overwhelming sentiment of our readers has always been that business should be fun. We agree. The small-business ideas contained within the following pages may not suit all tastes and personality types, but chances are that you'll hit upon one or two new ideas that strike your fancy and suit your budget.

CREATING YOUR OWN
ADVERTISING AGENCY

If you were bitten by the advertising bug while watching *Melrose Place's* Heather Locklear strut her micro miniskirted stuff at Amanda Woodward Advertising, then take our advice and invest your money elsewhere. If, on the other hand, you've been plying the ad trade for some years now, have a good sense of where to start and where you want to go, then far be it from us to try and dissuade you from going into this $138-billion business.

You can choose from a number of roads in this business; cross-promotional, direct mail, television, print, radio, just to name a few. Small businesses and mammoth conglomerates alike need all the help they can get in today's super-competitive market. If you've got creativity to spare, and really know how to turn a catchphrase, then advertising is where you ought to be!

RAKING IN THE DOUGH

Since you're working for yourself, your income is entirely up to you. Typically revenues fall someplace between $30,000 and $80,000 per year, before income taxes. But since no one's looking over your shoulder, your livelihood is at the mercy of your determination to get the job done.

START-UP COSTS

This is a business that is best begun in the home. Once you're making more money, you can safely expand into foreign territory, but that's at the growth stage. Start-up costs shouldn't exceed $15,000, and could even fall as low as $1,000 if you already own a computer system.

HELP IS ON THE WAY

New trends in the business, big events that signal changes to come, awards ceremonies, and industry leaders—these are all things with which you should be familiar. Associations and trade publications can help you do just that.

Associations:

- American Advertising Federation: 202/898-0089
  Washington, D.C.

- American Association of Advertising Agencies: 212/682-2500
  New York, New York

Trade Publications:

- *Advertising Age*: 312/649-5200
  Crain Communications; Chicago, Illinois

- *Adweek*: 212/536-5336
  New York, New York

- *American Demographics*: 607/273-6343
  Ithaca, New York

- *Creative Business*: 617/424-1368
  Boston, Massachusetts

Read All About It:

- *The Advertising Agency Business: The Complete Manual for Management and Operation,* by Eugene J. Hameroff, et. al. NTC Business Books, 1997.

- *How to Start and Run Your Own Advertising Agency* by Alan Krieff. McGraw-Hill, 1992.

MARKET RESEARCH

The best market research in the ad biz is fieldwork. Years of cutting your teeth on large corporate accounts should furnish you with a glossy portfolio and a list of connections. You'll also learn much about yourself, and your preferences, so when the time to go it alone has come, you'll know whether you're interested in pitching your services to auto mechanics, children's stores, or luxury day spas.

One-person ad agencies such as yours typically charge by the hour, by the project, or on a monthly retainer. Rates vary because of a number of factors, such as location, type of client, and whether you're working in radio, print, or television. The average billing rate is $35–$100/hour. That's some broad range—your best bet is to place calls to similar operations, and make some tactful inquiries.

EQUIP YOURSELF

- computer with desktop publishing and presentation software

- laser printer

- fax modem

- photocopier

- fax machine

- dual-line phone system

- expansive and comfortable workstation (desk, ergonomic chair)

- stationery and business cards

GETTING THE WORD OUT

If you're not sure about how to get noticed, then, oh, boy, are you in trouble. Fact is, you're probably an old hand at shedding that spotlight on others. But don't be surprised if you get a case of stage fright now that it's your turn to stand front and center.

Put all those savvy attention-grabbing devices to work for you by:

- listing your name with the local creative directory

- advertising in the Yellow Pages

- networking at trade associations and professional organizations

- putting out ads in trade magazines

- teaching a continuing education advertising course at a local college

BECOMING AN
ART/PHOTOGRAPHY
REPRESENTATIVE

Artists and managers don't often think alike. And if they did, they wouldn't need one another as much as they do. Whereas artists and photographers are high on creativity, they are often running on empty where business and negotiating skills are concerned. Why else would so many of them be starving?

By hiring an art and photography representative, artists can do their thing, secure in the knowledge that someone is looking out for their best financial interests. That's where you come in. As an artists' and photographers' rep, you'll be in constant touch with our society's more sophisticated echelons. But remember, while much of your day may be spent waxing poetic with your clientele and viewing beautiful images, just as much time, if not more, will go to teleconferences with the buyers. So if you're a very easygoing person, with a tough streak to match, you've got what it takes to sell your client's work to art directors everywhere.

RAKING IN THE DOUGH

The biggest determinant of income in this business is the quality of your client list. So select your illustrators and photographers with care. If just one person from your roster becomes a success, you're looking at an income of over $100,000 to $150,000 per year. Don't count on this kind of return in your first year. Since you'll be working on commission, your income during the "talent collection" phase of this business may not exceed $25,000. But just think how much you've got to look forward to.

START-UP COSTS

This business can begin in the home no matter what size your apartment is. You don't even need a jacked-up computer system to make this business tick. In short, you won't require more than $2,000 to start—just make sure you've saved up enough funds to keep food on the table and a roof over your head when times are tough.

HELP IS ON THE WAY

Who knows what constitutes good art? You had better, if you're going to make a serious run at this business. Get in touch with some of the following sources to learn all you can about your future enterprise.

Associations:

- Art Dealers Association of America: 212/940-8590
  New York, New York

- Society of Photographer & Artist Representatives: 212/779-7464
  New York, New York

- Visual Artists & Galleries Association: 212/808-0616
  New York, New York

Trade Publications:

- *Art Direction*: 212/889-6500
  Advertising Trade Publications Inc.; New York, New York

- *The Artist's Magazine*: 513/531-2222
  F & W Publications Inc.; Cincinnati, Ohio

- *Professional Photographer*: 404/522-8600
  PPA Publications & Events Inc.; Atlanta, Georgia

Read All About It:

- *The Photographer's Guide to Marketing and Self-Promotion* by Maria Piscopo, Allworth Press, August 1995

- *Photographer's Market*: 800/289-0963
  Writer's Digest Books, Cincinnati, Ohio

- *Sell and Re-Sell Your Photos* by Ron Engh, Writers Digest Books, May 1997.

MARKET RESEARCH AND LOCATION

Since most publishers, advertising agencies, and magazines are located in large cities, that's where you'll find most professional illustrators and photographers. Teleconferencing and telecommuting aside, you'll want to remain close to your clients and buyers to succeed in this field.

Check out the going rates for photography and illustrating services before you get involved. This is crucial information—never approach a bargaining table without it.

As a representative, charging your clients a flat fee is a no-no. "If you don't get paid, we don't get paid" is the basis for all legitimately successful agents. The exact percentage is something you'll have to determine based on your experience, track record, and the industry standard (usually 20 percent).

EQUIP YOURSELF:

- artist-representative agreement contracts

- high-grade telephone system with voice mail, speaker, and conference options

- fax machine

- slides and composite books filled with high-quality photos of your clients' work

GETTING THE WORD OUT

Artists are a cozy lot. Somehow, somewhere they manage to find each other. And when they get to talking . . . well, let's just say it's hard to stop them. This is why word of mouth plays a major role in your business. One satisfied client is just chatty enough to start a major trend in your direction.

If you're not in cahoots with any promising illustrators or photographers right now, you'll have to hustle to secure both the talent and the hiring squad. First, start building up your client list by advertising your services in their trade magazines and listing your name in their agents' directories. Once you've got a product, beat a hasty path to advertising, book, and magazine trade shows. Bring your artists' portfolio just in case, and give everybody your card. This is a good way to meet your future business contacts, since your work will often take you to art directors' offices as far-flung as New York and Los Angeles, just to peddle your clients' goods.

BECOMING A
BAND MANAGER

This business is perfect for anyone with musical appreciation and an ability to spot a headline act in the making. If you've been around the music scene long enough to know a hot new band from a garage or cover band, you may just have what it takes to make it big in the band management business.

And while it may sound glamorous and exciting to represent up-and-coming bands, you will have your work cut out for you. Dealing with temperamental band musicians, even more temperamental club owners, and having to constantly book new dates can take a toll on even the most energetic person. But if you can recruit top-notch performers with staying power and stick it out with them for the long haul, there's nothing stopping you from reaching gold.

RAKING IN THE DOUGH

As a band manager, you will be shaving around 15 percent off your band's total earnings. That can amount to a significant profit if you happen to represent several bands at a time. Depending on your drive, talent, and ambition, you stand to make anywhere from $15,000 to $100,000.

Another benefit to featuring numerous bands on your roster is that the more bands you represent, the more chances you have of signing with a record label. And 15 percent of those profits can bring in some serious cash flow.

START-UP COSTS

This business can and should be started out of the house at first. Since your primary responsibilities will be booking dates for your bands, you can easily cut costs by running the whole thing in your house. But since you will have to reach into your own back pocket for marketing purposes, expect to invest around $2,000 in the start-up of this business.

HELP IS ON THE WAY

Hopefully, you've taken our advice and learned something about this industry via work experience. But progress doesn't wait for us to catch up, so hear all the latest developments through:

Associations:
- The Recording Industry Association of America (RIAA): 202/775-0101
  Washington, D.C.

Trade Publications:
- *International Musician*: 212/869-1330
  New York, New York

- *Musician*: 212/536-5362
  New York, New York

Read All About It:
- *All You Need to Know About the Music Business* by Donald Passman. Simon and Schuster, 1997.

- *The Billboard Guide to Music Publicity* by Jim Pettigrew. Watson-Guptill Publications, 1993.

- *The Business of Artist Management* by Xavier M. Jr. Frascogna and H. Lee Hetherington. Watson-Guptill Publications, 1995.

- *How to Make and Sell Your Own Record* by Diane Sward Rapaport. Putnam Publishing Group, 1992.

- *This Business of Music* and *More About this Business of Music* by Sidney Shemel and M. William Krasilovsky. Watson-Guptill, 1995.

EQUIP YOURSELF
- computer for scheduling and accounting purposes

- phone system and cellular phone

- business cards and press kits

- fax machine

CAST AND CREW

In this business, you and the musicians you represent are working for each other. While band members like to believe that their manager works for them, you are still in control and will need to treat each musician as a valuable member of your staff.

When choosing a band, remember that musical ability is only the first consideration. You will have to evaluate the band's stamina, cooperation, and general attitude. Since you will be working very closely with these people, you have to make sure they are worth the investment.

GETTING THE WORD OUT

Once you've booked a band to play a venue, you cannot rely solely on the club owner to advertise the performance. You will earn a much better reputation in the business if you contribute to marketing your clients' gigs. You should also encourage band members to spread the word to their friends, family, and acquaintances.

One way to get the word out cheaply is to hang up posters all over town, advertising the band. Make sure you provide each band member with plenty of posters so that you're not stuck doing all the grunt-work.

STARTING YOUR OWN
BOOK PUBLISHING BUSINESS

The publishing business is tough. Competition between large publishing houses is growing, but many smaller publishers are making their way in the industry by selecting a small number of commercially viable titles and/or choosing to specialize in one particular area of interest.

There is absolutely no limit to what you can publish. You can focus on short stories, serious non-fiction, computer books, gift books, fiction from young writers, wedding books, picture books, or comic books. The choices are endless, so if you choose a niche, make sure you have what it takes to compete with other like-minded publishers.

Publishing involves many different jobs. There's acquiring new material, as well as taking care of production, distribution, and sales. So if you're serious about succeeding in this business, you've got your work cut out for you.

RAKING IN THE DOUGH

Depending on how many titles you release each year and your channels of distribution, you can make $20,000 to $120,000 per year. If you plan on distributing through the corporate channels, you can easily make up to $50,000 per year. For educational markets, your profits can total $30,000 to $60,000 each year. But if you're planning on distributing through retail outlets, you can make much more depending on your books' commercial success.

START-UP COSTS

You will need at least $10,000 to start your business. Printing and marketing costs will make up the majority of your expenses in the first year, and will grow considerably once you expand your book line.

HELP IS ON THE WAY

People who love to read do well in this business, especially those who love to read the trades. This multi-faceted business requires that you keep your eyes peeled for new developments. The following sources should prove immensely helpful to anyone trying to get a leg up in the book biz.

Associations:
- American Book Producers Association: 800/209-4575
  New York, New York

- American Booksellers Association: 800/637-0037
  Tarrytown, New York

Trade Publications:
- *Publisher's Weekly*: 800/278-2991
  Cahners Magazines, New York, New York

- *Small Press: The Magazine of Independent Publishing*: 401/789-0074
  Wakefield, Rhode Island

Read All About It:
- *The Book Publishing Industry* by Albert N. Greco. Allyn and Bacon, 1996.

- *How to Make Money Publishing from Home* by Lisa Shaw. Prima Publishing, 1998.

- *LMP: Literary Market Place: The Directory of the American Book Publishing Industry*: R.R. Bowker, Annual.

- *Making It in Book Publishing* by Leonard Mogel. Arco Publications, 1996.

- *You Publish It: How to Start a Home Publishing Company for Under One Hundred Dollars* by Margaret and Robert Cooper. Cooper House Publishing, 1994.

MARKET RESEARCH AND LOCATION
The type of books you plan on publishing will determine your customers' profile. Ask yourself: What kind of people would be interested in my publications? Once you've drawn a mental composite, you can begin planning your marketing campaign.

Your choice of location, however, will not be affected by your audience, since you will have to conduct national marketing campaigns—that is, unless your titles have a regional focus. You can even begin operating right out of your home.

EQUIP YOURSELF

- computer with layout, accounting, and record-keeping software

- copier

- fax machine

- laser printer

- phone system for orders

- office furniture

- promotional material (book catalog, letterhead, etc.)

CAST AND CREW

Many successful publishing companies were started by one person. But as your list of titles gets longer, you may have to hire an assistant to help with orders, distribution, and accounting.

You will also have to establish a working relationship with book distributors and printers who will quickly become an important part of your business's operations.

GETTING THE WORD OUT

Before you can see a profit, you will have to market your books to the right audience. Some basic marketing strategies for book publishers are:

- direct mail

- display ads in general-interest and trade publications

- co-op advertising with other publishers

- submission of books galleys to book clubs and reviewers

- prepublication articles in leading magazines

- television and radio appearances by the author

- press releases to potential buyers and media outlets

STARTING YOUR OWN
CAREER COUNSELING SERVICE

In today's highly competitive marketplace, companies have been cutting expenses left and right. Many people edged out of what were once secure jobs are now reevaluating their career plans. These days, it's no more unusual to find a middle manager changing courses in the midst of a successful career, than it is to find a college sophomore changing majors.

This turn of events has seen career counseling gain tremendous popularity. Besides helping others find financial stability, you will also help them find their true calling.

Counseling centers often offer instruction in interviewing procedures, create resumes, and administer personality assessments. The operators are usually licensed counselors, who teach and lecture on career placement in colleges and vocational services to build their reputation. If you are committed to helping others achieve career success, you are primed and ready to open your very own career counseling center.

RAKING IN THE DOUGH

The amount of money you make will vary depending on whether you lecture and how many clients cross your threshold on a yearly basis. A mid-size center can expect to make $50,000 to $90,000 per year.

START-UP COSTS

Because you'll most likely have to rent a space where clients will come to discuss career plans and target their search, you will need to shell out some shekels on office space. You will also have to market your services to colleges and job placement agencies, which can run you anywhere from $1,000 to $5,000. And when you factor in the cost of outfitting your establishment — couches, tables, carpeting, lighting, career books — you'll find that you'll need $15,000 dollars in start-up capital, at the very least.

HELP IS ON THE WAY

Career counselors have to stay ahead of every industry. You will be required to know the employment statistics for various locations, average salary, advantages and disadvantages, and advancement potential for almost every career imaginable. Seems like a daunting task? Well, don't worry, there following references will keep this information right at your finger tips.

Trade Publications:

- *Career Directions*: 608/884-3367
  Edgerton, Wisconsin

- *Career Success*: 816/781-7557
  Liberty, Missouri

- *Making It!*: 516/829-8829
  Great Neck, New York

Read All About It:

- *Career Choice and Development* by Duane Brown and Linda Brooks. Jossey-Bass Publishers, 1996.

- *Career Selector 2001* by James C. Gonyea. Barrons Educational Series, 1993.

- *The Pathfinder: How to Choose or Change Your Career for a Lifetime of Satisfaction and Success* by Nicholas Lore. Fireside Books, 1998.

EQUIP YOURSELF

Career counselors require the following items to kick-start their own careers:

- career finder software

- educational videos and audiocassettes

- computer for scheduling, bookkeeping, and storing client profiles

- laser printer

- office furniture

- phone system

- fax machine

- copier

MARKET RESEARCH AND LOCATION

We have already said that the majority of your customers will be college graduates and job placement services. But you can also see big profits from targeting high school seniors. Since picking a major is as fraught with difficulty as picking a career, you can help young people make informed decisions about the rest of their lives.

Your best chance of succeeding is to work in a large city. That way, you will gain access to a plethora of local high schools and universities as well as the many employment agencies usually situated in a metropolitan area.

GETTING THE WORD OUT

Once you're ready to begin counseling, you will have to inform local employment agencies, universities, and high schools of your availability. Make appointments with managers of counseling services and agencies, and inform them of the benefits of your service. Dazzle them with your expertise, and they may send a steady stream of business your way. You should also visit college preparatory centers and make sure to post up a flier describing your services.

Another solid customer-generator is to take out either a small ad or display ad in the classifieds. Job seekers will be sure to notice and will seek out your invaluable assistance.

BECOMING A
FULL-TIME CARTOONIST/ ILLUSTRATOR

Professional cartoonists have been struggling to amuse Americans for hundreds of years now. From the original political cartoons to Lichtenstein's comic-strip art works to today's "Far Side" and "Dilbert" mania, cartoons have proven that they have the power to both influence and entertain millions of people. Just ask which section most people first turn to when reviewing their daily paper. A majority will proudly admit to being avid comic readers.

As a cartoonist, you can either write and draw your own comic strip, or partner up with a writer, if your pen isn't exactly mightier than a sword. Besides syndicated cartoon strips, illustrators have a variety of opportunities to make a living. They can illustrate books and magazines, design T-shirts and company logos, or publish their own comic books. So if you can truly work wonders with pencil and paper, get ready to make this business into a miraculous success story.

RAKING IN THE DOUGH

The only downside to becoming a professional cartoonist is that your income may be unstable. You can make up to $60,000 one year and only $15,000 the next. The key to making this business work on a consistent basis is to try to obtain syndication or work for an established organization.

START-UP COSTS

To get your business up and running you will need at least $3,000 in start-up capital. Depending on your marketing needs, you may require up to $10,000 for a blitz campaign.

HELP IS ON THE WAY

You will have to network with many like-minded professionals to stay on top of new ideas and industry trends. Here are a couple to start you off:

Associations:

- Cartoonists Northwest: 206/226-7623
  Seattle, Washington

- National Cartoonists Society: 212/627-1550
  New York, New York

- Society of Illustrators: 212/838-2560
  New York, New York

Read All About It:

- *The Business of Illustration* by Steven Heller and Teresa Fernandes. Watson-Guptill Publications, 1995.

- *How to Be a Successful Cartoonist* by Randy Glasberger. North Light Books, 1996.

EQUIP YOURSELF

- computer with peripherals

- drafting table and stool

- drawing utensils

- graphic design software

- phone system

- fax machine

LEARN TO EARN

If you're looking to obtain permanent-resident status in the cartoonist marketplace, you will most likely have to undergo some professional design and art courses. Even the most innately talented cartoonist could benefit from formal training of some kind. Your work will probably reflect that extra bit of professionalism, and potential clients will be sure to appreciate that.

GETTING THE WORD OUT

You should also send samples of your work to greeting card companies, book publishers, T-shirt companies, magazines, and newspapers. The key to longevity in this business is to consistently sell your talent and ability to prospective employers.

There are no better places than publishing trade shows, seminars, and association events to market yourself. What's more, you will be able to exchange vital information with other cartoonists/illustrators and make key connections in your field.

CALLING THE SHOTS AS A
CASTING DIRECTOR

If you're looking for a high-powered position, you're in the right place. The people who gave rise to the infamous "casting couch" carry quite a bit of clout in the entertainment industry—at least as far as actors and their agents are concerned.

But there's also much responsibility and hard work that goes along with this business, as you're only as good as your last job. A solid reputation is no guarantee of success. There's always another casting agency only too happy to muscle in on your action. Constant finagling and finessing is required to make sure you're on the inside track to your next meal ticket.

In spite of the pressure-cooker atmosphere, this business is a great idea for anyone with a penchant for the entertainment industry. If you've worked in the field for some time—whether it be as a casting associate, a producer, or even a location manager—and can boast a Rolodex full of industry contacts, you're already off to an auspicious beginning.

RAKING IN THE DOUGH

Don't expect those contracts to start pouring in tout de suite. Doubtless you'll have to survive a dry season, but after a few years building your business you stand to earn as much as $80,000 or more each year.

START-UP COSTS

Surprisingly, you won't need a ton of cash to bankroll this business. If you snag your first contract before investing in office space, you can finance the whole operation with the money you're afforded up front. The entire outfit shouldn't take more than $20,000 to set up, and can cost as little as $10,000.

HELP IS ON THE WAY

If you're not reading the trades, you're not in on the late-breaking news stories. And in the cutthroat casting business, if you're not bidding for a contract from minute one, you're in a too-little-too-late situation. Don't get left out when the funds are being allocated; see these sources and pounce when the getting is good.

Trade Publications:

- *Hollywood Reporter*: 213/525-2000
  Los Angeles, California

- *Location Update*: 213/461-8887
  Hollywood, California

- *Variety*: 213/857-6600
  Los Angeles, California

Read All About It:

- *All You Need to Know About the Movie and TV Business* by Gail Resnick and Scott Trost. Fireside, Feb. 1996

- "Blu-Book Production Directory," *Hollywood Reporter*. Jan. 1999

- *Film Producers, Studios, Agents, and Casting Directors Guide.* Lone Eagle Publishing Comnpany, Sept. 1999

- *Starring John Wayne as Genghis Khan: Hollywood's All-Time Worst Casting Blunders* by Damien Bona. Citadel Press, 1996.

Web Resources:

- Extras Casting (*www.extrascasting.com*) Directory of extras for casting directors

- Cast-a-Head (*www.castahead.com*) Actors' headshots, resumes, audio and video files for casting

MARKET RESEARCH AND LOCATION

Since all of your income will come from film, video, and commercial production companies, don't even consider going into business in a remote location. Still, the movie business isn't just about "Hollywood or Bust." While this used to be the case, bigger budgets and higher audience expectations have led movie producers to Seattle, Chicago, and Miami, as well as a host of other show business–friendly towns. So it's possible for your business to thrive in any similar area.

But first you've got some work to do—namely, in the form of film and commercial production research. You'll have to come up with answers to questions such as: Which casting directors have local and out-of-state production companies and advertising agencies worked with in the past? Have they had any problems with previous contractors? What can you do to add value to the job of casting, and differentiate yourself from the competition?

As a casting director, you are in the position of an independent contractor. The producer, network, or ad agency will hire you on a flat fee basis (ranging from approximately $4,000 to $5,000). In return, you will be required to fulfill your contractual obligation, and cast the designated roles to the hiring company's satisfaction. But since initial assignments are hard to come by, don't balk at anything under $5,000 when you're first starting out. Old-proverb time: You must learn how to crawl before you can walk.

EQUIP YOURSELF
- computer with fax/modem and necessary software
- fax machine
- multiple phone lines
- video and camera equipment
- office and lobby furniture
- office equipment

GETTING THE WORD OUT
Work those connections! That's your only successful marketing strategy. A listing in the creative directory is all well and good, but trust us, no producer worth his million-dollar budget ever found a casting director flipping through the phone book. It just doesn't happen.

This is where the value of industry background comes into play. If you're a total stranger to this junior-high-clique-y field, an outsider looking in is all you'll ever be. Every contact is worth its weight in gold, so wine 'em and dine 'em, but make sure they put in a good word on your behalf. Often that's all it takes to get a fair hearing from the money man or woman.

OPENING UP A
CHILD DAY CARE CENTER

All those hours of babysitting in junior high don't have to go to waste. If you go gaga for cute little tots, then you may just have what it takes to make it in the child-care biz full-time. And when you consider that the demand for day-care services is growing with every passing year, your decision to open just such a facility may be a very sound one.

With the meteoric rise of the women's movement, more and more women are taking it to the work world. That's good news for you. Because when there's tikes to be cared for, you'll be just the person for the job.

RAKING IN THE DOUGH
Depending on whether you opt for a small, in-home day-care service or a large facility with a significant number of child-care workers, you can make anywhere from $20,000 to $90,000+ per year.

START-UP COSTS
This business can cost you a bundle if you're planning to open a large-scale facility. With the cost of recreation materials, space, insurance, and marketing being what it is today, you will need at least $30,000 on hand to get your center off the ground.

For smaller enterprises, you'll have to fork over much less. Somewhere from $2,000 to $10,000.

HELP IS ON THE WAY
Is taking candy from a baby really as easy as they say? Don't you believe it. Get the real dish from:

Trade Publications:
- *Day Care and Early Education*: 212/620-8000
  Northampton, Massachusetts

- *Early Childhood News:* 513/847-5900
  Dayton, Ohio

- *Early Childhood Today:* 212/505-4900
  New York, New York

Read All About It:
- *Profitable Child Care: How to Start and Run a Successful Business* by Nan Lee Hawkins and Heidi Rosenholtz. Facts on File, 1993.

- *Start Your Own Childcare Business* by Dawn Kilgore. Prentice Hall Trade, 1996.

FRANCHISE ALTERNATIVES

Opening a franchise can be a good way to begin your foray into child-care waters. Not only will you receive full training, you may also be eligible for financial assistance. These organizations will require you to fork over a small percentage of gross sales, but are fairly affordable, with start-up fees ranging anywhere from $20,000 to $40,000.

- Lollipop Lane, Inc.: 602/953-6682
  Phoenix, Arizona

- Primrose Schools Educational Child Care: 404/998-8329
  Marietta, Georgia

- Tutor Time: 800/275-1235
  Fort Lauderdale, Florida

MARKET RESEARCH AND LOCATION

The best way to determine the community's child-care needs is to call other child-care centers and ask them about enrollment. If the majority of centers have a waiting list or are booked solid, your facility may be just the answer to many parents' prayers. Another way to gauge the money-making potential of your target area is to call schools and other social organizations, asking about the number of working parents in their district.

Once you've settled on an area, you will have to find a space conducive to housing large groups of children. Spaces with an adjacent outdoor areas are prime child-care property. Parents will be more than comforted by the notion of their child playing in the fresh air.

LICENSE AND INSURANCE

When you're taking care of kids, protection is the name of the game. A general-liability package is a must-have for every child-care facility operator. Every state has different licensing requirements, so contacting your state's local licensing office is essential.

EQUIP YOURSELF

- computer system for accounting purposes, client database, and medical information

- child-sized furniture and cots for nap time

- toys and other safe games

- musical equipment

- mini-frigidaires for snacks

GETTING THE WORD OUT

The best time to start marketing your day-care center is in the summer, when the children are out of school. That will give parents ample time to check out your business and enroll their child before school begins.

Advertising in newspapers and hanging up fliers all over town is a good way to target the busy parent on the go. Once you are contacted, emphasize the center's safety precautions and the learning environment you plan to foster.

CAST AND CREW

Make sure there is at least one caretaker for every group of seven children. A well-trained staff is key to your company's success. And most importantly, educate your workers in accident prevention, first aid, and CPR.

STARTING YOUR OWN
DATING SERVICE

Classified ads, Internet chat rooms, and video dating all have one thing in common. Print, techno, video, and telecommunications mediums may be diverse as night and day, but all realize the fiscal felicity of nabbing a chunk of America's largest-growing demographic—single people. Even before the premiere of *Married . . . With Children*, the number of unmarried folk has been on the rise. When you consider that nearly 50 percent of the entire American population is living à la solitary confinement, is it any surprise that dating services have been raking in a steady stream of funds?

SWM, DWF, DBM, SBW, SWJM. Get the picture? Dating via special services has reached mammoth proportions. An entire language has been coined to serve these lovelorn throngs. There is ample room in the market for anyone whose got matchmaking on the mind. Imagine what fun you could have playing professional cupid: screening prospective clients, deciding who's best suited for whom, seeing the elation of a newly married pair you've brought together. What could be better? There are scores of people who live to set up their lonely-heart friends, with nothing but the couples' eternal gratitude as their reward. Well, thank-yous need no longer be your sole compensation. These days providing a dating service is an even more rewarding occupation, both financially and emotionally.

RAKING IN THE DOUGH
Annual revenues for a dating service can range anywhere from $50,000 to $500,000. Expect to break even in 4 months to 2 years, depending on the size of your initial investment. Sales will vary depending on the location of your office and number of clients.

START-UP COSTS
Depending on how ornate you want to get, or how snazzy a location you wish to occupy, your initial investment can be as low as $15,000 or as high

as $100,000+. Hint: Unless you've got a foolproof gimmick and financial backing galore, postpone investing in the deluxe office suite with panoramic views until your business proves profitable.

HELP IS ON THE WAY

So far as business go, matchmaking is a bit on the wacky side. A novice in the dating game can learn about ethical business practices through:

Associations:

- International Society of Introduction Services: 818/222-1367 West Hills, California

MARKET RESEARCH AND LOCATION

Where you pitch your tent will depend greatly on an area's concentration of singles. To find out the hottest zones for solo living check with the Census Bureau, the community newspapers, and the public library. Now what about the competition? How many dating services are located in that area? Is there enough business to fuel more than one service? And lastly, what will distinguish your dating service from the rest?

It's obvious that large metropolitan areas have a greater percentage of single dwellers, but an office in a posh neighborhood can cost a pretty penny. Those of you with a smaller stash of start-up capital who still want to target these areas should consider setting up shop in less expensive commercial zones. Yes, that means pounding the pavement to find the best deal. But don't go too far off the beaten track. A safe neighborhood and a nearby parking lot will make the majority of your clientele, namely women, feel more comfortable and, as a result, more apt to seek out your matchmaking services.

LICENSE AND INSURANCE

Contacting an accountant as well as a lawyer will save you oodles of time when it comes to meeting the federal and other tax requirements, filling out the requisite documents, and setting up an efficient accounting system. Once you've handled these matters, you'll need to find out about obtaining health and property insurance as well as a federal employer identification number. It may take some time to lay this dull business to rest, but when all is said and done, you won't regret what you did for love.

IMAGE MATTERS AND EQUIPMENT

Spare no expense in designing your office. Putting on the ritz may just pay off in the end. And if an affluent clientele is what you're after, there's just no other way to go. Aside from a large space, you'll also need state-of-the-art video and/or computer equipment, and a sophisticated interior design.

Another factor to consider when designing your office is the comfort levels of your customers. Most people may feel intimidated or frightened when joining a dating service for the first time. It will be your and the decor's job to make them feel right at home. Keep your video equipment safely tucked away in a separate room, so customers do not get scared at the prospect of being videotaped. The design of your office should make your clients comfortable. Rich velvet couches, muted wallpaper, and traditional furniture will enable them to relax. An assortment of magazines, from *The New Yorker* to *Elle*, should divert the anxiety-ridden, and get them breathing easier. To put your clients at the pinnacle of ease, you may even consider serving up tea and coffee.

THE PRICE IS RIGHT

Who can put a price tag on love? Well, you can, that's who. Some dating services charge a one-time registration fee, while others follow a pay-as-you-go policy. If you charge a one-time fee of $700 to $2,500, you can be sure to attract wealthy individuals. But if not enough upper-bracket singles reside in your area, you may just have to go back to setting up your friends. The most effective method of setting a price for your services is to check out the competitors' rates in your area.

CAST AND CREW

A dating service can easily be operated with a small staff. Most services are run by the owners themselves with only a few other employees. To give your service a first-class feel, you should look into hiring a friendly receptionist to meet and greet your clients upon arrival. An assistant to help with filing and other clerical tasks will also come in handy. But don't attempt to fly solo if you're going to be offering videotaping services to clients. You'll have to hire individuals with technical expertise to create professional-looking videos. Your clients will expect top-drawer clips for their money.

GETTING THE WORD OUT

A steady stream of recruits is the lifeblood of your business. In the world of dating services, reputation and reliability are the buzzwords of success. But you'll have to attract your initial group of clients in order to display your matchmaking prowess. First, decide on the target age; there are the twenty- and thirtysomething sets, divorced singles, and senior citizens. Remember not to spread yourself too thin by trying to cater to every group. If you're chasing down the young single, you'll have to advertise in different publications than if you were going after the senior citizens. Your marketing campaign will have to be tailored to a specific demographic in order to bring in results.

Generating interest can be difficult, especially when you're first starting out. Special membership deals are a popular method of acquiring a clientele. A free trial membership, a "pay half now, half when married" offer, or two-clients-for-the-price-of-one specials are all solid ways for you to get your dating service noticed. Once you've roped some converts into benefiting from your know-how, you can let your matchmaking skills go to work and prove, once and for all, that if singledom is the problem, you're the solution.

START A
DETECTIVE AGENCY

Sure, Mike Hammer was cool, and boy, did Agatha Christie have her clues together, but if your ideas of detective work are even remotely similar to those of Sir Arthur Conan Doyle, your pursuit may prove nothing but a wild-goose chase.

Private investigation no longer centers around the romance of Scotland Yard fieldwork. Most of it involves the very technical, very practical PC. Yes, skillful turns on the Web and a sweet-talking phoneside manner can get you info even J. Edgar would have bugged for. So, if you can adjust your *Moonlighting*-inspired fantasy to working on cases of insurance fraud, missing persons, and background checks, then you're on the right track.

RAKING IN THE DOUGH

The money you make will depend upon the type of service you provide. Because private investigation can range from actual surveillance work, stake-outs and all, to things as simple as credit checks, the fees can vary dramatically. Once you establish a loyal clientele, you can expect to see a take-home of $25,000 to $100,000 per year.

START-UP COSTS

Here's the real good news since you don't need a lot of fancy equipment, and can work from your home sweet home, your business can be up and running for under $10,000. HELLO?! Did anyone just hear "credit limit"?

HELP IS ON THE WAY

Need a crash course in detecting, or just looking to lay your paws on some newfangled, James Bond–style gadgets? Get the whole skinny from these associations, trade zines, and guidebooks.

Associations:

- Council of International Investigators (CII): 215/540-0528
  Ambler, Pennsylvania

- National Association of Investigative Specialists (NAIS): 512/719-3595
  Austin, Texas

Trade Publications:

- *Database Directory*: 914/328-9157
  White Plains, New York

- *Directory of Online Databases*: 800/347-GALE

Read All About It:

- *Be Your Own Dick: Private Investigating Made Easy* by John Q. Newman. Loompanics Unlimited, 1993.

- *Entrepreneur's Start-Up Guide: Private Investigator*. Entrepreneur Publications.

- *How to Make $100,000 a Year as a Private Investigator* by Edmund J. Pankau. Paladin Press, 1993.

- *Introduction to Private Investigation: Essential Knowledge and Procedures for the Private Investigator* by Joseph Travers. Charles C. Thomas Publications, 1997.

- *Private Investigation: Methods and Materials* by Frank J. MacHovec. C.C. Thomas, 1991.

- *Undercover Operations: A Manual for the Private Investigator* by Peter Anderson. Citadel, 1991.

MARKET RESEARCH

This will be your first mission as a private investigator. But this time you'll be working for yourself. You'll need to dig around in your own backyard to determine what sort of specialization will be most profitable. Would the private sector prove most lucrative, or should you limit your work to background checks for large corporations and attorneys? You'll find that most affluent areas can fill your plate with assignments from both companies and individuals.

LICENSE AND INSURANCE

While not all states will throw the book at you for not getting licensed, you should look into it ASAP if you're serious about running a successful business. Lawyers and the government will most often steer clear of unlicensed investigators, as will educated consumers who expect professionals to come complete with some form of certification.

EQUIP YOURSELF

The Basics

- computer with printer and fax/modem

- photocopier

- business telephone line with voice mail

- ergonomically correct work space (desk, chair, keyboard)

Surveillance Necessities

- state-of-the-art camera

- tape recorder

- camcorder

- binoculars

- some clever disguises (phony mustache, shades, and the like)

GETTING THE WORD OUT

Once you settle on your specialization—be it finding facts, people, or indiscretions—you must decide how to lure the prospective customers to your den. The Yellow Pages is always a good start. Neither will fair-pricing practices hurt your business any. This is your cue to hop to it, and check the fees of competing private investigators. There is no harm in slightly underselling yourself at the beginning—once you've hooked yourself some takers, you can up the ante considerably.

But don't stop there. Direct-mail advertising can work wonders. Networking with other PI's may just net you some referrals. What's more, you can work some public-relations magic by calling the media and informing them of what it is you do, and why it is of human interest.

STARTING YOUR OWN
MOBILE DISC JOCKEY SERVICE

Weddings, anniversaries, bar and bat mitzvahs, night clubs . . . imagine all the fun you can be having cracking your tunes for a festive crowd of party-goers. Besides the obvious perks—flexible schedule, meeting new people, and playing your music as loudly as you want—starting your own disc jockey service with one or more DJ's can be an exciting way to make a living.

Provided you have a knack for mixing it up and have been practicing your DJ skills for several years, you can expect to become a successful entrepreneur. Effective marketing, a killer presentation, and state-of-the-art equipment are really all that are standing between you and a thriving DJ enterprise.

RAKING IN THE DOUGH

Solo DJ's with a steady stream of business can expect to make from $25,000 to $50,000 per year. Organizations with two or more DJ's can handle more events, and will, as a result, reap more money. These multi-DJ companies can bring in anywhere from $70,000 to $130,000 per year.

START-UP COSTS

The high price of stereo equipment will be reflected in your start-up costs. You should be ready with at least $10,000 on hand to spend on start-up necessities. If you already have a large inventory of music, reliable equipment, as well as a trusty vehicle that will get you from one gig to the next, your start-up costs can total as low as $1,000 for office equipment and promotional literature.

HELP IS ON THE WAY

You may know all there is to know about dance music, but the following sources pick up where your repertoire leaves off:

Association:

- American Disc Jockey Association: 609/978-2180
  Manahawkin, New Jersey

- Disc Jockey Association: 610/929-4315
  Reading, Pennsylvania

Trade Publications:

- *DJ Times*: 516/767-9335
  Port Washington, New York

Read All About It:

- *Mobile DJ Business Guide*, Entrepreneur Publications.

- *The Mobile DJ Handbook: How to Start and Run a Profitable Mobile Disc Jockey Service* by Stacy Zemon. Focal Press, 1991.

MARKET RESEARCH AND LOCATION

The relatively low cost of starting your own DJ service can be attributed to low overhead. To run your musical enterprise, you will only need a small room in your house with an extra phone line for business calls. You will, however, have to find an area to store your sound system. A used van can do double duty by housing your equipment and getting you where you want to be.

No matter where you're located, one thing is always a given—people will always have parties. So unless your services are out of the prevalent price range, there won't be any shortage of business. Make sure you're not on the exorbitant side of the fee spectrum by calling successful DJ's and asking about their rates.

EQUIP YOURSELF

Depending on how much cash you have to invest, you can buy used equipment or lease it until your business is on surer footing. Equipment you just can't do without includes:

- turntables

- mixers

- amplifiers

- speakers

- a variety of music selections; on either records or CD's

Optional equipment includes:

- An advanced light system to complement your music

GETTING THE WORD OUT

Listing your service in the Yellow Pages is a good start. But the majority of your customers will come from word-of-mouth advertising. To secure your first group of loyal customers, leave your card with wedding consultants, flower shops, banquet halls, and synagogues.

You can also send out a direct-mail package describing your DJ expertise and reliability. Promise them an event they'll never forget, include a special discount coupon, and wait for the phone to start ringing.

STARTING YOUR OWN
EDITORIAL SERVICE

A knack for the written word and the ability to catch even the subtlest of printed errors is all you'll need to start your own writing/editorial service bureau. There is an enormous amount of opportunity for communication-savvy entrepreneurs in today's market.

Once you think about the amount of printed material being produced every day—newsletters, direct-mail packages, annual reports, sales letters, training manuals, press releases, book-packaging copy—you'll understand why a well-positioned editorial service can become very successful.

RAKING IN THE DOUGH

A well-established service with several corporate accounts can bring in any-where from $40,000 to $100,000 per year. You should also consider that certain projects pay better than others. For example, you can charge much higher prices for a marketing piece than a regular editorial project. Some veteran direct-mail writers make up to $25,000 per project.

START-UP COSTS

Since many start-up editorial services operate from a home office, your initial investment will be very low. Depending on the equipment you already own and your client prospects, you can start for as low as $3,000. Those of you who'll need to start from scratch—buying equipment and launching a marketing campaign—will require around $7,000 to get your business off the ground.

HELP IS ON THE WAY

While much of your business may be conducted in solitary confinement behind closed doors, you'll not have anything to occupy your time with if you don't know how to network. Picking up key contacts is an art form all its own, and here's where you can start:

Trade Associations:
- Association of Editorial Business: 202/543-1800
  Washington, D.C.

- Editorial Freelancers Association: 212/677-3357
  New York, New York

Read All About It:
- *Chicago Manual of Style: The Essential Guide for Writers, Editors, and Publishers.* Univ. of Chicago Press, 1993.

- *Copy Editing: A Practical Guide* by Karen Judd. Crisp Publications, 1992.

- *Editorial Freelancing: A Practical Guide* by Trumbell Rogers. Aletheia Publications, 1995.

- *How to Start and Run a Writing and Editing Business* by Herman Holtz. John Wiley and Sons, 1995.

- *The Literary Marketplace: The Directory of the American Book Publishing Industry.* R.R. Bowker.

- *The Writer's Market.* Writer's Digest Books.

EQUIP YOURSELF
- a computer system with fax/modem and word processing software

- business phone line

- fax machine

- business cards

- desk and ergonomically correct chair

GETTING THE WORD OUT
Before you determine your marketing strategy, you should decide which writing and editorial niche you wish to fill. If becoming a freelance writer is your main concern, you should decide whether you want to write articles for magazines, books, or promotional material for other companies. Once you've settled that issue, proceed to mail pitch-letters to each company with samples of your writing.

If you plan on running a strictly editorial business, you should strive to secure customers such as catalog producers, publishers, and advertising firms. You can make calls to the head of each creative department and/or send your promotional material and resume.

For technical writers and editors, you will be targeting specific industries and organizations. Make sure you're up on any relevant terminology before you try handling these often complex assignments.

While direct-mail and schmooze campaigns are often most effective, there's still more you can do to generate business. Listing your service in the Yellow Pages, the local creative directories, and *The Literary Marketplace* can also bring paying customers to your door.

LEARN TO EARN

- Work at an advertising firm, PR firm, or publishing house to enhance your writing and editorial skills.

- Enroll in copywriting and editorial courses.

- Develop a portfolio of your best work to pique the interest of clients.

OPERATING YOUR OWN
EXECUTIVE SEARCH FIRM

Entrepreneurs with hearts of gold, listen up: Finding jobs for out-of-work executives is a task worthy of Mother Teresa herself. And boy, is this business ever booming! With the nineties' downsizing frenzy, there are more displaced VP's needing your services than ever before.

But that's not all. Corporations are also realizing the value of executive-search firms. Now that their human resources departments are streamlined to bare-bones status, companies are outsourcing the recruitment work to head-hunters just like you.

So there you have it—a verifiable need for your services. All that's left is to take the plunge, and watch the hearty compensation catapult you straight into the arms of an early retirement.

RAKING IN THE DOUGH

Are you ready for this? A self-motivated entrepreneur can easily make six figures running with the headhunters. The average salary will fall someplace in the range of $90,000 to $150,000.

START-UP COSTS

You've heard the rule: "It takes money to make money." But every rule has its exceptions—and this one is no exception. You can actually set up this mint of a venture on minimal capital, right out of your studio apartment. Start-up costs start at $2,000 (assuming you already own a computer system) and max out at $15,000.

HELP IS ON THE WAY

You probably know who's hot in Hollywood; unfortunately, that's none of your business. Your work lies in the realm of job placement, so get to know it! Find out which areas of the market are growing, and you may just find yourself a breadwinning niche.

Associations:

- The Association of Executive Search Consultants: 212/398-9556
  New York, New York

- National Association of Executive Recruiters: 800/726-5613
  Altamonte Springs, Florida

- National Association of Personnel Services: 703/684-0180
  Alexandria, Virginia

Trade Publications:

- *Executive Recruiter News*: 603/585-2200
  Kennedy & Kennedy, Inc.; Fitzwilliam, New Hampshire

- *Recruitment Today*: 714/751-1883
  Costa Mesa, California

- *Recruiting Trends*: 312/332-3571
  Chicago, Illinois

Read All About It:

- *The Executive Search Collaboration: A Guide for Human Resource Professionals and Their Search Firms* by Janet Jones-Parker. Robert H. Perry, 1990.

MARKET RESEARCH AND LOCATION

Before you start hunting, take some time for gathering. You'll need to lay your hands on some serious information before you can pass go and collect your $200. Take working from your home as an example. Sure it's fine if you live in or around a metropolis, but it's far from satisfactory if the only business within fifty miles of you is a highway oasis that includes both a Shell and a McDonald's. You get the picture? Population size counts. As does its profile, so hit the books to see where your area stacks up.

Another reason to hit those books is the fee scale. Picking numbers at random is liable to land you right back at the Department of Employment Security. Call other headhunters to get a sense for what you should charge. While some recruiters work for their client companies on a retainer, you'll most likely find that most executive search firms work on contingency. This means that they charge a percentage-based finder's fee—usually between 25 to 30 percent of the new-hire's first year's salary—which is only paid upon the client company's acceptance of the candidate.

And while we're on the subject, it is a wise fledgling entrepreneur who uses the resources provided in this book. It is imperative that you know your industry inside out and upside down, so sidle up to a trade magazine and peruse the night away.

EQUIP YOURSELF

- computer, fax modem, printer, Internet server hookup

- accounting and database management programs

- fax machine

- two phone lines and voice mail

- ergonomically correct office furniture

- company stationery, business cards

- promotional material

GETTING THE WORD OUT

Calling prospective clients and pitching your services via telephone is just one popular means of finagling business. Others include:

- advertising in the telephone directory, the Internet, and any existing business directories

- networking at trade shows

- putting out help-wanted ads

- direct mail of pamphlets/brochures to potential client companies

STARTING YOUR OWN
FACSIMILE TRANSMISSION SERVICE

Communicating by fax is definitely here to stay. A faster, more reliable, and cheaper method of exchanging information has yet to be developed. The reduced prices of fax machines have ensured that no office need go without one.

Practically any document, whether it be a graph, report, photo, or order form can be processed by fax. Opening your own fax service bureau can reap substantial profits for any entrepreneur. In 1995, fax service revenues reached an astounding $1.2 billion, and analysts predict consistent growth in the future. And since most people couldn't live without their trusty fax machine, your business is bound to thrive.

RAKING IN THE DOUGH

A facsimile transmission service can provide up to $100,000 per year, with average profits coming in at $35,000 for smaller operations. Business-to-business services can reap even a larger, steadier income, since you'll be handling a large bulk of transmissions over longer periods of time.

START-UP COSTS

Depending on whether you choose to set up a conventional copy/fax service shop or work out of your home or a small office providing only mass faxing services to businesses, your start-up costs can range from as low as $5,000 to $50,000.

HELP IS ON THE WAY

Joining a trade association will allow you to receive up-to-date information on your chosen industry. When it comes to new developments in facsimile technology, you want to stay as far ahead as possible.

Associations:
- American Facsimile Association: 215/875-0975
  Philadelphia, Pennsylvania

- International Facsimile Association: 602/453-3850
  Lake Havasu, Arizona

Trade Publications:
- *Fax Facts*: 513/772-5057
  Cincinnati, Ohio

- *Faxreporter*: 201/488-0404
  Hackensack, New Jersey

MARKET RESEARCH AND LOCATION

When you're contemplating an ideal locale for your fax service, consider the three options available to fax service entrepreneurs. You can either set up a fax station (at a copy shop, hotel, airport, or convenience store), use your house, or open your print/copy shop and conduct your business from there. Your strategy will be determined by how much start-up capital you have to invest.

If you do opt to open a copy shop, highly trafficked commercial zones will bring in a good share of walk-ins. Local residents will also get in on the act. Help get these long-term customers in the door by hanging up a large, bold sign bearing your company logo, and offering competitive prices for all facsimile and copy services.

EQUIP YOURSELF

If you're planning on offering mass fax services out of your home, you'll require special faxing software as well as a high-speed modem. You may also require multiple phone lines or a T-1 line for faster transmission.

For a small copy/fax shop, you'll need a cash register, a variety of paper, several computer systems, at least two fax machines, and laser copiers. If you're worried about exceeding your start-up budget, you should consider leasing copiers and fax machines until you can afford to buy.

GETTING THE WORD OUT

Mass faxing services tend to target large businesses that market heavily over the fax. Telemarketers, social organizations, and PR firms rely on mass fax broadcasting servers to spread the word about their products, clients, and services. Contacting large companies such as these, and offering reasonable rates for large broadcasts, can secure you several lucrative corporate accounts. Many industry newsletters are also sent out via fax. Contact the owners of these publications with an offer they can't refuse. Once you're established, you can raise your prices to reflect the quality of your service.

A small shop or a fax booth can be advertised effectively with a catchy logo and slogan. Hire a graphic designer to create an eye-catching sign. You can also advertise your shop by hanging large "special offer" signs in the windows and using conventional print methods.

STARTING YOUR OWN
GENEALOGY SERVICE

Have you ever wondered about the identity of your ancestors, or wanted to trace the origins of your family several centuries back? More and more, people are looking to find out where they came from. Whether it's a need for a cultural affiliation or just a nagging curiosity about their family tree, people are signing up with genealogists in order to trace their lineage. Even major corporations are looking to trace their roots, and are hiring professional corporate genealogists to trace the history of their parent founding companies.

Writing ability is key in this business. If you want to succeed in the future, you must know how to write clear and interesting reports about what you found in the past.

While writing is certainly a top-drawer concern, a love of research is the first golden rule of genealogy. You'll have to dig through archives for hours on end—often in decidedly deluxe-less accommodations. But who needs the light of day? If you truly enjoy this type of work, every moment spent searching the annals will constitute a step towards enlightenment.

RAKING IN THE DOUGH

If you have steady business from individual customers, you can make up to $30,000 per year. But if you're lucky enough to secure valuable corporate accounts, that figure can skyrocket all the way up to $55,000.

You can also make more money by creating attractive presentations for your histories, and charging extra for this added benefit.

START-UP COSTS

This business has work-at-home written all over it. As most genealogists conduct their business right out of the house, start-up expenses can be fairly low—around $3,000 to $10,000.

HELP IS ON THE WAY

An aspiring genealogist would do well to take some professional courses in library sciences. But if you're in need of a quick solutions to any problem, consult these reliable resources.

Trade Publications:
- *Family Chronicle*: 800/FAM-CHRO
  Lewiston, New Jersey

Read All About It:
- *Becoming an Accredited Genealogist: Plus 100 Tips to Ensure Your Success* by Karen Clifford. Ancestry Inc., 1998.

- *The Everything Family Tree Book*, by William G. Hartley. Adams Media, 1998.

- *The Genealogists Companion and Sourcebook* by Emily Anne Croom. Betterway Books, 1991.

- *The Researcher's Guide to American Genealogy* by Val D. Greenwood. Genealogical Publishing, 1990.

- *Writing Family Histories and Memoirs* by Kirk Polking. Betterway Books, 1995.

EQUIP YOURSELF
- computer with modem and internet software

- fax machine

- office furniture

- promotional material

GETTING THE WORD OUT

You will have to be as thorough in your marketing as your family and corporate research. Some tactics that have worked for other like-minded genealogists include:

- direct-mail promotions to corporate executives and families

- distribution of flyers and brochures

- sending press releases and obtaining editorial coverage

BECOMING A
GIFT-BASKET RETAILER

Gift baskets make for great presents when making a good impression is important, but the time to shop around for that perfect gift is scarce. Not only are such gifts a feast for the eyes, they also contain a variety of goodies that's sure to please even the toughest customers. Gift-basket retailers have been making a killing in the market for the past 15 years.

Running your own gift-basket service can be an interesting and rewarding experience. If you have an eye for clever arrangements, have a small start-up fund, and a little marketing savvy, you can turn this venture into the little business that could.

RAKING IN THE DOUGH

As a gift-basket provider you have two options: You can either work out of the house through mail order, or set up a small shop where customers can select the items they want included. Working out of the home, you can expect to gross around $35,000 to $70,000 per year, making more as you learn more about the art of selling your wares.

But even these ample figures are dwarfed by the profits reported by retailers with shops in busy commercial thoroughfares. These storefront owners report grossing anywhere from $150,000 to $400,000 per year.

START-UP COSTS

Home-based business owners can start their business on $2,000 to $10,000. Shop owners will need at least $40,000 to begin operating.

HELP IS ON THE WAY

There are several helpful resources available for your gift-basket needs. Consult these valuable advisors, and you'll have the lowdown on vita trade secrets.

Associations:
- Gifts and Decorative Accessories Association of America: 212/689-4411
  New York, New York

Trade Publications:
- *Gift Basket Review*: 904/634-1902
  Jacksonville, Florida

- *Gifts and Decorative Accessories*: 212/689-4411
  New York, New York

Read All About It:
- *Gift Baskets for All Seasons: 75 Fun and Easy Craft Projects.* Abbeville Press, 1996.

- *Great Ideas for Gift Baskets, Bags and Boxes* by Kathryn Lamancusa. TAB Books, 1992.

- *How to Start a Home-Based Gift Basket Business* by Shirley Frazier. Globe Pequot Press, 1998.

- *Start and Run a Profitable Gift Basket Business* by Mardi Foster-Walker. Self-Counsel Press, 1995.

MARKET RESEARCH AND LOCATION

While you may think no one could survive without gift baskets, many pockets of the American population prove that's not the case. Truth be told, gift baskets are not popular with everyone. Many sections of the country would laugh out loud at the thought of buying wares to put in a basket—especially since they can both grow the wares and weave the baskets themselves. No, these folks won't be impressed by your ribbons and bows, and won't buy into your high markup. Needless to add, they are not your target consumer.

If it's a store you have your sights set on, then a busy, affluent area is your best bet. As is the case with most gift-centered stores, you're on the lookout for a high-foot-traffic quotient.

EQUIP YOURSELF

If you're homeward-bound, you will need to invest in the following supplies:

- wicker baskets of all shapes, sizes, and styles
- inventory
- wrapping supplies
- computer system
- a toll-free business line for orders
- packaging materials
- office furniture
- fax machine

For store owners, the following items are vital to your business's success:

- display fixtures
- wicker basket of all shapes and sizes
- inventory
- wrapping supplies
- packaging materials
- computer system
- industrial refrigerator for perishables
- office furniture
- lighting

STOCKING UP

You will have to establish a good working relationship with gift wholesalers and make frequent visits to industry trade shows to maintain a popular list of products. The following items, however, will get you started in creating an inventory.

- a variety of coffee beans
- several cheeses
- chocolates and other confections
- imported meats

- fruits

- candles and decorative holders

- body lotions and other toiletries

- mugs

- stuffed animals

- cloth napkins and rings

GETTING THE WORD OUT

Brochures displaying your most attractive gift-basket selections are a great way to market your business. Distribute these to corporations, through direct mail, and to nearby shops. You should also list your shop/gift service in the Yellow Pages, and advertise heavily in newspapers and local magazines during holiday seasons.

People working out of the house should put together a catalog displaying their baskets and try to secure customers through mail-order.

START YOUR OWN
GRAPHIC DESIGN BUSINESS

If you're no stranger to graphic artistry and pride yourself on being on the cutting-edge of technology, a desktop publishing firm may just be the ticket to your success. In the privacy of your home, you can begin designing brochures, pamphlets, magazines, Web pages, CD-ROMS, and books for companies.

The growing demand for private desktop publishing firms has incited many an entrepreneur to consider this low-cost business alternative. There are about 3 million desktop publishers working in the U.S. And established companies are getting in on the action, because at a much lower price tag, they can receive the same services from a solitary designer as they would from a large design firm.

RAKING IN THE DOUGH

Since you'll probably want to charge no less than $50 per hour, a one-person graphic design firm can bring in an average of $50,000 each year. A company with a steady clientele and several savvy designers can expect annual profits of over $140,000.

START-UP COSTS

Graphic designers have it made, since this profitable business comes complete with a low investment requirement. If you work from home, a staggeringly low $5,000 is all it will take to get the ball rolling.

HELP IS ON THE WAY

Look into these associations created especially for people involved in high-tech enterprises. Many provide members with informative newsletters dealing with the latest trends in design and technology.

Associations:

- Association of Desktop Publishers: 619/279-2116
  San Diego, California

- Graphic Artist Guild: 212/463-7759
  New York, New York

- National Association of Desktop Publishers: 800/874-4113
  Boston, Massachusetts

Trade Publications:

- *Graphic Arts Monthly*: 212/463-6834
  Cahners Publishing Co., New York, New York

Read All About It:

- *Starting Your Small Graphic Design Studio* by Michael Fleishman.
  North Light Books, 1996.

LOCATION

A small room is your own house may be all you need to start up your design firm. This translates to low overhead, no commuting, and a tax deduction on your house. If you have to meet clients, arrange to meet them at a restaurant or coffeeshop. You can bring your portfolio along and if the quality of your work is impressive, your customers will never notice the lack of formal office space—in fact, many will enjoy the free lunch.

EQUIP YOURSELF

- a powerful computer system (equipped with at least 16 MHz and 1-GB hard drive)

- a large monitor (at least 17 inches)

- fax/modem

- graphics, layout, and word processing software programs

- photocopier

- fax machine

- multiple phone lines

- promotional materials, business cards, letterhead

GETTING THE WORD OUT

Letting others know about your flair for layout and design will require you to create a unique marketing strategy. Large corporations are the best customers around. When approaching them, make sure to find out who is in charge of company communications. Most companies have a vital need for designers, whether it be for promotional materials, Web pages, shareholder communications packages, or corporate newsletters and magazines. One way to secure these valuable clients is to design a customized brochure or flyer for each company. The director of communication is bound to notice your unique and thoughtful approach.

If you're interested specifically in Web design, create an impressive site and advertise your design services on the Web.

Good networking skills can also generate a steady stream of business. Make sure to call publications, public relations firms, and advertising agencies, which are most in need of continuous graphic-design support.

STARTING YOUR OWN
GROCERY DELIVERY SERVICE

For as long as we can remember, grocery shopping has been viewed by many as a necessary evil. Pushing around the large cart, spending hours searching for that elusive item, waiting in a long line at the deli and checkout area.

Wouldn't it be great to send your customized shopping list to a company, and have them fulfill your order and deliver your products directly to your doorstep. For hundreds of thousands, this scenario is a dream come true. More and more consumers are asking: Who has time for grocery shopping anyway? Grocery-shopping services think they may have the answer.

As the baby boomers age, there will be a greater need for shopping services. Since the 1980's, the number of food delivery services has grown to an estimated 1,500. For the elderly, shopping for food is not simply just a waste of time, it can be a great burden. By simply taking it to the supermarket, you can fulfill all your customers' orders and your own financial needs.

RAKING IN THE DOUGH

Food-delivery-service companies, depending on their marketing costs and staff size, can bring in anywhere from $30,000 to $120,000. This number can also be augmented, should you decide to cut overhead by running the business right out of your home.

START-UP COSTS

If you begin your business out of your home and hire a moderately sized staff and pay them a small hourly rate plus tips, you can start your company on as little as $10,000. Marketing costs will make up the bulk of your start-up investment.

But if you plan to go all out, leasing a large office and hiring a staff of 10 or more employees, you can expect to shell out around $30,000 before launching your service-based company.

MARKET RESEARCH

If you plan on working from home, check out the profile of local residents. Find out if there are many households consisting of four or more individuals—because large families are often short on time, and big on appetite.

Then, check out the number of elderly people living in your area. Senior citizens often have disabilities that keep them housebound, and your service may come in handy to people in this position. One way to determine the number of elderly residents is to check out adult day-care centers and local nursing homes, since they may have already tabulated this figure.

EQUIP YOURSELF

- computer system

- four telephone lines

- office furniture (desk, filing cabinets, chairs)

- pagers for each of your staff members

- signs bearing your company logo for each driver's car

CAST AND CREW

Your company will not only be hiring drivers, it will be hiring people that can perform the job of shopping for others with skills and supreme care. The one reason some people still opt to do their own shopping is because they don't feel they can trust strangers to pick out just the right apple, or the ripest of melons. Training your employees will include thorough training on how to be a discriminating shopper. Because in this business, one bad apple will in fact spoil the bunch.

When hiring your team members, you should make sure they have a valid driver's license and a spotless driving record to boot. Since you will have to count on them to transport the groceries in a timely and reliable fashion, put your mind at ease by checking into their backgrounds.

GETTING THE WORD OUT

The grocery-shopping service lends itself to many inexpensive marketing tactics. Obtain permission from supermarkets to post up your flyers. Try to post them around the checkout aisles where weary shoppers congregate. You should also make sure to contact any adult and children's day-care centers and tack up your brochures on their premises. Older people and mothers with their hands full can provide you with consistent business and once the word spreads, will refer your business to others.

HEAT UP YOUR FINANCES WITH AN
HERB FARM

With the ban on butter, and the war on salt, the time is ripe for growing your own herb garden. Consumers and restaurants are in hot pursuit of this savory commodity, so there's no time like the present to harvest the herbal cash crop.

The organic craze will also feed into your corporate account. People are willing to pay top dollar just to go au naturel. Chefs have also gone wild over the great taste of herbs, and since the food-service industry is experiencing a period of unprecedented growth—in 1996 Americans actually spent more money on dining out than on groceries—that means more clients for your business.

But the yum-yum factor isn't all that herbs have going for them. There's also the holistic healing movement to take into account. A large percentage of the population is turning its back on conventional medicine and following the advice of Deepak Chopra all the way to the General Nutrition Center. All this hoopla about getting back to nature bodes well for all you up-and-coming herb farmers.

And best of all, you don't even have to cart your fanny all the way to Green Acres country to make your herbal dreams a reality. Nuh-uh, you can grow your business right from your very home. So, if putzing around in soiled overalls is your idea of seventh heaven, an herb farm will make every day a Sunday.

RAKING IN THE DOUGH

Be prepared, because unless you strike oil in the process, working the land isn't necessarily going to make you a wealthy landowner. Depending on the size of your crop, you stand to make anywhere from $30,000 to $150,000 per year in this business.

START-UP COSTS

The herb farmer's ante can run the gamut from a paltry $3,000 to a staggering $300,000. But since it's highly unlikely that your plan includes hundreds of acres in Heartland USA, expect to invest an average of $40,000. Many herb farmers are indeed able to start up on the cheap by buying a small greenhouse, and expanding only after there's a solid client list in the works.

HELP IS ON THE WAY

Your may have the greenest thumb this side of the Continental Divide, but when it comes to farming for profit, you're still a beginner. Here's how you can make others' experience work for you.

Associations:
- American Herbal Products Associaton: 301/951-3204
  Washington, D.C.

- Herb Growing and Marketing Network: 717/393-3295
  Silver Spring, Pennsylvania

- International Herb Association: 708/949-HERB
  Mundelein, Illinois

Trade Publications:
- *Botanical and Herb Reviews*: 501-253-7309
  Eureka Springs, Arizona

- *HerbGram*, American Botanical Council: 512-331-8868
  Austin, Texas

- *The Herb, Spice, and Medicinal Plant Digest*: 413/545-2347
  Amherst, Massachusetts

Read All About It:
- *Growing Herbs* by Deni Brown. DK Publishing, 1995.

- *The Herb Book* by John B. Lust. Bantam Books, 1983.

- *The Potential of Herbs as a Cash Crop* by Richard Alan Miller. Ten Speed Press, 1992.

MARKET RESEARCH

You can live the high life growing herbs, but only if you come prepared. After all, this isn't the Dark Ages. While crossing your fingers and vibing to the beat of a rain dance isn't going to make you an overnight sensation, plowing through those books and digging for the right figures certainly will.

Deciding which takers to target is no jaunt through the countryside. The botanical market is a diverse lot that includes the following:

- restaurants

- supermarkets

- health food stores

- medical industries

- holistic healing shamans

- manufacturers of herbally enhanced products

- wholesalers

- brokers

Your job is to decipher what it is these buyers need, and as the song says, give them what they want.

GETTING THE WORD OUT

Now, as for getting these buyers to come to you, keep dreaming! No way is that mountain ever coming to Mohammed! All upstart herb farmers must learn how to sell themselves. While cold calling will certainly become one of your many talents, you won't always have to go the door-to-door route— farmers' markets, for example, are a great place to meet restaurateurs and other industry professionals face-to-face.

If you're going to give a winning pitch, one that will convince the buyer that your product will be there in due time and in good shape, you must bring plenty of product samples, and make sure that your presentation is:

- smooth and confident

- well-researched and accurate

- more economically viable than the competition's

EQUIP YOURSELF

- greenhouse or a plot of land

- seeds, fertilizer, soil, gardening tools and supplies

- computer system

- transportation for pickup and delivery of product and supplies

- business cards and stationery

LEARN TO EARN

Work on a farm for a few months and you'll see, a weed-wacker only gets you so far. Since agriculture is a highly technical industry, what you don't know can hurt your business prospects. The general consensus on small-scale farming is that the would-be entrepreneur should study agriculture and horticulture before going at it alone.

BECOMING AN
IMAGE CONSULTANT

The growth of the image-consultant business is astounding. And it's no wonder. Many company executives are at a loss when it comes to grooming, wardrobe, proper speech, and etiquette. And who can blame them. If they had spent all their time honing their images, they probably wouldn't have had time to climb so high in the ranks of the corporate elite.

The global market has also helped boost the number of image consultants. Proper international business etiquette and professionalism can make or break a deal, and no company is willing to lose billions of dollars over a minor *faux pas*.

To become a successful image consultant, you will be required to serve as an example of your instruction. If you're planning on being a wardrobe and style consultant, you will have to look like a million dollars. Hair, nails, clothes, and makeup will have to be immaculate. If communication is your area of choice, be prepared to perfect your body movements, eye contact, and voice. The success of your service will depend on both you and your clients making the right impression.

RAKING IN THE DOUGH

Because the majority of your clients will be affluent business people, you can expect to make $30,000 to $40,000 per year in the beginning. Once you've established your reputation and have garnered stable corporate accounts, you can easily bring in anywhere from $80,000 to $200,000 per year.

START-UP COSTS

Although this business may seem ultra-affordable, the education costs will offset the low overhead. On average, the image consultant can begin operating with $10,000 to $15,000 in the bank.

HELP IS ON THE WAY

If you could use an few extra pointers to make a dazzling first impression, these resources are bound to get your image and career on the fast track.

Associations:

- Association of Image Consultants International: 800/383-8831 Washington, D.C.

Read All About It:

- *How to Gain the Professional Edge: Achieve the Personal and Professional Image You Want* by Susan Morem. Better Books, 1997.

- *The Language of Color* by Dorothee L. Mella. Warner Books, 1988.

- *Looking Good: A Comprehensive Guide to Wardrobe Planning, Color, and Personal Style Development* by Nancy Nix-Rice. Palmer Pletsch Publishing, 1996.

- *The New Professional Image: From Business Casual to the Ultimate Power Look* by Susan Bixler and Nancy Nix-Rice. Adams Media, 1997.

- *Say It Right: How to Talk in Any Social or Business Situation* by Lillian Glass. Putnam, 1991.

MARKET RESEARCH AND LOCATION

Since your main clientele will consist of corporate executives, make sure you situate your service in a large city. You will also get a fair amount of work from affluent women. Make sure your location and marketing campaign takes this customer profile into account.

EQUIP YOURSELF

An image consultant requires a minimal amount of equipment. Once you begin getting more clients, you may have to invest in additional office equipment and supplies.

- a pager or cell phone for easy customer access

- a computer for bookkeeping and scheduling

- promotional material—brochures, instructional booklets, and business cards

- a camera
- a portfolio of successful makeovers
- a business phone line

GETTING THE WORD OUT

To get your business the attention it deserves, you will have to contact human-resources departments of local corporations and/or distribute direct-mail pieces to executives explaining your services in detail. When it comes to making a great impression, follow-up is everything. So check in with your recipients about a week after you've mailed your brochures.

Advertising in business and social magazines will also do wonders for your business. You can either take out classified ads, or make an even more dramatic impact with a professionally designed display ad.

STARTING YOUR
INTERIOR DESIGN FIRM

Have you ever wondered why some of your friends have beautifully decorated houses or apartments and others couldn't decorate to save their lives? It all comes down to a matter of taste and flair for interior design. Some people are just born with an instinctive knowledge for coordinating the right fabrics with the right colors, and purchasing that perfect centerpiece item that sets the ambiance for the rest of the place.

The interior design industry is competitive, and many companies have been reporting a gradual decline in the market. But if you start small and build a loyal clientele, there's no reason why you couldn't make your business a success.

If you have what it takes to make your living quarters a pleasant sight to behold and love to offer suggestions to design-challenged friends, then you may have what it takes to transform your hobby into a lucrative design studio.

RAKING IN THE DOUGH

Depending on the size of your projects and the number of clients you have, design firms can make anywhere from $30,000 their first year to $150,000 with a small staff and several years of solid design practice,

START-UP COSTS

Start-up expenses for an interior-design studio can be pretty low. The majority of your expenses will go toward marketing your studio and investing in design software. This amount can range from $3,000 to $10,000.

HELP IS ON THE WAY

Interior designers are always evolving in their design philosophies and strive to stay on top of modern design trends. The following resources will provide you with the basic knowledge of design theory, point you in the right direction for professional training courses, and provide valuable networking opportunities.

Associations:

- American Society of Interior Designers: 202/546-3480
  Washington, D.C.

- Interior Design Society: 800/888-9590
  High Point, North Carolina

- International Interior Design Association: 312/467-1950
  Chicago, Illinois

Trade Publications:

- *Interior Design*: 212/645-0067
  New York, New York

- *Interiors and Sources*: 800/833-9056
  North Palm Beach, Florida

Read All About It:

- *How to Prosper as an Interior Designer: A Business and Legal Guide* by Robert Alderman. John Wiley & Sons, 1997.

- *How to Start a Home-Based Interior Design Business* by Suzanne Dewalt. Globe Pequot Press, 1997.

- *How to Start and Operate Your Own Design Firm*. McGraw-Hill, 1993.

- *Interior Graphic and Design Standards* by S.C. Reznikoff. Whitney Library of Design, 1986.

MARKET RESEARCH AND LOCATION

Depending on your specialty, private residences, commercial spaces, or businesses, you will have to begin operating in an area that will provide a significant number of clients in your area of specialization. Big cities are a good bet for those designers planning to break into the corporate or commercial market, while a location near affluent suburban areas can bring in clients wishing to spruce up the appearance of their homes.

Since you will be meeting with clients in their homes or businesses, you can start your interior-design firm out of your home. Once you're established, you can open up a small office in your target area.

EQUIP YOURSELF

Interior designers can get away with owning very few pieces of relatively inexpensive equipment. To get the best deals on software, contact industry associations and look through trade magazines.

- drafting table

- drawing tools

- business phone line and phone with voice mail options

- fax machine

- computer system

- CAD system or other design software

GETTING THE WORD OUT

Design firms attract the majority of their clients from word-of-mouth advertising. When first starting out, you can obtain referrals by offering your services at special discount rates. That way you can secure more professional experience, and will have samples of your work to show prospective clients.

If you're hoping to break into the corporate image market, contact facility managers of various corporations and try to set up interviews. Bring samples of your work and your most professional demeanor.

The best-kept secret among interior designers is that the majority of your business will come from networking with affluent executives and home owners. Schmooze is the name of the game. Attend functions where you can hobnob with the rich if maybe not-so-famous. Dinner parties, gallery openings, and auctions can win you valuable clients and security in the long run. And never leave home without promotional material displaying your best work.

BECOMING AN
INVENTOR

Ever wonder who came up with the first Beanie Baby? Or who masterminded that whole water-as-an-expensive-bottled-beverage phenomenon? It probably wasn't some mad scientist with a Rube Goldberg device set up in the garage. The answer is simple—creative people just like you. Right now, the only difference between you and run-of-the-mill inventors, or product developers as they are known to corporations, is that inventors have the skills and determination to put their thoughts into action.

Ideas are everywhere. You've probably been struck with quite a few yourself. But selling your concepts to the people who can develop and manufacture them is a full-time job. Once you learn how to go about marketing your brainstorms, you'll be making more money than you ever thought possible without a law degree.

RAKING IN THE DOUGH

What with companies starved for new ideas, you don't have to be an optimist to predict a sunny financial future. After you establish yourself in this field, you can make anywhere from $30,000 to $100,000+ per year in advances and royalties.

START-UP COSTS

There's good news and there's great news. The good news is that this business shouldn't require more than $4,000 in start-up capital. The great news is that if you already call a computer system your own, your whole investment need not exceed $1,000.

HELP IS ON THE WAY

Be aware that this is a tricky business. Concepts are easy things to swipe. After all, ideas are actually just so much thin air. Many a product developer will tell you that when you meet with interested companies, you almost have no guarantee that your idea will not be swept out from under you. So all inventors agree that legal assistance is a must-have, as is notifying all companies that you would like them to sign a non-disclosure agreement prior to divulging any confidential information.

But you can get all this information firsthand from the people at:

Associations:
- Inventors Assistance League, International: 818/246-6540
  Glendale, California

- Inventors Clubs of America: 404/355-8889
  Atlanta, Georgia

- National Congress of Inventor Organizations: 213/878-6952
  Los Angeles, California

Trade Publications:
- *Inventors' Digest Magazine*: 800/838-8808
  Boston, Massachusetts

- *Inventors Resource Guide*: 716/359-9310
  Rochester, New York

Read All About It:
- *Adventures of an Inventor: Or How to Survive and Succeed in the Inventing Business* by Jacob Fraden. Hurricane Books, 1996.

- *Eureka!: The Entrepreneurial Inventor's Guide to Developing, Protecting, and Profiting from Your Ideas* by Robert Gold. Prentice Hall Trade, 1994.

- *Inventing Small Products for Big Profits, Quickly* by Stanley Mason. Crisp Publications, 1997.

- *Stand Alone, Inventor! And Make Money with Your New Product Ideas* by Roger G. Merrick. Lee Publications, 1998.

MARKET RESEARCH
As any product developer will tell you, trade shows are the best places to conduct your market research. Once you get a feel for your area of expertise — be it toys, candy, or electronic gadgets — you can visit the appropriate trade shows to see whether your ideas are in tune with what various companies attempt to bring to the marketplace. These are also the very places to make

the right corporate connections and embark upon profitable relationships with future clients.

EQUIP YOURSELF
- computer system with graphic design software

- fax machine

- stationery, envelopes, and business cards

- contracts

GETTING THE WORD OUT
You can contact corporate research and development (R&D) departments directly by phone. Chances are they will at least give you a fair hearing. As mentioned earlier, you can also meet clients at trade shows. Another attention-getting device is direct-mail advertising. If you target the right corporations and send the materials along to key decision-makers, you may just get a few meetings out of the bargain. Once your foot is in the door, let your boundless enthusiasm, self-confidence, and ingenious ideas seal the deal.

BECOMING A
JEWELRY DESIGNER

Do you dream of becoming the Kenneth Lane of the new millennium? Has Arts & Crafts always been your strong suit? Has the pursuit of art been your raison d'être all along? Or have you simply made a bundle selling beads at a Grateful Dead show? If so, then designing jewelry may be just what the financial planner ordered.

Whether you're a longtime student of this discipline, or just have innate talent, the business of jewelry design has a wealth of money-making opportunities for people who know how to sell their wares. But whereas knowing your craft is one thing, selling it is something entirely different. So be prepared; if you're to outshine the competition, you'll have to spend at least as much time peddling your product as you did making it.

RAKING IN THE DOUGH

The profits can vary drastically from one designer to the next. If you hook up with a large distributor, you're looking at profits of $70,000 to $80,000. But you can still score a pretty penny by marketing yourself. Typical revenues hover around the $25,000 mark.

START-UP COSTS

Most of your capital will go towards jeweler's materials, supplies, and promotional brochures. But all in all, the start-up equation need not total up to more than $5,000.

HELP IS ON THE WAY

It don't mean a thing if you can't bead that string, but reading up on the custom-made jewelry industry can give your talents a much needed direction.

Associations:

- Independent Jewelers Organization: 800/624-9252
  Westport, Connecticut

- Jewelers of America: 800/223-0673
  New York, New York

Trade Publications:

- *Fashion Accessories*: 201/384-3336
  Bergenfield, New Jersey

- *Jewelry Crafts Magazine*: 800/528-1024
  Los Angeles, California

Read All About It:

- *The Art of Jewelry Design* by Maurice Galli, et al. Shiffer Publishing, 1994.

- *The Design and Creation of Jewelry*, 3rd ed., by Robert von Neuman. Chilton Book Company, 1982.

- *Handmade Jewelry: Simple Steps to Creating Wearable Art* by Carol Grape. North Light Books, 1996.

- *Inspirational Guide to Beads and Jewelry Making* by Janet Coles and Robert Budwig. Simon and Schuster, 1990.

- *Jewelry & Accessories: Creative Designs to Make and Wear* by Juliet Bawden. North Light Books, 1995.

Learn to Earn:

- Gemological Institute of America: 310/829-2991
  Santa Monica, California

MARKET RESEARCH

Much of your research will be right at the market—the flea market, that is. You'll also find plenty of jewelry on display at craft shows, jewelry trade shows, and artisan galleries. Hit all these hotbeds of baubles to check which designs and materials are the most popular.

Use this research to determine the going prices. If you undercut the value of your wares, they'll go from priceless keepsakes to cheap trinkets faster than you can say "tacky."

EQUIP YOURSELF

- materials incorporated in your designs

- vises

- pliers

- molds

- melting equipment

- cleaning supplies

- photo brochures and business cards

GETTING THE WORD OUT

As alluded to earlier, selling your goods means you're gonna have to work it. Put on your most avant-garde garb, your most comfortable shoes, and step to the street. Pound that pavement from gallery to counter and back again. Talk to the purchasing directors, and ply them with your samples. No matter what happens, never leave without at least passing along your business card and brochure.

You can meet the head honchos at jewelry trade shows, where you can set up a table and display to your heart's content. Your company literature should include a clever story of what your jewelry signifies, how you got started in the biz, and some schmaltzy tale about the priceless one-of-a-kind nature each piece has to offer.

DEVELOPING YOUR OWN
LITERARY AGENCY

No doubt about it, you're a bookworm. You've never resorted to *Cliff's Notes*, or judged a book by its cover. Good thing too, because once you become a literary agent you can say good-bye to ever reading anything with a cover on it again. You'll be skimming one manuscript after another, and editing pages upon pages of text, but if you're a truly enamored with the written word, you'll love every second of it (okay, maybe every other second).

A literary agency is a viable enterprise for anyone who knows what's up in the publishing industry. That means industry contacts, as well as an understanding of the trends and currents taking place within the literary marketplace. If you have these prerequisites down cold, there's nothing to stop you from making a killing in the book trade.

RAKING IN THE DOUGH

Your prospects are bright. Once the business is on its feet, you stand to earn anywhere from $35,000 to $100,000 per year (and even more if you can net yourself a best-seller). But because much of your income will come from royalties, which don't begin to pour in until after a work is published, don't expect to see the big bucks until after at least a year of operation.

START-UP COSTS

The literary agency is an ideal home-based business op. You'll save loads by choosing the spare bedroom over the power office suite and the p.j.'s over the power business suit. In short, you can get the whole shebang going for as little as $1,500.

HELP IS ON THE WAY

While they won't tell you how to start up a literary agency or give you all the knowledge necessary to succeed, the following sources and trade mags can keep you informed on all the late-breaking developments and key contacts in the field.

Associations:
- Association of Authors' Representatives: 212/353-3709
  New York, New York

Trade Publications:
- *Publisher's Weekly*: 800/278-2991
  New York, New York

Read All About It:
- *Be Your Own Literary Agent: The Ultimate Insider's Guide to Getting Published* by Martin Levin. Ten Speed Press, 1996.

- *How to Be Your Own Literary Agent: The Business of Getting a Book Published* by Richard Curtis. Houghton Mifflin and Company, 1996.

- *Literary Agents: What They Do, How They Do It, and How to Find and Work with the Right One for You* by Michael Larson. John Wiley & Sons, 1996.

- *LMP: Literary Market Place: The Directory of the American Book Publishing Industry*. R.R. Bowker.

- *What Book Publishers Won't Tell You: A Literary Agent's Guide to the Secrets of Getting Published* by Bill Adler. Citadel Press, 1997.

MARKET RESEARCH

In your research, pay special attention to the pricing policies and commission charged by other agents. The standard percentage is 10 to 20 percent of your clients' deals. Investigate all the details carefully—not only do you stand to earn on your authors' domestic sales and foreign book rights, but you've got film and audio possibilities to boot.

Specialization is another aspect you may want to look into. Non-fiction is a very broad category, and believe it or not, there are agents out there who are striking it rich by just dealing in cookbooks or how-to's.

EQUIP YOURSELF
- computer system

- fax machine

- photocopier

- telephone

- desk, chair, filing cabinets

- personalized stationery, business cards

GETTING THE WORD OUT

Who are your primary clients? If you were thinking the publishers, you were sorely mistaken. Sure you want the publishers' attention, but that's not paramount to your business. Authors are the lifeblood of any literary agency. You won't see so much as one red cent from a publishing house until you have a stable of quality writers with good ideas to spare.

Get the talent's attention by:

- listing your agency in the *Guide to Literary Agents* and the *Literary Market Place*

- advertising in writers' trade magazines

LAUNCHING YOUR OWN
MAIL-ORDER BUSINESS

For many, mail order is the best way to start a business with the lowest possible risk in terms of time and money. Mail-order businesses have recently experienced a great deal of coverage. Everyone's trying to get in on the action. In 1993, it was estimated that five to six million people were working in the mail order industry. And who can blame them. Proper management and organization can make a mail-order enterprise very profitable and will not require as much work as most businesses.

How does it work? Simple. A well-targeted advertisement, a post office box, and . . . voila! you're in business. There are of course other important details to take care of. Such as picking the product, arranging for shipment, and processing the orders. But when all is said and done, this is the lowest-maintenance business on the entrepreneurial block.

RAKING IN THE DOUGH

On average, a mail-order business can bring in around $40,000 per year. Depending on the number of products you plan on selling, that number can increase dramatically. As you expand and develop a catalog showcasing a wide range of fine products, you can see profits ascend as high as $150,000 per year.

START-UP COSTS

This business can be started on as low as $10,000. This low start-up won't require much cost-cutting if you start slow, working with one product out of your own home.

HELP IS ON THE WAY

These trade magazines will provide you with vital news regarding direct-mail practices, catalog, and other mail-order strategies. Once your business is off the ground, a yearly subscription is recommended to keep you in step with the competition.

Trade Publications:
- *Catalog Age*: 203/358-9900
  Stanford, Connecticut

- *Direct Marketing Magazine*: 516/746-6700
  Garden City, New York

- *Target Marketing Magazine*: 215/238-5300
  Philadelphia, Pennsylvania

Read All About It:
- *101 Great Mail-Order Businesses: The Very Best (And Most Profitable) Mail Order Businesses You Can Start* by Tyler Gregory Hicks. Prima Publishing, 1996.

- *Building a Mail Order Business: A Complete Manual for Success* by William Cohen. John Wiley & Sons, 1996.

- *How to Start and Operate a Mail-Order Business* by Julie Simon. McGraw-Hill, 1993.

SELECTING A LOCATION
One of the biggest bonuses of starting a mail-order business is that it can be done right out of your comfy, cozy house. Because you will be dealing with customers by phone or processing orders through the mail or fax, you can maintain your records and conduct all your operations from your home base.

If you're planning to start a larger company, with a moderate staff, a small office will provide you with ample space to run your business.

EQUIP YOURSELF
- computer system with fax/modem

- credit card merchant status

- fax machine

- office furniture

- postage meter, envelopes
- promotional material

GETTING THE WORD OUT

Since mail-order businesses generate all of their sales from advertising, you will have to pay close attention to your marketing strategy. A very popular method of advertising your wares is the direct-mail method. To mail directly to your customers, you will have to rent a mailing list. This can set you back initially, but you can always conduct a preliminary test of the list's effectiveness before investing. To create a high-powered direct-mail campaign, you will have to produce a colorful brochure featuring your product. You can hire a professional designer to customize your mailing pieces to your specifications.

Taking out an ad in the classifieds section is a relatively cheap method, and you can easily track the success of your ad. Keeping close tabs on all your advertisements, whether it be display, classified, or direct mail, will keep you from throwing your money away on ineffective advertising space.

BECOME A
FREELANCE MAKEUP ARTIST

Makeup artists like Max Factor, Bobbi Brown, and Trish McEvoy made the world of makeovers look glamorous, but the reality is that it takes hard work and talent to become makeup artist to the stars—famous enough to launch your own line of beauty products. That's not to say that thousands of beauticians aren't making a decent living beautifying the rest of the population. But only a few make it to the elite ranks of celebrity makeup artists.

Professional instruction may also be in the future for any makeup artists wannabes. If you have a real interest in turning ordinary people into covergirl contenders, then you will find this business both lucrative and fun. The key to making your services vied after is to create dramatic results and listening to your customers. If your clients love the way they look, they will come back year after year for a repeat performance.

RAKING IN THE DOUGH
Artists working out of their homes can expect to make a profit of $20,000 to $50,000 per year. The latter sum will come once you establish a solid reputation with photographers and other important clients.

START-UP COSTS
The majority of your start-up funds will be allotted to a savvy marketing campaign. The rest of your capital will be divided between makeup tools, products, and transportation. Overall, the investment should fall between $4,000 and $10,000.

HELP IS ON THE WAY
Beauty technicians have to keep up with the latest in makeup trends and glamor looks to keep their clients happy. There are dozens of beauty magazines lining the shelves of every bookstore. Make sure you read as many as

possible. But for some professional assistance like financing options and networking opportunities, consider joining the following associations.

Associations:
- National Beauty Culturists' League: 202/332-2695
  Washington, D.C.

- National Cosmetology Association: 800/527-1683
  St. Louis, Missouri

- World International Nail and Beauty Association: 714/779-9883
  Anaheim, California

Trade Publications:
- *Make-Up Artist Magazine*: 818/504-6770
  Sunland, California

- *National Beauty News*: 918/583-5708
  Tulsa, Oklahoma

- *Shop Talk*: 312/978-6400
  Chicago, Illinois

Read All About It:
- *Cosmetology Career Starter: Express Your Creativity in a Rewarding Career* by Lorraine Korman. Learning Express, 1998.

- *Making Faces* by Kevin Aucoin and Gena Rowlands. Little Brown & Company, 1997.

- *The Technique of the Professional Make-Up Artist* by Vincent Kohoe. Focal Press, 1995.

MARKET RESEARCH AND LOCATION
The location of your business will depend on the type of occasions you will be providing makeup services for. Should you choose to work for area photographers, commercial shoots, or department fashion shows, you will have to travel to certain destination and be available on-site as long as you are needed.

If you're planning to provide private makeovers for everyday occasions like parties and informal gatherings, your best bet is to have the clients come to your home. In that case, you will have to reserve a space in your house for your business with adequate lighting.

LICENSE TO STYLE

Many states require that makeup artists receive a cosmetologist license before practicing professionally. In most cases, you will have to enroll in beauty school before you are allowed to work on your own. Getting some extra training, however, can be a great asset to any makeup artist. You will learn all the tricks of the trade, including hair-styling techniques, color selection, and proper methods of application. Since the majority of your business will come from a repeat clientele, you will have to become as skilled as possible to insure your business's ongoing success.

EQUIP YOURSELF

- beauty supplies (cosmetics, brushes, eyelash curlers, etc.)

- carry-all bag

- transportation

GETTING THE WORD OUT

There are a myriad of opportunities for makeup artists to spread the word about their services. But first you must build a professional portfolio to show prospective clients. This is the point at which you'll have to shell out bucks for professional photographs for your book. But you can also be thrifty by arranging to do the makeup for models of start-up photographers who are also in the process of putting together their books.

Make sure to practice on anyone for free — in order to expand your artistic range. Once you've taken this step, visit successful photographers, talent and modeling agencies, and party planners in you area, leaving your card and work samples.

Other marketing strategies include direct-mail promotion, listing yourself in the Yellow Pages, and advertising in women's publications.

THE BUSINESS OF
MASSAGE THERAPY

A nice long massage has long held the venerable distinction of being the "Number One Way to Unwind." The tired, huddled masses that pour out of the commuter trains each and every day of the work week need to relax. Whether it's boredom, exercise, or actual overwork that ties knots in our backs, this physical tension isn't doing anything to help our rapidly escalating stress levels. But then you probably already know this; why else would you be seriously considering a business in massage therapy?

If you think you have what it takes to handle the manual labor (extensive muscle strain and many hours of standing) while gaining satisfaction from your work . . . then get ready, because you're going back to school. Most states will require that you become certified, which means you'll need study the fine art and science of massage for months on end. But once school's out, there's nothing to stand in the way of certified massage therapists and sizable sums of profit.

RAKING IN THE DOUGH

As a massage therapist you are in the driver's seat where profits are concerned. If you market your services well, the final word on profits will be your own endurance—how many hours of massage do you have in you each day? Once you have an established clientele, your annual profits should fall someplace between $20,000 and $50,000.

START-UP COSTS

Minimum financing is another reason to feel good about the business of massage. For well under $4,000, the whole operation can be well underway.

HELP IS ON THE WAY

Let's face it, much of the massage industry is sustained by fads. There's Swedish massage, shiatsu, and a myriad of other means to iron out the kinks in a weary back. Stay in touch with new developments by contacting the following sources.

Associations:
- American Massage Therapy Association: 847/864-0123
  Evanston, Illinois

- Associated Bodywork and Massage Professionals: 800/458-2267
  Evergreen, Colorado

- International Massage Association: 202/387-6555
  Washington, D.C.

Trade Publications:
- *Massage Magazine*: 408/477-1176
  Santa Cruz, California

Read All About It:
- *Healing Massage Techniques: Holistic, Classic, and Emerging Methods* by Frances Tappan. Appleton and Lange, 1992.

- *Mosby's Fundamentals of Therapeutic Massage* by Sandy Fritz. Mosby Year Book, 1995.

- *Save Your Hands: Injury Prevention for Massage Therapists* by Lauriann and Robert Greene. Infinity Press, 1995.

MARKET RESEARCH
While massage is a popular form of stress-reduction in many areas, the single-beauty-parlor-and-bar town is probably not one of these. If you hail from some such godforsaken utopia, a move is as crucial to your business as a pair of strong, healthy hands.

A preponderance of health clubs is a good sign that an area can support an independent massage therapist. Just make sure that your prices are in sync with those of other massage professionals. Then develop some truly outstanding services, such as house calls or a complimentary power bar after every massage, and you'll pull ahead of the competition in due time.

EQUIP YOURSELF
- massage table

- portable radio and relaxation music

- aromatherapy massage oils

- appointment book

- business cards, promotional material

GETTING THE WORD OUT

There's two types of masseurs/masseuses—and the nice ones aren't found through the back pages of a newspaper. Before you decide to advertise your services, check the newspaper to make sure you are listed with the legitimate bodywork therapists. Look for the words "hot" and "erotic," and ask to have your ad placed elsewhere.

The good old phone book is still one of the most popular sources of business. A tastefully designed display ad in your city's Yellow Pages should score you more than a few clients each year.

If you like the idea of pocketing corporate funds in exchange for rubbing the necks of tense employees, then direct mail will serve you well. Put together a persuasive sales kit that tells it like it is (e.g., a relaxed employee is a productive employee), and send it out out to the various department heads. Then watch corporate execs allocate big portions of budgets to your worthy cause.

BECOMING A
MEETING PLANNER

As anyone whose ever worked in the corporate strata will tell you, meetings are the building blocks of the work week. The actual administrative functions can and are delegated to minions such as assistants and other underling "team" members. You yourself have probably felt the sting of the outgoing voice-mail message which perpetually informs you that your contact is in a meeting.

All this has led you here—to the meeting-planner chapter of this book. Fine thing too, because since we have entered the age of the never-ending meeting, the business world has elevated the conference, committee meeting, convention, etc., to an art form. Increasingly elaborate and expensive events put you in a position to reap handsome rewards. But that's only if you have what it takes.

Pitching your business strategy and negotiating contracts will be your first orders of business; thus, communication skills are a must. This means chucking filler words such as "like" and "you know." A head for business and budgets is also a top consideration. These aren't the eighties; companies are still leery of wanton spending. What they want, and what you have to provide is an smooth and interesting meeting background for a reasonable price. If you can't get that down, you'll be out on your bankrupt bootie in no time.

RAKING IN THE DOUGH

Since you can work in the glow of your very own fireplace, you won't have to part with any greenbacks for rent purposes. What's more, you can charge your expenses straight to the client company. All this translates into high profit margins ranging anywhere from $30,000 to $80,000+ per year.

START-UP COSTS

The jewels don't have to go into hock, and neither does that vintage Mustang, because starting this business is a cinch where start-up capital is concerned. No hotsy-totsy equipment to invest in and no big-time stock purchases to be made; all you need is your wits and approximately $8,000 to cover the incidental equipment and expenses, as well as any business start-up legal fees you may incur.

HELP IS ON THE WAY

Face it, no matter how many business meetings you planned in the past, no matter how well-traveled you are, and no matter how many trade shows you've been finagled into attending, making a business of this experience is another thing altogether. Why make your own mistakes when you can learn from the veterans at:

Associations:

- Association Network: 916/393-9290
  Sacramento, California

- Association of Meeting Professionals: 703/549-0900
  Alexandria, Virginia

- Connected International Meeting Professional Association: 703/978-6287
  Fairfax, Virginia

- International Society of Meeting Planners: 320/763-4919
  Alexandria, Minnesota

- Meeting Professionals International: 214/702-3000
  Dallas, Texas

Publications:

- *Association Meetings*: 978/897-5552
  Maynard, Massachusetts

- *Corporate Meetings*: 212/827-4736
  New York, New York

- *Meeting News*: 212/615-2829
  New York, New York

- *Meetings & Expositions*: 202/626-2789
  American Society of Association Executives, Washington, D.C.

- *Successful Meetings*: 212/592-6263
  Bill Communications, New York, New York

Read All About It:

- *Big Meetings, Big Results: Strategic Event Planning for Productivity and Profit* by Tom McMahon. NTC Publishing, 1996.

- *The Comprehensive Guide to Successful Conferences and Meetings* by Leonard and Zeace Nadler. Jossey-Bass Publishers, 1987.

MARKET RESEARCH

In order to arrive at a realistic estimation of your business prospects you're going to have to go to the phone book. Call other meeting planners to find out how much they charge, as well as how much business comes their way. While you're at it, don't leave out the caterers and hotels. Talking to these people can clue you into how much business they get through meeting planners. If the numbers are on the high side, you know you're surveying the right field.

You can also call the corporations in your area to find out what percentage have in-house meeting planners and what percentage chooses to outsource. Also call your city's Chamber of Commerce for a list of all the trade shows that are held in your locale. Use this information to call the trade show organizers and find out the names of the companies attending. Then whip up your ingenious pitch and drum up business by calling the bigger names directly.

EQUIP YOURSELF

- computer with printer and fax/modem and necessary software

- fax machine

- telephone with voice mail and conference features, and headset

- photocopier

- ergonomically correct work space (desk, chair, keyboard)

- promotional materials: brochures, business cards, letterhead

GETTING THE WORD OUT

If you don't already know how to blow your own horn, it's high time you took to practicing. Self-promotion is what sells service and the following ideas should start you well on your way:

- direct-mail advertising to corporate executives

- networking with local business organizations

- advertising in trade magazines catering to corporate executives

- finding out about trade shows and conventions by calling area convention and visitors bureaus

BECOME A
MYSTERY SHOPPING SERVICE
PROVIDER

The cold war is over, and many covert operatives are out of business. Or are they? Now that communism is pretty much out of commission, isn't it about time the U.S. took on the poor state of customer service? Business executives sure seem to think so. After all, managers can't be around all the time, and security cameras are too "Big Brother," not to mention expensive, so how on earth can business owners keep customer-service personnel on their toes? You don't have to be a rocket scientist to figure it out, especially now that mystery shoppers have taken on the customer-service departments at thousands of American businesses.

Still, something's not clear... what in the world is a mystery shopper? Simple, this is a customer like any other in every respect but one—it's not the merchandise they're sizing up, but the customer service. These under-cover evaluators take copious mental notes and fish for specified information. Then they write up a report, and woe to those who get "reported." Boy, are they in for a training session!

In short, this business is for anyone with a gripe against modern customer service, a yen for intrigue, and a history of volunteering for hall-monitor duty back in junior high. Sound familiar? Well, welcome to your life!

RAKING IN THE DOUGH

Your profits will depend on the value your services provide. For instance, you can simply report your findings on a case-by-case basis, or you can add overall service summaries that give employers a bird's-eye view of the big picture. While the latter will involve more work, it will also net you a heftier bundle of profit. A mystery shopping service can bring in anywhere from $30,000 to over $90,000.

START-UP COSTS

Even though you'll be dealing with corporate clients, you don't have to open an office right away. You can even hire a team of part-time mystery shoppers, all of whom must work off your premises and in the field. You can even begin operations while you're still employed. All in all, figure start-up capital between $10,000 and $20,000.

Read All About It:

- *Mystery Shopping* by James Poynter, Kendall Hunt Publishing, 1996.

MARKET RESEARCH AND LOCATION

Interviewing other mystery shoppers is crucial. There's no better way to find out what really goes on in this relatively new business. If you ask the right questions, you can learn about fees, about working across county and state lines, about marketing strategies guaranteed to grow your business, and about the ethics and etiquette that go with the job.

Studying your future clients will also prove beneficial. You won't believe how many retail-oriented businesses are in need of your assistance. Restaurants, banks, cable and Internet access providers, Fortune 500 corporations, you need only shut your eyes and throw open the Yellow Pages to find a business with customer-service complaints. Focus on a certain type of business, and go to work. Find out what their problems are, how they are presently dealing with them, how much the problems and the solutions are costing, then step in and offer to save them—a lot of time and money, that is.

LICENSE AND REGISTRATION

Because certain states may require that you have a private detective's license before practicing in the lucrative field of mystery shopping, it is our recommendation that you hire an attorney. Your legal counsel will not only check out the state's rule and regulations, but will also help you register your business and wade through the bureaucracy.

EQUIP YOURSELF

- computer with printer and fax/modem

- quantitative analysis software

- photocopier

- business telephone line with voice mail

- fax machine

- ergonomically correct work space (desk, chair, keyboard)

- promotional materials: brochures, business cards, letterhead

GETTING THE WORD OUT

Your best bets for bringing in the bread and butter clients are:

- direct-mail advertising

- networking with local business organizations

- advertising in trade magazines that target your focus industry, as well as in newsletters that are put out by the very companies you wish to reach and distributed to their franchises

- public-relations campaigns targeting the above magazines, local business newspapers and television/cable access programs

- cold calling or telemarketing

CAST AND CREW

You'll need an army of on-call mystery shopping professionals. Screen the applicants to make sure that they will blend in with their surroundings. Also, keep in mind that the mystery shopper's pen is mightier than the supervisor's ax. Look for people with a balanced disposition, and don't hire anyone with a chip on his or her shoulder—people's jobs are at stake.

PUBLISHING YOUR OWN
NEWSLETTER

In the past twenty years, newsletters have become a great way to make money and disseminate information about a variety of topics. There are around 1.5 million newsletters published in North America. Newsletters began as variations on company brochures. But these days, the best newsletters, like *Bottom Line*, resemble magazines more than newspapers. Actually, a newsletter is a cross between a magazine and a newspaper.

Entrepreneurs who start their own newsletters focus their subject matter on a specific industry or consumer group. There have been newsletters for entrepreneurs, alcoholics, Mr. Moms, fugitives from the rat race, and anything else you can think of. The possibilities are endless; all you have to do is come up with a good newsletter idea and be ready to take subscriptions.

Writing ability is a definite bonus, since in the beginning you may have a hard time paying writers. But even if you're not a writing virtuoso, you can still become a first-class newsletter publisher.

RAKING IN THE DOUGH

Depending on whether you're writing corporate newsletters or taking individual subscriptions, you can garner between $35,000 and $80,000 each year. Keep in mind that while corporate outfits usually pay bigger bucks, if your newsletter becomes popular enough with subscribers, you can bring in just as much, if not more, moolah by putting out an independent publication. It all depends on the quality and effectiveness of your marketing strategy.

START-UP COSTS

You can begin working right out of your own home, but your marketing and production costs will add up. Try to have at least $5,000 in the till to cover those expenses.

HELP IS ON THE WAY

You may have story ideas aplenty, but if you're not tuned in to the customers' needs, you may just find your circulation plummeting. Learn how to keep abreast of what the public wants to know by consulting the following sources.

Associations:
- International Association of Business Communicators (IABC): 415/433-3400
  San Francisco, California

- Newsletter Publishers Association (NPA): 703/527-2333
  Arlington, Virginia

Trade Publications:
- *Newsletter on Newsletters*: 914/876-2081
  Rhinebeck, New York

Read All About It:
- *Home-Based Newsletter Publishing: A Success Guide for Entrepreneurs* by Susan Rachmeier. Prentice Hall Trade, 1997.

- *Making Money Writing Newsletters* by Elaine Floyd. EF Communications, 1994.

- *Success in Newsletter Publishing: A Practical Guide*. Newsletter Publishers Association, 1993.

MARKET RESEARCH

Many corporations use employee newsletters to keep their workers informed about company activities. To secure corporate accounts, you should contact the Director of Communications at each company for which you'd like to write. If you secure an account, you will have to conduct interviews with spokespeople at the company and generate your own story ideas from the information provided. This type of newsletter can be very lucrative.

You can also begin a general industry newsletter—restaurant, fashion, or automotive—and then market to all professionals within that industry, regardless of what company they work for. To succeed here, you will have to provide timely information on a weekly basis.

If you plan on targeting individual readers, you will have to come up with an idea mainstream enough to get the attention of your customers. Think about why readers would like to subscribe to your newsletter over another magazine or journal, and plan on providing interesting articles to keep your readers coming back for more.

EQUIP YOURSELF

- a separate phone line for new subscriptions

- a modem, fax software, and internet access with an e-mail account

- database software like filemaker to keep track of customer activity

- laser printer

- copier

- a high-end computer system

- office furniture

GETTING THE WORD OUT

To generate interest in your newsletter, you may have to seek national exposure. The best way to do this is to write articles about your newsletter and its benefits, and try to get a write-up in nationally distributed publications. Once you've accomplished this feat, you will be surprised at how many orders you receive. One newsletter publisher reported an influx of 500 orders after receiving editorial coverage in a large magazine.

BECOMING A
PROFESSIONAL NUTRITIONAL CONSULTANT

Health, fitness, physical well-being . . . few of us can say that we don't care about any of this. Living a healthy lifestyle has become a major concern. Ever since the phrase "you are what you eat" came into vogue, many of us have been treating our bodies as temples, and loading up on the healthy-diet hype.

With all this emphasis on eating right, avoiding fast-food outlets, and staying at a good weight, the nutritional industry is making big profits off of American's obsession with healthiness. In the mid-1990's, the number of registered dietitians nearly doubled. And the demand is growing as well.

Considering the myriad of health problems plaguing the nation—high cholesterol, hypertension, etc.—it makes sense to seek counsel from an experienced, licensed nutritional professional. If you want to help others start healthy eating habits and educate people about the benefits of a balanced diet, then this business is perfect for you.

RAKING IN THE DOUGH

Since most private nutritional counselors charge at least $60 per hour for their services, the amount of money you make can add up quickly. Prepare to see pretax profits add up to anywhere from $40,000 your first year to $120,000 after you've amassed a bevy of nutritionally challenged clients.

START-UP COSTS

If you start work from your home address, you shouldn't need more than $3,000 to $10,000 to get your business up and running.

HELP IS ON THE WAY

Whether you need information about nutritional courses, new developments in the industry, or marketing techniques, you'll find it all through the following resources.

Associations:
- American Association of Nutritional Consultants: 702/361-1132
  Las Vegas, Nevada

- Dietary Manager's Association: 603/775-9200
  St. Charles, Illinois

- Nutrition Institute of America: 212/799-2234
  New York, New York

Trade Publications:
- *Journal of Nutrition:* 301/330-7050
  Bethesda, Maryland

Read All About It:
- *The Dietitian's Guide to Vegetarian Diets* by Mark and Virginia Messina.
  Aspen Publishers, 1996.

- *Opportunities in Nutrition Careers.* VGM Career Books, 1991.

LICENSING
Besides the basic business license, nutritional consultants are required to maintain a special license. Depending on what kind of educational background you have or are planning to pursue, you will have to secure information regarding becoming an accredited and licensed nutritional consultant.

MARKET RESEARCH AND LOCATION
Individuals that fall into the middle- to upper-class income brackets will be your best source of stable business. You should also try to find areas replete with the aging baby-boomer set. This demographic has been known as having a preoccupation with healthy eating and living.

If you're planning to operate a consulting service for individuals, rather than corporations or restaurants, you can begin working from a small office. Because you'll have to be meeting with clients on a regular basis, you should consider this alternative rather than working out of the house.

EQUIP YOURSELF
- computer system

- nutritional software programs

- office furniture

- business cards, stationery, letterhead

GETTING THE WORD OUT

The best way to advertise your business to the public is to write informative articles about nutrition for local papers. If your article is accepted, you will be viewed as a foremost authority on the subject matter, and can include your phone number for people who want to learn more.

You can jump-start your client list by advertising in local papers and on the radio. Stress the importance of eating right as well as your credentials. When it comes to health, most people want to know they're dealing with an expert.

STARTING A
PERSONAL SHOPPING SERVICE

Pop quiz: What was it that they meant by "shop till you drop"? Those of you who never tire of the chase probably have yet to figure that one out. You are the apple of America's eye—the carefree consumer. Mind you, we're not talking care*less*, which is largely pejorative, and suggests the unsavory image of a house full of junk. No, that doesn't describe you in the least.

The ideal candidate for this venture is an impresario of style. The model personal shopper is always the focus of positive attention, and has the perfect gift for every occasion. But what's more, these entrepreneurs are not selfish with their talents. So if you'd like to teach the world to dress in perfect flattery, you may have found your calling.

But a personal shopping service is not for the tight-fisted. Having fun is a key component of squandering other people's money. Procuring trunk loads of merchandise without a moment's fear, guilt, or regret requires complete unfamiliarity with buyer's remorse. You must buy with joy in your heart, and peace in your mind. If such has been your experience all along, you're a natural. So take that jacket by its lapel and blithely proceed to . . . CHARGE IT!

RAKING IN THE DOUGH

In all honesty you're probably not going to make a mill in the garment district. But who cares? With your spending habits, you probably couldn't amass so much as a dime. Wait and see. The money you save by purging that urge to splurge will add up in no time.

A realistic assessment of your potential salary will fall someplace between the $20,000 to $40,000 range. It all depends on your ambition, and the staying power of your drive to keep on shopping.

START-UP COSTS

Are all you young entrepreneurs listening? Well then, hear this opportunity knock: Your investment need not exceed $1,000. Why so paltry? No need for office space or any high-tech equipment means no need to impress the loan officer.

HELP IS ON THE WAY

You probably know full well about the fashion magazines, the home-accessory catalogs, as well as the layout of every shopping center in your time zone, but have you heard about the following business boosters? If not, then . . .

Read All About It:

- *Chic Simple Men's Wardrobe* by Kim Gross and Jeff Stone. Knopf, 1998.

- *Chic Simple Women's Wardrobe* by Kim Gross and Jeff Stone. Knopf, 1996.

- Entrepreneur's Start-Up Guide: "Personal Shopping Service": 800/421-2300

MARKET RESEARCH AND LOCATION

A city bubbling over with activity is an ideal locale for a personal shopper. Your target customer is someone without a second to spare and with money to burn (why else would they actually be paying you for a day at the mall?!). How do you find these sugar mamas and papas? Here's what to look out for:

- high-end household income

- traveling habits

- corporations & executives

- dual-income families

- affluent single parents

- tourists

Parceling through the odds and ends of your target area is not as daunting a task as it appears. The following sources can provide you with a mountain of invaluable demographic information:

- U.S. Census Bureau

- Local Chamber of Commerce

- An ever-obliging librarian

While you're at it, determine what your pricing policy is going to be, and put it in writing. Because there are a lot of tough customers in this racket, most personal shoppers charge by the hour, not by purchase. Call several personal shoppers in your area to find out where they stand on fees. People still believe that you get what you pay for, so don't sell yourself short just because you're new to the scene.

EQUIP YOURSELF
- a car to tool around the shopping districts

- daily planner to keep track of appointments

- Rolodex with clients names and phone numbers

- business cards to expand your clientele

- beeper and cellular phone, for last-minute cancellations and consultations

- subscriptions to several magazines and catalogs

GETTING THE WORD OUT
Now comes the fun part! Here's your chance to get creative. How are you going to attract a clientele that won't have you rifling through Dumpsters come New Year's Day. Let's pretend you're short on connections, what now?

- write your own press release and mail away

- advertise in popular city publications

- list yourself in the Yellow Pages

- cold-call, brutal yet effective

- strategically post fliers (in hotels and corporate lobbies)

- get free-handed with your business cards

STARTING YOUR OWN
PET SITTING SERVICE

Hear ye! Hear ye! Animal lovers, listen up! Entrepreneurs with a soft spot for furry creatures are a lucky lot. Getting paid to feed and play with other people's pets, what could be better? Besides the obvious perks of never having to wear a suit and absolutely no human supervision, there's the matter of very low start-up costs. A pet sitting service can easily be started right out of your own backyard, and you can bring in substantial currency as your reputation and customer base grow.

We all like to go on vacation every now and then. For some of us, it's a simple process of pack up and go, but for poor Fluffy, the issue is fraught with controversy. Pet owners understand their charges' concern, and are almost always grappling with the horns of a major dilemma: what to do with the dog, cat, or python, as the case may be. Dropping Fifi off at a friend's is too much of an imposition, but the kennel is so impersonal, it's downright cruel. That's where you come in. Not only will you be providing care for the pet, you can also water the plants and get the mail. But since trust is of paramount importance, just you leave that disco ball where you found it. That's right, while the customers are away the pet sitters will not play. The peace of mind your service has to offer will keep your clients coming back time and time again. So get out your pooper-scooper, and get ready to make a pretty profit sitting pets.

RAKING IN THE DOUGH

On average, a pet sitting service can expect to bring in a pretax net profit of $52,000. But that's just for starters. Some pet sitting service businesses report profits of $110,00 to $200,000 annually. You may have to contend with a few difficult critters now and again, but what's a few barking canines when we're talking this kind of money.

START-UP COSTS

Here's the best part of all. Pet sitting services can be started on virtually nothing. You can even house the entire operation under your own roof, saving yourself tons of cash in the meanwhile. The whole kit and caboodle can be set up on a measly $500. Some business owners report a start-up cost of $4,000 or even $5,000. But even at the high end of the start-up spectrum, a thrifty capitalist could do much worse than this small-stakes/high-profit venture.

MARKET RESEARCH

While it's true that pet owners abound, you're far better off researching the local market before opening for business. Are there a lot of young, single professionals residing in the area? What about the about the well-to-do? These groups tend to log on more frequent-flier miles than any other, and are bound to spawn more potential patrons than you'll know what to do with. You should also keep an eye out for competition. Check out the local Yellow Pages and call up any contenders. Ask them about what kind of services they offer, which kinds of pets they sit for, and what territorial region their services cover. A robust interrogation may get you thinking about how to differentiate yourself in the marketplace, or reveal that all competition is null and void.

HELP IS ON THE WAY

Registering for membership with one of these associations can considerably boost your business. Besides serving as referral services and resource centers, they will provide access to inexpensive insurance plans and offer discounts on certain products and services.

Associations:
- National Association of Professional Pet Sitters: 202/393-3317
  Washington, D.C.

- Pet Sitters International: 910/983-9222
  King, North Carolina

Trade Publications:
- *Pet Age*: 312/663-4040
  Chicago, Illinois

Read All About It:
- *Pet Sitting for Profit.* Howell Book House/Macmillan, 1991.

- *The Professional Pet Sitter: Your Guide to Starting and Operating a Successful Service.* Paws-itive Press, 1994.

- *Sit and Grow Rich: Petsitting and Housesitting for Profit.* Upstart Publishing, 1993.

LICENSE AND INSURANCE

You don't have to be a vet to succeed in this biz, but you will have to have some familiarity with the basics of pet care. You'll also have to look into obtaining a standard business license and various permits, as well as meeting certain tax requirements. If the home-based route is for you, check with a professional about city zoning laws before stocking up on plastic cushion covers.

Insurance is a top-dog issue in the pet industry. Forget the weak humor, and concentrate on the scary side of animal care for a moment—not all pets are friendly to strangers. That's where a reliable insurance salesperson comes in. You'll need bonding and liability insurance, as well as automobile insurance that covers you while transporting pets for business purposes.

Finally, don't even think about saving money on lawyer's fees by drafting up the client-pet sitter agreement yourself. In case something goes horribly wrong, you'll need the added protection that only a well-thought-out contract can offer. You shouldn't be held accountable for every little problem that arises, so protect yourself and your business by having a lawyer draw up an airtight contract.

EQUIP YOURSELF

The beauty of the pet sitting business is that it requires very little space and only the most basic equipment for operation. Anyone with a spare room can start a sitting service.

Mandatory Office Equipment
- office desk and chair
- fax machine
- two-line phone
- filing cabinet
- possibly a computer system to maintain a client database.

Since you will have many appointments to keep and a good deal of tooling around to do, invest in a few local maps and a scheduling aid. And don't forget . . .

Pet Supplies

- pet carrier
- first-aid kit
- extra leash

SERVICES AND PRICES

Determining which services you'll be providing to customers and what you will charge is your next step. In addition to pet care, some pet sitters offer the deluxe home-maintenance package: bringing in the mail, starting the client's car once a day, collecting newspapers, and watering the plants. Your rates will depend on the services you provide.

When setting prices, keep geographic considerations in mind. Calculate the total amount of gas expended for each trip and figure that expense into your total bill. It may seem like a drop in the bucket, but drip, drip, drip, and before you know it you're dry.

You should also factor in the number of pets per household. The more pets, the merrier your pocketbook. Twenty bucks is the average going rate per call, but it's always a good idea to check out where the competition stands. And don't forget to ask about the services being provided when getting the cash breakdown. Sure, you're providing a humanitarian service, but that's as far as your resemblance to non-profit goes. You can't survive on applause, even if you are willing to jump through hoops for your customers.

GETTING THE WORD OUT

Your first couple of self-employed years will see a large portion of time spent in the pursuit of advertising and promotion. Once your customers are hooked and feel that you can be relied upon, you'll have enough business to last you a lifetime. There's no need to invest your life savings into a marketing campaign. Get your creative juices flowing, and you'll be surprised at how quickly the word will spread. Your first goal is to get as much free press as you can. Leaving your business cards or posting fliers at your local veterinarians' offices, pet grooming salons, and pet shops will get you noticed by pet owners all over the county.

Another great way to generate business is to write up a press release about your company. You'll want to make it as newsworthy as possible. Create a press release that reads like a newspaper article, citing the popularity of pet sitting services. Local newspapers and radio stations will be more likely to feature your release free of charge if the promotional aspects are toned down. Don't offer special deals or discounts, save that pitch for when you've got prospective clients on the line.

If you have a few tokens left to invest in marketing, consider renting bench space at local parks for your advertisement. Since parks are piled high with people walking their pets, this marketing strategy may be the soundest initial investment you can make.

OPENING YOUR OWN
PHOTOGRAPHY STUDIO

Have you ever wanted to get into showbiz? Do you dream of trading places with the paparazzi when you see them at work? And how about those exotic scenes so strikingly depicted in the pages of *National Geographic*, do you ever wish to claim credit? Or maybe it's danger you crave, and the opportunity to capture those shocking images of carnage in war-torn lands?

Even if you've never taken so much as a photography class, it's never too late to begin studying up for this business venture. Those of you lugging your cameras around, in search of that perfect image, will be glad to know that your long-time hobby can pay off big as a full-time occupation. There are many opportunities for a photography business owner. There are approximately 125,000 photographers currently working in the U.S. And it's no wonder, since photography was a $5 billion business throughout the nineties.

Weddings, corporate parties, entertainers, and young kids can all be a solid source of revenue. All you'll have to do is learn enough to create high-quality pictures for any person, on any occasion.

RAKING IN THE DOUGH

Large-scale studios with moderately sized staffs have been known to generate gross profits in the $300,000 range. But even a small, house-bound studio can bring in anywhere from $40,000 to $85,000 gross per year.

START-UP COSTS

Once again, the amount you spend on a small studio in your house will be much smaller than opening a large photo studio in a commercial location. One photographer working out of her home reported starting her business on a budget of $3,000. If you plan on renting space in a shopping mall for your studio, you'll need anywhere from $70,000 to $170,000 in start-up capital — depending on the location of the mall, and the dimensions of your space.

HELP IS ON THE WAY

When you're looking for marketing information, suppliers' directories, and other vital pointers, you can't go wrong with these valuable resources.

Associations:
- Photographic Society of America: 405/843-1437
  Oklahoma City, Oklahoma

Trade Publications:
- *Camera Arts Magazine*: 916/441-2557
  Sacramento, California

- *Photo District News*: 212/536-5222
  New York, New York

- *PhotoMarket*; 715/248-3800
  Osceola, Wisconsin

- *The Photo Review*: 215/757-8921
  Longhorne, Pennsylvania

Read All About It:
- *The Basic Book of Photography* by Michelle and Tom Grimm. Plume, 1997.

- *The Business of Commercial Photography* by Ira Wexler. Amphoto, 1997.

- *The Business of Studio Photography: How to Start and Run a Successful Photography Studio* by Edward Lilley. Amphoto, 1997.

- *How to Start a Home-Based Photography Business* by Kenn Oberrecht. Globe Pequot Press, 1996.

- *How to Start and Run a Successful Photography Business.* Images Press, 1993.

- *The Photographer's Guide to Marketing and Self-Promotion* by Mario Piscopo, Allworth Press, 1995.

- *Profitable Photography: Start and Run a Money-Making Business* by Gezas Szurovy. TAB Books, 1995.

LAYOUT AND DESIGN

Whether you're planning on opening a home-based studio or renting a larger space for a large studio, you will need to reserve at least 200 square feet for your darkroom. Studios located in a commercial area should also make allowances for a waiting room and a separate, enclosed area for the actual shoot.

EQUIP YOURSELF

Photographers need to stay current with the latest technology breakthroughs in the industry. But for starters, you will need these basic items to run a successful studio:

- several studio lights
- tripod
- seamless paper
- a high-end camera
- darkroom equipment
- computer for accounting purposes and creating a customer database

GETTING THE WORD OUT

Photographers can provide services for a variety of events. If you're planning to become a party and wedding photographer, make sure you send your card and samples of your work to wedding consultants and party planners in your area. If you're planning on providing headshots for actors, you would do well to list your business in acting trade magazines and directories. You can also leave your card with nearby talent and modeling agencies.

Advertising in traditional media outlets can also serve you well in the long run. By doing this, you are likely to secure a wide variety of clients and that can translate into a better payoff.

STARTING A
PLANT MAINTENANCE SERVICE

Ever wonder who tends to all those plants housed by large corporate buildings? Or what brand of Santa Claus shows up three weeks before Christmas to decorate your lobby with a truckload of poinsettias? Chances are it's not the executives. And if you think the inundated administrative assistants have no more pressing demands, you're sorely mistaken. No, the job of plant maintenance usually falls in the lap of an interiorscaping service, one that's specifically designed to do the job right.

If your home is a regular warehouse of chloroform-producing life forms, then this business opportunity may be just what you're looking for. A love for plants is crucial in this business, so if you enjoy whispering sweet nothings to your ferns, serenading your African violets, and generally spending quality time with all of your shrubs and flowers, then you're ready to watch your profits grow in the interiorscape field.

RAKING IN THE DOUGH

Plant maintenance technicians can bring in quite a bountiful harvest come billing time. Depending on the size of your business (the number of employees and clients) your gross annual income can range from $50,000 to $150,000.

START-UP COSTS

You won't need to spend a penny on office space, as this is one business that you can run from your very own home. But since you will need to invest in marketing, office equipment, employee salaries, and plant maintenance supplies, you will incur some costs. $15,000 should be more than enough to get you ready for business.

HELP IS ON THE WAY

To succeed in this industry, you'll need to know what design ideas have taken the corporate office world by storm. You'll also benefit by learning about the newest techniques in plant care and getting sales tips from industry professionals. The following sources should satisfy all of your most urgent concerns.

Associations:
- American Horticultural Society: 703/768-5700
  Alexandria, Virginia

- American Society for Horticultural Science (ASHS): 703/836-4606
  Alexandria, Virginia

Trade Publications:
- *Interior Landscape*: 312/782-5505
  Chicago, Illinois

- *Interiorscape*: 813/796-3877
  Clearwater, Florida

Read All About It:
- *The Complete Guide to Indoor Gardening* by Jenny Raworth and Val Bradley. Abbeville Press, 1998.

- *Interior Plantscapes: Installation, Maintenance, and Management* by George Manaker. Prentice Hall Press, 1996.

- *The Secret Life of Plants* by Peter Tompkins and Christopher Bird. HarperCollins, 1989.

MARKET RESEARCH AND LOCATION

Arm yourself with important knowledge before venturing into this competitive industry. Because you won't be the first horticultural technician on the block, you'll need to weed out the competition by doing quite a bit of cold calling. Call it a fishing expedition, call it a fact-finding commission, but get out there and make those phone calls. Survey every large company and property management firm. Find out what they like about their plant maintenance service, as well as what extra touches they'd want to have included in the service. Then tailor your business to their fondest wishes, and you'll have a chance to edge out your opponents.

Where you're located is another important factor to take into consideration. Is your area attractive to new companies or is the business community heading for the hills? If the corner drugstore is the closest thing to a Fortune 500 company that your area has to offer, then either you move your plant maintenance service to Boomtown USA, or this business isn't in your stars. Better you find out sooner than later.

EQUIP YOURSELF

- computer system with fax/modem and special software

- fax machine

- photocopier

- multiple telephone lines

- car or van for driving technicians to site

- plant care supplies (watering cans, biodegradable soap, hand pruners, plant paws, etc.)

GETTING THE WORD OUT

First call companies to find out who makes their building and grounds-maintenance decisions. Make sure to get this person's name and mailing address. Once you compile a database, you'll be able to get your direct-mail campaign under way. Send out brochures asking, "How are your plants doing?" every four or five months. Include all the benefits your business has to offer, and you're bound to get some interested callers.

Of course, you should also list your company in the Yellow Pages. Finally, don't forget to make those cold calls, and engage in plenty of networking to secure your initial client list.

BECOMING A
PROFESSIONAL PSYCHIC

If you are endowed with a reliable sixth sense, why let it go to waste? Ask yourself: Can you accurately guess a person's occupation before meeting them, have you ever predicted a strange event, do you believe that planetary alignments determine the course of our lives? If the answer is yes, then you may very well be right on the cusp of a supernatural career.

The psychic business has boomed in recent years. Whether it's for purposes of entertainment or police investigation, psychics are being called upon to predict people's destinies all over the country. And psychics are finding that they can make a good living foretelling the future.

But fortune-tellers have to take their craft very seriously, and are most successful when they can provide a variety of psychic services like palm readings, tarot readings, as well as creating elaborate astrological charts. If you're serious about this fun occupation, then get ready to reap the benefits of an amazing financial forecast.

RAKING IN THE DOUGH

Psychics with their own shops and a substantial amount of party engagements can make $20,000 to $80,000 per year.

START-UP COSTS

Promotion and advertising will require that you invest at least $5,000 in this business right off the bat. This figure can climb to $20,000 if you're dead set on a storefront office space in a busy commercial borough.

HELP IS ON THE WAY

To become a successful psychic, you will need to become well versed in psychic terminology and practices. There are many resources that will help you establish yourself as a leading psychic practitioner.

Associations:

- American Federation of Astrologers: 602/838-1751
  Tempe, Arizona

- Association for Astrological Networking: 800/578-AFAN
  Beverly Hills, California

Read All About It:

- *The Complete Book of Palmistry* by Joyce Wilson. Bantam Books, 1998.

- *Psychic Development for Beginners: An Easy Guide to Developing and Releasing Your Psychic Abilities* by William Hewitt. Llewellyn Publications, 1996.

- *Psychic Explorer: A Down-to-Earth Guide to Six Magical Arts* by Jonathan Cainer and Carl Rider. Piatkus Books, 1998.

- *The Psychic Pathway* by Sonia Choquette. Crown Books, 1996.

LOCATION

Store-front psychics who are most successful report having set up their shops in large cities, in areas that attract a lot of tourists. Targeting tourists is a good bet since traveling puts people in the mood to spend money on things they normally wouldn't.

The corporate psychic often out-earns any of the retail variety. By going in strictly for the major functions, these soothsayers make one big score after another.

LAYOUT AND DESIGN

Your psychic shop should exude an aura of mystery and fantasy. It is very important to get your customers in the mood. Your success will depend on helping people believe in your abilities.

You can begin designing your store from the outside. Create a unique sign and incorporate lanterns and wrought-iron gates to heighten the public's suspense.

The inside of your store should have a waiting area and a virtually soundproof room for readings. Make sure to hang a curtain over the front door, so customers will feel like they're entering a new world of unlimited possibilities. The inside should have comfy couches and plenty of charming antiques to give your enterprise that old-world feeling.

GETTING THE WORD OUT

An effective marketing strategy for psychics can include:

- advertising in Yellow Pages
- special-interest articles in local publications
- on-premises signage listing prices
- direct-mail pieces to corporations for corporate events
- ads in astrology magazines
- Web site

HEADLINE YOUR OWN
PUBLIC RELATIONS AGENCY

Getting into the public eye is all-important to large businesses, authors, actors, philanthropic organizations—in short, to everyone who needs to tap into a mass market or sway public opinion. No one would spend millions on advertising if spreading word of their activities wasn't absolutely crucial.

But media attention carries advantages that advertising doesn't. First of all, people have a tendency to doubt commercial claims. But they aren't nearly as cynical about what they see on TV, hear on the radio, or read in the papers. What's more, public relations is also cost effective—often saving a company thousands of dollars. And finally, no amount of advertising can do the job of just one good publicist when it comes to damage control.

If you have journalism or PR experience, and can get along with a variety of people, then you're a prime candidate for starting your own public relations agency. Our advice is to jump to it, because there's no time like the present to go into business. In the wake of downsizing, more and more companies are opting to cut their in-house PR staff. This explains why outsourcing is at an all-time high, and why you can really make some noise as a PR specialist.

RAKING IN THE DOUGH

Be prepared to see some tough times in your business's infancy stages. It takes a while to show your mettle, but once you prove that you can deliver more than the allotted 15 minutes of fame, a powerful client list won't be a long time coming. Expect to see gross revenues in the $40,000 to $80,000 range.

START-UP COSTS

Entrepreneurs just starting out in the public relations business need not blow their entire wad on a spiffy office suite. This venture lends itself to a home office. You need little more than your phone and your computer system to get the ball rolling. Depending on how much you already have to go on, figure start-up costs range between $1,000 and $10,000.

HELP IS ON THE WAY

Even if you've worked public relations on the corporate front before, you're on your own now, and that can be a little daunting. But don't worry, this isn't exactly where no man has gone before—there are plenty of venues to try for advice, just take a stab at the following.

Associations:
- International Association of Business Communicators: 415/433-3400
  San Francisco, California

- Public Relations Society of America: 212/995-2230
  New York, New York

Trade Publications:
- *Bulldog Reporter*: 510/596-9300
  Emeryville, California

- *Inside PR and Reputation Management*: 212/245-8680
  New York, New York

- *Tactics Monthly Newspaper*: 212/995-2230
  New York, New York

Read All About It:
- *Effective Public Relations* by Scott Cutlip, et al. Prentice Hall Press, 1994.

- *Managing a Public Relations Firm for Growth and Profit* by A. C. Croft. Haworth Press, 1997.

- *Practice of Public Relations* by Fraser Seitel. Prentice Hall Press, 1998.

- *Public Relations Agency*: 800/421-2300; Entrepreneur's Business Start-Up Guide.

- *The Public Relations Writer's Handbook* by Mary Aronson and Dan Spetner. Lexington Books, 1993.

MARKET RESEARCH

There's work to be had in just about every sector of commerce; everyone from not-for-profit organizations to investment corporations needs to reach a broad audience at one point or another. In order to promote effectively, you'll have to become familiar with the ins and outs of the various industries you're involved in, whether that be banking, food service, or publishing.

Also consider your pricing policies. As long as it's reasonable, you can charge according to the income you want and the expenses you'll incur. This can be done either by the hour or on a retainer basis. If you're not sure about your prices, arrange informational interviews with other agencies and see what the fair going rates are.

EQUIP YOURSELF

- computer with fax modem, laser printer, and appropriate software

- two phone lines with voice mail

- fax machine and photocopier

- desk and filing cabinet

- stationery and business cards

- CD-ROM media directories, such as *Bacon's* or *Burrelle's*

GETTING THE WORD OUT

You're going to have to bring in a steady stream of business, by any means necessary, to survive in the public relations hood. But if you're going into this business on your own, chances are this is already your strong suit.

The best way to get noticed is through word of mouth. Satisfied customers either will recommend you to other businesses, or can be used as references when you're making a proposal. There's no overestimating the value of a good rep in public relations, so never burn your bridges.

Getting involved in your community is also worthwhile. Volunteering can be a great opportunity to grab the attention of important people who have the power to expand your business.

STARTING YOUR OWN
REMINDER SERVICE

For busy people who hate to miss a loved one's birthday or fear to miss a loved one's anniversary, reminder services have come as a welcome relief to the ongoing anxiety. Why is it no matter how hard we try to remember, a relative's or friend's birthday inevitably escapes us? It becomes especially difficult for people with large families.

And birthdays are just the beginning. You can expand your services to include business meetings, important events, and even contact information. If you have penchant for creating loving memories and making order out of chaos, you can make this business a veritable success.

You will have to be very well organized to run this business, since your customers will rely on you to keep their acts together.

RAKING IN THE DOUGH

While this business is fun, profit potential is rather low. You can make from $10,000 to $30,000 per year. You will be charging a per-month fee, and the longer your customers subscribe the better your chances are of making more money.

START-UP COSTS

Equipment and marketing will account for the majority of your start-up expenses. You will have to invest no less than $2,000 to get this business up and running. Most likely your investment will fall close to the $6,000 average.

EQUIP YOURSELF

Reminder services can either be operated by manually or automatically by phone, by e-mail, or via fax. These products will come in handy for any method of communication:

- computer with modem

- fax software

- phone software

- organizer software

- fax machine

- copier

- dual-line telephone

- marketing material

SELECTING A LOCATION

This business can be started anyplace. But because your service is a luxury, make sure the townspeople have the discretionary funds to throw your way.

Since this business requires only one person to operate, and involves no face-to-face client contact whatsoever, it's just the thing for entrepreneurs of the homeward-bound persuasion. You can automate your database to call your customers and leave them messages, or cut costs by making good use of e-mail.

GETTING THE WORD OUT

An inexpensive way of marketing your business is to post your advertisement in newsgroups and electronic bulletin boards. You can also set up a Web page to describe your services to new visitors.

Another way to enlist busy people into your reminder program is to call corporations and ask if they would be interested in setting up a service for their busier employees. With today's gentler leadership systems, big companies are willing to go out of their way to keep their more valuable employees happy and frazzle-free.

LAUNCHING YOUR OWN
RESALE ENTERPRISE

Who says you only go around once? By taking the secondhand-store route, you can breathe new life into bygone fashions and resuscitate your finances. Just because grunge has gone the way of the powdered wig doesn't mean that retro chic has lost its hold over pop culture. Look around. The runways are chock full of eighties regalia. The resurgence of Hush Puppies and Candies are just a taste of what's in store. Window displays are lined with threads pulled straight out of *Charlie's Angels.* Hip huggers, platforms, halter tops and stringy T's . . . relics of the seventies? No longer. Young trendsetters and big-name designers alike are recycling styles like there's no tomorrow.

Secondhand stores have been flourishing since the recession of 1987. So, while you're a bit late to get in on the ground floor of the resale action, the market is nowhere near the point of saturation. You'll provide an invaluable service to the fashion-conscious and penny-wise by supplying today's looks at yesterday's prices. Even though the economy is looking up, bargain hunters show no signs of slowing down. In short, there's still a bundle to made in thrift.

RAKING IN THE DOUGH

Of course, before you fish through the piles of castaway duds, you'll want to know what manner of profit you stand to net. The first several months will be a struggle, but once you pull through, you're well on your way to drawing anywhere from $30,000 to $120,000 per year.

START-UP COSTS

As stocking your shelves will cost next to nothing, you won't need to break the bank trying to pay your suppliers. Thrift/consignment store start-up costs are some of the lowest around. In fact, you can begin operating on as little as $1,000. And even if you do go all out, you'll find yourself hard pressed to spend more than $15,000. Opening a thrift shop is much like shopping at one—even if you buy out the entire store, you still won't have exceeded your credit limit.

HELP IS ON THE WAY
Joining forces with others in your field can prove a great boon to business. As a newcomer to the game of thrift, you'll benefit to no end from getting in touch with those who have weathered the storms of the biz.

Associations:
- National Association of Resale and Thrift Shops (NART): 800/544-0751 St. Clair Shores, Michigan

- National Retail Federation (NRF): 212/551-9260 New York, New York

Trade Publications:
- *Too Good to Be Threw*: 614/487-0709 Columbus, Ohio

Read All About It:
- *Start and Run a Profitable Second Hand Store* by Richard Crop, et al. Self Counsel Press, 1997.

- *Thrift Score: The Stuff, the Method, the Madness* by Al Hoff. Harper Perennial, 1997.

MARKET RESEARCH AND LOCATION
If you've heard it once, you've heard it a thousand times—location, location, location! Proximity to foot traffic, parking, and other secondhand stores is a good indicator of future success.

The nature of bargain hunting is store-hopping, so don't worry about the competition. Instead of muscling in on your sales, other thrift shops in the area will actually expand your clientele.

If you choose your site wisely, a little market research will go a long way. Pile a few bags of old duds into the trunk of your car and head on over to the site of your new store. Offer your wares to the neighborhood shops, and make sure to check out their consignors' contracts and merchandise prices. This thorough investigation should be all the market research you need to get your own enterprise under way.

LICENSE AND INSURANCE

Unless you want to be up to your neck in paperwork, contact an accountant and a lawyer to sift through the ordinances and fine print. There will be plenty of business licenses, tax permits, and contracts to keep your hired guns busy. If, on the other hand, you don't have the capital to pay these pros, contact the local Chamber of Commerce for information on how you can handle these pesky technicalities yourself.

DESIGN AND EQUIPMENT

First things first. Before you send out the call for old clothes, you should consider where you're going to put them. Since you're not in the rummage-sale business, hangers and racks are a good place to start. Price tags may also prove useful. Keep in mind that yours is a retail establishment. You will therefore require the services of a cash register and a computer to keep track of accounts.

When it comes to apparel, mirrors and dressing rooms are the name of the game. A full-length mirror and a good lightbulb will transform any closet into a star-quality changing area. If all you have is an alcove, hang up a velvet curtain and voila! a dressing room is born.

Of course, you'll not want to leave your store bare of that certain something known as panache. Paint the walls a rich color. Consider using steel wool to give them that popular aged look. Look around some antique stores for inexpensive wood shelves, cabinets, and lighting fixtures. Attend a starving artists' sale or raid the walls of your fave coffeeshop for dirt-cheap art. Low cost and high quality *can* peacefully coexist— let your decor say it all.

And now, for the final pièces de resistance, the sign and window display. Never underestimate the importance of a fetching facade. If your sign is clever and eye-catching, and your window showcases your most stellar products, your shop is sure to take first place on every bargain hunter's hit list.

STARTING YOUR OWN
RESUME SERVICE

Try to remember the first time you sat down to write a resume. The painstaking thought process, the desperate thesaurus searches, the full waste basket . . . wasn't easy, was it? Nonetheless, twenty jobs and resume revisions later, you can finally say you're the resume champion of the world.

You now know that there is an art to constructing a professional resume — and we're not talking about lying. Anyone who can take a few qualifications and stretch them into an impressive full-page resume can offer his or her services to people just starting out or starting over in the work force.

Emphasizing the right points and adorning them with those action verbs can make even the most inexperienced candidate sound like management material. If you have had tremendous success crafting your as well as your friends' resumes, you may be able to put those powers to use. Some design experience may also put your services at the top of many clients' lists. A resume is after all a presentation, and it is up to you to make your clients' resumes stand out from the rest.

RAKING IN THE DOUGH

Resume crafters can expect to make anywhere from $20,000 to $60,000 per year. If you can constantly generate a steady flow of clients, and produce quality work that will get you valuable referrals, you can maintain this business for many years to come.

START-UP COSTS

For resume service owners working out of their house, this business can require a start-up investment as low as $3,000. If looking to branch out and open up shop in a small office, you will need at least $8,000.

HELP IS ON THE WAY

The look of resumes is constantly changing. And different industries can have different resume requirements. Make sure you're prepared to handle any job by reading up about resumes:

Associations:
- Professional Association of Resume Writers: 800/822-7279
  St. Petersburg, Florida

Read All About It:
- *The Adams Resume Almanac* by Robert L. Adams. Adams Media, 1994.

- *How to Start a Home-Based Resume Business* by Jan Melnik. Globe Pequot Press, 1997.

- *Knock 'Em Dead 1998* by Martin Yate. Adams Media, 1997.

- *Start Your Own Resume Writing Service* by JoAnn Padget. Pfeiffer & Company, 1994.

- *The Upstart Guide to Owning and Managing a Resume Service* by Dan Ramsey. Dearborn Publications, 1994.

MARKET RESEARCH AND LOCATION

College students, people in career transition, and immigrants will make up the majority of your clients. Many resume service owners swear by a college-town location, while others prefer operating in large cities. Wherever you choose to settle, remember to call around to other resume services to check out how much bang they give for the buck.

EQUIP YOURSELF
- computer system

- fax machine

- office furniture

- page layout and word processing software

- laser printer

GETTING THE WORD OUT

Besides traditional advertising strategies—telephone directories, career magazines, classified ads near the jobs section—you can distribute pamphlets and samples of your work to career counseling centers in nearby universities. You can even send out fliers, with a rate sheet, to out-of-town colleges. You will not have to meet with clients, so take advantage of this by making vital contacts all over the country.

You should also distribute your information to employment agencies around your area. When clients come in, they can refer them to your service. And once you're saddled with your first batch of customers, encourage them to refer their friends and acquaintances.

STARTING YOUR OWN
ROOMMATE MATCHING SERVICE

Finding the right roommate can often be as difficult as finding a needle in a haystack. Compatibility problems and a reticence to move in with complete strangers has forced most people to join forces with friends and/or acquaintances. But what about when a person relocates to a new city or doesn't know anyone looking for a roommate?

With the rising cost of housing, many people just can't afford to live alone. If they do go out in search of roommates through ads in the paper, they often become more distressed with every passing meeting. Unable to find satisfactory roommates, many people end up settling for less — and wind up relocating every time a lease expires.

In recent years, the role of the roommate matching service has become very important, especially in large cities. It will be your job to match roommates based on common interests, personalities, and budgets. An eye for compatible roommates and a certain amount of preparation can make running this business a rewarding and lucrative experience.

RAKING IN THE DOUGH

In this line of work, you will have to rely on a steady stream of clients to make a good living. During your first year, profits may be low, since you will be establishing yourself in the marketplace. But after you've attracted a variety of qualified applicants, you can expect pretax net profits of $35,000 to $70,000 per year.

START-UP COSTS

This business can be started out of the home, but since you will have to meet with clients on a daily basis, we recommend leasing a small office space in a commercial area. This will raise start-up costs, but will pay off in the long run.

An effective marketing campaign will also swallow up most of your initial start-up loot, but it always pays to get the word out. You can expect total start-up costs of $20,000 to $30,000 if you go out-of-house. Cut those figures in half if you decide to conduct business from the home.

MARKET RESEARCH AND LOCATION

Large and mid-sized cities are the ideal places to start this business. Such areas are bursting at the seams with your target customers—single, divorced, and widowed men and women, recent college graduates, and professionals who have had to relocate for work reasons.

To make sure your pricing policy is on the money, place some calls to similar services in your city, and check to see how much they charge. Then pick an upscale commercial zone to set up your headquarters, so that it's convenient to your desired clientele.

IMAGE MATTERS

Your space should have room enough for a private office, where you'll interview and screen your clients. There should also be a reception area where clients can wait to meet with you (just don't leave them waiting too long, lest they hook up and are never heard from again).

In terms of general decor, you may want to take pictures of your happy roommates and hang them up around the waiting area to underscore the effectiveness of your service to prospective customers.

CAST AND CREW

Since you will have to interview all of your clients, you may want to hire a part-time or full-time office assistant to help with accounting and other administrative tasks. Make sure the person you hire has a pleasant demeanor, is responsible, and understands his or her role. You will also want to rely on the assistant to conduct interviews from time to time, so make sure he or she has a professional appearance to give your business the proper image.

GETTING THE WORD OUT

A good way to bring in new business is to leave your name with relocation and real estate companies. If a need for your service comes up, and it will, you will be the first one they call.

You should also advertise in the local newspapers' real estate sections, paste up fliers throughout the neighborhood, and list your business in the Yellow Pages.

BECOMING A
SEMINAR LEADER

Speaking in public may scare the pants right off the majority of the population, but those brave enough to speak their minds can make quite a living instructing seminar-goers in anything from forming lasting relationships to improving their financial outlook. Conventions, corporations, universities, and community centers are constantly on the lookout for creative speakers with fresh ideas. To keep their members occupied, many of these organization schedule speakers to come in and lecture their members.

You don't need a Ph.D. or an MBA to become a bona-fide public speaker; all you need to do is to become an expert in your chosen field. Whether it's through writing articles for local papers and magazines or just doing that extra bit of research, if you're an effective communicator, you can launch your speaking career almost immediately and the reap its amazing benefits.

RAKING IN THE DOUGH

Seminar leaders make anywhere from $30,000 to $100,000 per year, with some of the most popular speakers even bringing in as much as $200,000 per year. But don't expect to make big money at first. Be patient, and as your reputation grows, so will your net worth.

START-UP COSTS

This business involves a relatively low price tag. You can start operating with as little as $3,000, and in some cases even less.

HELP IS ON THE WAY

You are never too young too learn the ins and outs of the seminar business. From polishing your speaking skills to marketing your enterprise, these helpful resources are bound to keep you on the right track.

Associations:
- American Seminar Leaders Association: 800/801-1886
  Pasadena, California

- National Speakers Association: 602/968-2552
  Tempe, Arizona

- Toastmasters International: 949/858-8255
  Misson Viejo, California

Trade Publications:
- *Marketing Seminars and Conferences*: 913/539-5376
  Manhattan, Kansas

- *Professional Speaker Magazine*: 602/968-2552
  Tempe, Arizona

- *Sharing Ideas*: 818/335-8069
  Glendora, California

Read All About It:
- *The Art of Public Speaking* by Stephen Lucas. McGraw-Hill, 1997.

- *How to Make a Fortune from Public Speaking* by Dr. Robert Anthony. Berkley Publishing Group, 1988.

- *How to Make It Big in the Seminar Business* by Paul Karasik. McGraw-Hill, 1991.

- *Speak and Grow Rich*, 2nd ed., by Dottie Walters. Prentice-Hall, 1996.

- *Success and Secrets of Motivational Superstars* by Michael Jeffreys. Prima, 1996.

MARKET RESEARCH AND LOCATION

Prior to zooming in on your target audience, you will have to select an area of expertise. Your best bet is to choose a subject you are genuinely interested in. Once you've completed this initial step, you will have to determine which audience would welcome your presentation. If you plan on targeting women, then you'll have to contact women's groups in your search for the perfect venue. If your bread-and-butter customers will most likely be comprised of business professionals, try to schedule seminars at corporations.

You won't have to invest in a spiffy office to make this business idea a huge success. Since you'll be doing a lot of traveling, you can skimp on overhead and save lots of money in the process.

EQUIP YOURSELF

All professional public speakers will need to invest in the following items:

- computer with modem
- fax machine
- cellular and/or phone system
- deluxe press kit and brochures
- training products, like videos, books, or audiocassettes

GETTING THE WORD OUT

Success in this business means blowing your own horn till you're blue in the face. Unless people know about your services and superior speaking abilities, they won't hire you. The more visible you become, the more money you will make. It's that simple.

You will need top-of-the-line promotional material to send out to prospective clients. Make sure your pamphlets are bright, professional, and accurately depict the content matter of your presentation. Try to get coverage in any publication or reviewed by various group leaders. Then, you can insert their testimonials into your press kit.

Seminar leaders just starting out should consider speaking free of charge. Not only will you get invaluable practice, you will begin to build a name for yourself, and that's what this business is all about.

OPENING YOUR OWN
SKATE RENTAL SHOP

From the beach, to the streets, everyone is strapping on a pair of in-line skates. Since the early 1990's, Rollerblades® have become as ubiquitous as roller skates used to be in the '70s and early '80s. Except for one small difference — these skates are much, much pricier. That's why rollerblade rental shops have been reporting hefty profits for several years now. While there're plenty of die-hard bladers with a pair of skates to call their own, many people prefer to rent theirs on special occasions. That's where you come in.

This business is a great financial solution for anyone who loves the outdoors. You will be responsible for matching the right skates with the right customer, collecting security deposits, and making sure everyone is equipped with the requisite safety gear. And when all is said and done, you'll be thrilled with the knowledge that not only are you making a good buck, you're also helping people enjoy a healthy and entertaining pastime.

RAKING IN THE DOUGH

Small in-line skate shops make anywhere from $30,000 to $70,000 per year, depending on whether you're situated in region that allows for year-round skating. You can also bring in extra funds by buying a cooler and selling beverages (at a healthy profit) to thirsty athletes after a hard day's skate.

START-UP COSTS

Since you'll be working outside you can do away with expensive overhead costs by setting up a booth with a bold sign. But you will also have to market your services and invest in at least 20 pairs of skates. So expect to spend no less than $10,000 to get up and running.

HELP IS ON THE WAY

You can read about trends in sports in all your favorite consumer magazines, and while you're at it, give the following a look-see.

Trade Publications:

- *City Sports*: 415/626 1600
  San Francisco, California

- *Fitness and Speed Skating Times*: 954/782-5928
  Pompano, Florida

LICENSE AND INSURANCE

While it is a fun sport, in-line skating can also be dangerous. You will have to secure liability and theft insurance before opening for business.

Also, make sure to check with the local authorities before setting up house. You may have to register and pay a standard fee before you can legally open up for business.

MARKET RESEARCH AND LOCATION

This one's simple. You should set up shop in a sunny and warm climate, with plenty of active people enjoying it. While you can run your business in any city during the summer, you will stand to make more if you migrate to a tropical clime.

EQUIP YOURSELF

- at least two sets of in-line skates in every size—more in the most common sizes

- safety gear

- a large van for transportation of goods

- a mobile cart to display your services

- a lockbox to keep your cash

GETTING THE WORD OUT

The best way to attract customers is to create a bold corporate identity and watch the outdoorsy types flock to your stand. You should also hang fliers near your station and in local sports shops for even better results.

Another way to attract customers is to offer in-line skating lessons for novices. You can either hire an instructor or do it yourself after hours.

OPERATING YOUR OWN
SOFTWARE PUBLISHING FIRM

Software publishers and designers are coming out of the woodwork in droves. Everyone from young hackers to experienced computer programmers are getting in on the lucrative software action, and are seeing their efforts amply rewarded. You can choose to hire designers, and take care of the publishing and distribution end, or just become a full-time consultant to companies in need of assistance. There are many opportunities in this business and they're not all in Silicon Valley either! The software publishing industry has been on a steady rise during the nineties, and shows no sign of slowing down.

If you have creativity, an ability to spot a gap in the software applications market, and have the technical expertise to boot, you are a prime contender for becoming a successful software publisher.

RAKING IN THE DOUGH

Just as there are no limits to your imagination, there are no limits to how much money you can make. The software field is ripe with opportunities, and one good idea can set you up for life. Successful software designers report making $60,000 to $300,000 per year.

START-UP COSTS

The appeal of this business for young people lies in it being a very cost-effective business alternative. You can start working right out of your house, and you may even have all the necessary equipment already set up. Marketing your programs will most likely be the costliest factor in your business plan. If you already have top-of-the-line computer equipment, you can start for as low as $3,000. For people whose computer needs are yet to be provided for, you'll need around $10,000 to get this business off the ground.

HELP IS ON THE WAY

To keep up with what's going on in the software publishing industry, you'll need to look to professional resources. You never know when a new program will come out that can make your work easier.

Associations:

- Information Technology Association of America: 703/522-5055
  Arlington, Virginia

- Software Publishers Association: 202/452-1600
  Washington, D.C.

Trade Publications:

- *IEEE Software*; 717/821-8380
  Los Alamitos, California

- *Soft-Letter*; 617/924-3944
  Watertown, Massachusetts

Read All About It:

- *Building a Successful Software Business* by David Radin. O'Reilly & Associates, 1997.

- *Dynamics of Software Development* by Jim McCarthy and Denis Gilbert. Microsoft Press, 1995.

- *Making Money with Multimedia* by David Rosen. Addison-Wesley, 1994.

- *Software Project Survival Guide* by Steve McConnell. Microsoft Press, 1997.

MARKET RESEARCH AND LOCATION

Because most software publishing companies can be run by one person and rarely receive visits from customers, they are often started in the home. Even very successful publishers prefer to work out of their home, claiming it's more comfortable and fosters creativity.

Before developing any software programs, research as many business industries as you can. Focus on each one's needs and limitations, and then consider what kind of program would fulfill these needs. You can create games and other general programs, but most software creators believe targeted niche programs are most lucrative in the end.

EQUIP YOURSELF

- phone system for technical support

- computer system

- modem

- peripherals

- software applications

GETTING THE WORD OUT

Once you've developed a software program that you think has what it takes, begin to compile promotional material that will set it off in the most favorable light. Make sure to include a product shot in eye-catching packaging. Once you've created brochures, determined the price you wish to charge, and have a toll-free number set up for orders, you can begin distributing information about your new product.

Direct mail can get you the results you want. Send each promotional package to professionals in your target industry. Make sure to emphasize the benefits they stand to gain by using your program. Another solid choice for marketing your program is to set up a booth at all industry-related trade shows. You can use this opportunity to demonstrate your software's capabilities and appearance.

ESTABLISHING YOUR OWN
TALENT AGENCY

Oh, those impish thespians! Don't you just adore their earnest, soul-searching ways? And with their ephemeral beauty and statuesque physiques, models aren't so bad themselves. Bag this attitude, and you're already halfway to being best friend (as well as worst nightmare) to talent everywhere, namely an agent.

Other talent agent qualifications include an ability to negotiate contracts, break bad news, schmaltz on the schmooze, discern a dud from a stud, and give moral support with the best of them. Once you're packing these esteemed credentials, you're ready to say hooray for Hollywood.

RAKING IN THE DOUGH

Doubtless you've heard about the kind of money Michael Ovitz was clearing during his heyday as talent rep extraordinaire. Well, rest assured that your chances of seeing such lofty sums are about a million to one. You'll have to content yourself with a spiffy, if not inspirational, profit margin—something between the lines of $20,000 (in the initial business stages) and $80,000+ (once the business is more established) per year.

START-UP COSTS

This type of work doesn't take much in the way of office space, employees, and equipment. Your main capital outlays will probably go to marketing schemes, so it's perfectly reasonable to get the whole kit and caboodle under way for under $20,000.

HELP IS ON THE WAY

You go to theaters, you watch TV—heck, you've even sat through three VH-1 *Fashion Television* marathons. What more can you possibly need to know about the entertainment industry? Plenty. And you'll find out exactly how much after you get a peek at the following:

Trade Publications:

- *Agent & Manager Magazine*: 212/532-4150
  New York, New York

- *Backstage*: 800/437-3183
  New York, New York

- *Hollywood Reporter*: 323/525-2150
  Los Angeles, California

- *Variety*: 213/857-6600
  Los Angeles, California

MARKET RESEARCH AND LOCATION

Any large city will provide a nice backdrop for your operation. Aside from local venues for showcasing talent, such as theaters, comedy clubs, and musical auditoriums, you've also got nationwide opportunities in the form of movie studios and casting directors knocking down your doors. Not to mention the throng of hungry talent that springs up at every turn. Hicksville USA isn't big enough for the next Pitt or Paltrow—no matter what that old contrarian John Cougar has to say about it.

Before you sign your very first act, you'll need to see a teacher about some students. Reputable actors workshops, dance studios, voice instructors, modeling schools, as well as solid university theater and dance programs should provide you with fertile grounds to conduct your talent search. You simply can't waste your time on any riffraff that may pass your threshold. If that P.C. sensibility of yours gets all hot and bothered by such blatantly elitist tactics, wait until you see what happens to you after you've lived through one hatchet job of Hamlet's soliloquy too many. Perish the thought!

Finally, never you mind about determining your fees. To protect the talent's inalienable rights, all agents' fees have been created equal. Thus, be you ever so humble, you still deserve the standard 10 percent cut. Good news for an upstart!

LICENSE TO REP

No representative's agreement between you and your clients will ever be binding until you've completed the small matter of passing a test. Every state will require that you get your agent's license. To do so, you'll need to register for the exam, buckle down, and hit the books.

You may also have to fill out lengthy applications to register as an agent with labor unions such as SAG, AFTRA, AEA, and SWG. If these acronyms are all Greek to you, hie your way to the nearest library—you've got mass quantities of learning to catch up on.

EQUIP YOURSELF

- work space: a few spare rooms in your house or a leased office space

- computer with database and accounting software, printer, fax/modem

- telephone system

- photocopier

- fax machine

- cameras and videotaping equipment

- office furniture

- promotional brochures, business cards, stationery

GETTING THE WORD OUT

The game of an agent is all about key contacts. These are, of course, none other than the people who do all the hiring. The local casting agents and directors, for example, are the cats that the big guns of Hollywood seek out when shooting at a location near you. Advertising agencies also handpick talent, announce auditions, and dispense with tremendous budgets. Here are some methods that will get you into their consciousness, if not immediately into their good graces:

- a display ad in the local production directory, as well as a listing in the Yellow Pages

- send promotional material announcing your new agency directly to casting agents, production companies, photography studios, department stores, and any other potential clients

- list your name with the talent unions in your area

OPENING YOUR OWN
TEMPORARY EMPLOYMENT AGENCY

It's plain to see that we are living amidst a fluctuating market; a time when corporate restructuring is as ubiquitous as McDonald's restaurants. It comes as no surprise then that the popularity of temporary employment services has risen sharply in these rapidly changing times. In fact, this service field has a projected growth rate of 5 to 10 percent well through the year 2000. Everybody is looking for a temporary solution to their everyday work-related dilemmas, and are finding that the new wave of temp services are meeting their particular needs.

Although experience in human resources is helpful, it is not absolutely necessary to the success of your enterprise. All you'll have to do is recruit an army of dedicated temps and then play matchmaker. Finding willing and able workers for your army of temps shouldn't be a problem, since many people are being restructured right out of their jobs, and are not willing to part with their incomes, steady or not. The only challenge will lie in snagging those lucrative corporate contracts that will have your recruits filing away come Monday morning.

RAKING IN THE DOUGH

Well-conceived and organized temporary services with a large office and a staff of five and up can make as much as $600,000 per year. But before you start getting too excited, the majority of moderately sized services make from $50,000 to $100,000.

Profits can be boosted by savvy marketing, a large force of eager recruits, and a reliable permanent staff.

START-UP COSTS

You'll need at least $25,000 to meet the advertising, office space, equipment, and payroll expenses.

If, on the other hand, you have enough space in your home, and plan on doing all the work yourself, you can start up on as little as $10,000.

HELP IS ON THE WAY

Much of your success will be based on top-notch networking skills. And what better place to start making connections than among your own peers?

Associations:

- National Associations of Temporary Services: 703/549-6287
  Alexandria, Virginia

- National Staff Leasing Association: 703/524-3636
  Arlington, Virginia

Read All About It:

- *Fastrate: The Temporary Employment Service Project Management System* by Darrell Griffin. Lawrence Publishing, 1992.

- *Start Your Own Temporary Employment Agency.* Prentice Hall Trade, 1996.

LOCATION

Overhead costs can be considerably downsized by running the service out of your home. If you plan on being house-bound, make sure to set a room aside for meeting with clients and screening prospective employees.

For those who wish to move into a traditional office space, a business district will allow your corporate clients to meet with you without going too far out of their way. Also, your temps can check in quickly and won't have far to travel from your office to their assignment.

RECRUITING

Your employees have to be reliable, skilled, and professional. Your business's success depends on the quality of your team members. You will have to conduct interviews, administer basic tests, like typing, spelling, and filing, and match the right job with the right workers. Ads in the classifieds section are a good way to get the attention of the unemployed. You can either take on all these responsibilities, or hire a permanent staff member to take charge of these duties.

CAST AND CREW

Running a temporary employment service may require you to hire a reliable team of permanent employees. Train your workers to hire new recruits, deal with clients, oversee payroll, and coordinate assignments. However many permanent employees you choose to hire, you will have your hands full with the many day-to-day responsibilities of running a temp service.

GETTING THE WORD OUT

Heavy client contact and selling will keep your business running on course. A good strategy used by many agency owners is to contact human resources departments at companies throughout your chosen location. Make an appointment and use that time to pitch your service.

If you are planning to run a specialized temporary employment service — engineers, graphic artists, computer programmers, etc. — take out advertisements in trade publications, and once again, make sure to contact clients in your industry of choice.

OPERATING A
TRANSLATION SERVICE

Go ahead, ask yourself: What does the global economy mean to you? It could mean a whole lot, depending on whether or not you are thinking about operating a language translation service. With corporations expanding as far as the four corners of the earth, qualified translators are quickly becoming an inexpendable expenditure. Translators who are proficient in several languages have a good chance of making a great living in the years to come.

Would-be entrepreneurs deficient in required language proficiency, take heart. You can hire skilled translators who can do the work for you. All you'll have to do is arrange their appointments and keep track of accounting. As a manager, you will have full control of this lucrative business idea. So, if you've ever wanted to move with the jet set, get ready to be whisked away on a business adventure you'll never forget.

RAKING IN THE DOUGH
A translation service business with a variety of translators covering many different languages can see a pretax net profit of $60,000 to $120,000. If you choose to operate on your own and know several "in demand" languages, expect to make around $25,000 to $45,000 per year.

START-UP COSTS
Start-up costs for this business are relatively low. A single-person, home-based operation can be started on $3,000. But a full office with several staff members can bring your start-up costs to $20,000 to $40,000.

HELP IS ON THE WAY
You don't need to obtain a translator's license to start your business, but you will need to brush up on your language skills. You can enroll for language courses at local community colleges and universities.

Associations:
- American Association of Language Specialists: 301/986-1542
  Washington, D.C.

- American Translators Association: 703/683-6100
  Alexandria, Virginia

Read All About It:
- *Guide for Translators* by Morry Sofer. Schrieber Publishing, 1995.

MARKET RESEARCH AND LOCATION

Big business and international politics is the name of the game, and the amount of corporate and government clients you secure will have a lot to do with your bottom line. To get your hands on these players, you'll have to set up operations in a large city where you're bound to find a steady stream of clients.

While you can open this business right out of your home and cut costs dramatically, some business owners choose to create a cosmopolitan image by having a facility that's on a grand scale. Either option can work, but you'll have to decide which suits you based on the amount of start-up capital you have to invest.

EQUIP YOURSELF

Your translation service will go nowhere without these key elements:

- computer with peripherals

- fax machine

- copier

- work stations (desks, chairs, etc.)

- tape recorders

- phone system

- promotional material (brochures, business cards, etc.)

GETTING THE WORD OUT

To inform prospective clients of your services, you will have to network for several years to develop a steady supply of business. Call on hotels, governments agencies, travel agents, and corporations to inform them of your wide range of interpreting services. Follow up this call with a brochure listing the companies you've worked for, contact information, and rates.

You should also list your service in the Yellow Pages, and mail postcards to any clients you wish to work with in the future.

STARTING YOUR OWN
TREND FORECASTING FIRM

Did you predict the Spice Girls' meteoric success? Were you buying out large supplies of Beanie Babies before the hysteria set in? Are you currently sporting a pair of Hush Puppies you discovered before their resurrection? If your answered yes to two questions, you may just be a prime candidate for making a profit off the new science of trendology.

If you're skeptical about the legitimacy of this business, consider that the top trendologists are making millions of dollars off their insider information. Large corporations and marketing firms are paying through the nose for reports citing the latest trends in youth culture. Your insight into what today's pop-culture phenomenon means for the future can bring in a windfall to last you for many years to come. So, if you've always been ahead of your time, we predict that your day has finally come.

RAKING IN THE DOUGH

It's no wonder trend watchers are cropping up all over the nation; the financial rewards are well worth engaging in the competition. The top agencies report incomes of $500,000+ per year, but don't expect to make over $20,000 your first year out.

START-UP COSTS

Your main expenses will be marketing your service to companies, and proving that your organization has its eye on the leading trends. While this industry is by no means saturated, several trend-spotters have already made their indelible marks. Establishing an equally high profile will require several months to two years of ceaseless effort.

You will also have to have enough capital to produce a newsletter reporting your fad findings. So, even if you cut costs by working part-time out of a home office, you'll still need at least $5,000 to $10,000 to tide you over until you secure the backing of major clients.

HELP IS ON THE WAY

Since this is a relatively new field, you will often have to rely on your own resources. But leading trend-spotters are coming out of the woodwork with several books citing their findings. Once you scan these trend treasure troves, you will have a better grasp of what it takes to build your own trendspotting business.

Trade Publications:
- *Trend Journal*: 914/876-6700
  Rhinebeck, New York

Read All About It:
- *Clicking* by Faith Popcorn. HarperCollins, 1997.

- *How to Turn Trends into Fortunes* by Stu Taylor and Tom Biracree. Birch Lane Press, 1993.

- *Predicting the Future: An Introduction to the Theory of Forecasting* by Nicholas Rescer. State University of New York Press, 1997.

- *Street Trends: How Today's Alternative Youth Cultures Are Creating Tomorrow's Mainstream Markets* by Janine Lopiano-Misdom and Joanne DeLuca. HarperBusiness, 1997.

- *Trends 2000* by Gerald Celente. Warner Books, 1997.

EQUIP YOURSELF
- dictaphone

- computer with fax/modem, word processing and internet software

- subscriptions to music and lifestyles publications

- VCR for screening flicks

CAST AND CREW

Besides your own marketing skills, you will want to hire an avant-garde fashion force to scout out the latest in street trends. For a nominal fee, you can recruit young people to go and search out new ideas, slang, and clothes trends of young trend-setters. Make sure each of your sleuths has basic writing skills, since you will require them to write up one-page reports to express their findings.

GETTING THE WORD OUT

Marketing your forecasts to major corporations will take some skills and a considerable amount of time. Some of the options available to you are:

- creating a sample newsletter, and mailing it to the marketing departments of prospective clients

- putting together a thorough proposal outlining the benefits you offer and mailing it off to the marketing department heads of prospective clients

- writing a press release about your cutting-edge business and sending it out to newspapers and business magazines across the nation

Don't expect these communications to work wonders. Missives alone won't send employers racing to your door; follow up with phone calls and letters if you want to secure a business meeting.

START YOUR OWN
TUTORING SERVICE

Finally, a money-making venture even the idealist in us can admire. Picking up where the insufficient educational system leaves off is what tutoring services are all about. And whether you're helping students keep up with their schoolwork, surge to the head of the class, or prepare for standardized tests, you'll be able to satisfy your most altruistic wishes as well as your most material needs.

Think back to your own experience. Those high school days when all anyone wanted was to never hear those three dreaded little letters S.A.T. ever again. Or the day the word "act" was morphed into all-caps and saddled with all sorts of fatal connotations. Then recall the time that half of your college consorts suddenly dropped you like a two-headed stepchild for the guys at Kaplan and Princeton Review.

Yes, the learning centers have been there all along. And parents have been ponying up the big bucks to enlist their progeny in these tutoring programs with a "price is no object" zeal. A patient and intelligent entrepreneur with great leadership skills can make out like an insider trader in this business—only instead of subpoenas, you'll be seeing notes of gratitude from hundreds of satisfied customers.

RAKING IN THE DOUGH

Whether you choose to buy into a franchise or go the indie route, the popularity of tutoring services with the education-minded set will ensure an income that's between $30,000 and $90,000 each year. And if you later decide to grow your business—opening up additional locations and expanding your bases of operation—you may be looking at revenues in the multi-millions.

START-UP COSTS

You can start your own company for as little as $2,000. If you work with neighborhood schools, you can gain access to their classrooms and learning-lab equipment (tape recorders, headsets). The only thing you'll have to provide is tapes that explain the reasoning behind the correct answers, practice tests, and advertising dollars. The start-up costs will climb if your operation involves a separate facility with a staff of trainers.

You'll have to part with at least $100,000 if you buy into a franchise. The upside of going with an established name in teaching is that you'll benefit from a solid reputation and receive guidelines for obtaining a business loan and assistance in running your organization. The downside: forking over a percentage of your earnings each year for the privileges that come with membership.

HELP IS ON THE WAY

Parents are a prickly lot. But you can't blame them for their concern. All these educated consumers want to know is that you are the right person for the job. You know you're in trouble when your customers know more about the field than you do. So learn all about the industry by following up with these sources.

Associations:
- American Society for Training and Development: 703/683-8100
  Alexandria, Virginia

- The Association of Independent Tutors: 204/255-4251
  Winnipeg, Manitoba, Canada

Trade Publications:
- *Teaching Exceptional Children*: 703/620-3660
  Alexandria, Virginia

- *Training and Development Magazine*: 703/683-8100
  Alexandria, Virginia

Read All About It:
- *500 Tips for Tutors* by Sally Brown and Phillip Race. Stylus Publications, 1993.

- *Becoming an Effective Tutor* by Lynda Myers and Phil Gerould. Crisp Publications, 1990.

- *A Handbook for Personal Tutors* by Sue Wheeler and Jan Birtle. Open University Press, 1993.

MARKET RESEARCH AND LOCATION

Short of a retirement community or a housing project, this type of business can thrive in any locale. The more expensive franchise courses will not survive in lower-middle-class neighborhoods. Still, if there are numerous schools in the area, a large percentage of students will be looking for academic success. Thus, you would be able to stay in business by opening up a reasonably priced, independent tutoring service.

Franchise operations that often charge as much as $1,400 for an eight-week course tend to draw a ritzier clientele. College towns, affluent suburbs, and "gentrified" urban areas will prove to be veritable customer breeding grounds.

EQUIP YOURSELF

- desks and chairs

- tape recorders with headsets

- practice tests and workbooks

- computer with database software

- letterhead, stationery, envelopes

- promotional materials: brochures, personalized pens, etc.

GETTING THE WORD OUT

While word of mouth is crucial to your continued success, as an upstart you'll have no access to this business generator unless you're running a franchise. Independent operators need to work extra hard for client attention by:

- advertising in parenting sections of local newspapers

- conducting direct mail campaigns

- posting fliers at schools and at recreational centers

CAST AND CREW

If your operation includes more than one tutor, or if you'd rather let someone else teach while you handle finances, marketing, and the like, you'll have to interview, hire, and train candidates. While teaching experience may be helpful, it is not always necessary. Plenty of teachers could put the Energizer Bunny to sleep. What you need are people with a fresh approach, superb communication skills, and stupendous reserves of patience.

STARTING YOUR OWN
WEB DESIGN/CONSULTING BUSINESS

The information superhighway is going full speed ahead. While sales may have been slow in the past, they are expected to double in the next ten years. It's simple: People are getting more and more comfortable shopping via the Web, and companies are falling all over themselves to get involved.

And as the demand for effective and professional home pages rises, Web page designers and consultants will also increase in number. Most companies not only hire designers to create their pages, they also continue to using their service for maintenance purposes. Because the content of pages should change on a monthly basis, the role of the designer/consultant has become a more permanent occupation. And while many companies have begun to hire in-house Web gurus to design and manage their pages on a full-time basis, most still prefer to outsource.

RAKING IN THE DOUGH

Depending on how many accounts you secure, you can make $20,000 to $80,000. The former number will most likely be your profit during the first year of operation. After you develop a strong portfolio and an equally reliable customer base, you can look forward to an income closer to the latter figure.

START-UP COSTS

The cost of running this business is fairly low, provided you already have the technical support necessary. Since most designers/consultants work out of their homes, blowing your wad on office space shouldn't be an issue. All said, a Web site–developing business can be yours for $3,000 to $10,000.

HELP IS ON THE WAY

The World Wide Web is changing every day. New software, procedures, and developments have Web stylists and consultants looking for information

wherever they can find it. Get a clue by digging into these important resources.

Associations:

- Independent Computer Consultants Association: 800/774-4222:
St. Louis, Missouri

- Internet Business Association: 703/779-1320
Reston, Virginia

- Internet Society: 800/468-9507
Reston, Virginia

Trade Magazine:

- *Internet World*: 203/226-6967
Westport, Connecticut

Read All About It:

- *Creating Killer Web Sites* by David Siegel. Hayden Books, 1997.

- *Hotwired Style: Principles for Building Smart Web Sites* by Jeffrey Veen.
Hotwired Books, 1997.

- *The Internet Business Primer* by Wayne Allison. Sourcebooks, 1997.

- *The New Internet Business Book* by Jill Ellsworth. John Wiley & Sons,
1996.

- *Secrets of Successful Web Sites: Project Management on the World Wide
Web* by David Siegel. Hayden Books, 1997.

EQUIP YOURSELF

- computer with at least a 2-GB hard drive

- phone system

- separate phone line for Internet access

- modem

- peripherals

- Web design software

- fax software

- promotional material with Web page samples

GETTING THE WORD OUT

There are many ways to advertise your Web designing and consulting abilities. A very effective way to showcase your talents is to create a striking home page for your own business. Companies in search of qualified assistance might very well stumble upon your page. Once they're hooked by the quality of your work, they can contact you by e-mail or regular phone. Because serious customers usually prefer to negotiate, it is not necessary to advertise your prices on the Web.

Another way to generate more business is to mail promotional material to the directors of communications at a variety of local corporations. Explain the value of a stunning home page in your brochure, and include sales of previous work.

OPEN YOUR OWN
WEDDING CONSULTANT SERVICE

According to the guys at *Forbes* magazine, the wedding-planning business rakes in around $34 billion a year. And when you consider the elaborate and lavish nature of today's weddings, it's no wonder these businesses are cropping up all over the country.

It will be up to you to take care of the many details that will go into making each and every wedding an affair to remember. Everything from planning the seating arrangement to orchestrating the rehearsal dinner will fall right into your realm of responsibility. A wedding is one of the most complicated events to plan. It's no wonder that more and more people want to concentrate on their exciting new life together, rather than what will be served as the main course. If you have great coordinating skills and love to make others happy, then roll up your sleeves and start planning those weddings.

RAKING IN THE DOUGH

Full-time consultants with an established clientele can bring in about $60,000 per year. To achieve or even surpass this financial goal, plan on charging a minimum of $3,000 to $4,000 per event.

START-UP COSTS

Because you can start your business right out of your house, and will require a limited amount of equipment, a $2,000 investment should be enough to get started.

HELP IS ON THE WAY

Traditional weddings are more and more being surpassed by unusual and different wedding arrangements. If you want to keep up with the latest in photography, floral arrangements, themes, and menu options, these bridal resources will keep you ahead of the competition:

Associations:
- Association of Bridal Consultants: 203/355-0464
  Westport, Connecticut

- Association of Wedding Professionals: 916/482-3010
  Sacramento, California

- National Bridal Service: 804/355-6945
  Richmond, Virginia

Trade Publications:
- *Bride's*: 212/880-8800
  New York, New York

- *Modern Bride*: 800/777-5786
  New York, New York

Read All About It:
- *Secrets of a Bridal Consultant: A Wedding Workbook* by Joyce Hartmann and Loretta Staff. Dorrance Publishing, 1997.

MARKET RESEARCH AND LOCATION

Affluent neighborhoods or metropolitan areas are regular gold mines of opportunity for bridal consultants. To determine the number of people tying the knot in any given area, call your local county clerk. Since all marriages must be accompanied by a license, you can call and ask how many licenses were issued that year.

Another tactic is to find out the number of existing wedding-planning services in the area. Next, call each service and pose as a prospective client, asking how many events they coordinate each year. If the number is high, then there's a good chance you will be provided with your fair share of the wedding business profits.

EQUIP YOURSELF
- computer for accounting and record-keeping

- desk and file cabinets for storage of important contracts and receipts

- fax machine

- business phone line and/or cellular for easy access

GETTING THE WORD OUT

In the wedding biz, your work can speak for and sell itself. Wedding consultants often attract the majority of their customers from referrals. Here's how it works: You've arranged a spectacular wedding extravaganza. Several guests remark what a lovely celebration it is, and ask about the identity of the coordinator. These guests may have young daughters and sons poised on the brink of marriage. So guess whom they'll turn to when it comes to hiring a reliable and creative wedding planner? That's right, you.

Another way to spread the word about your service is to leave your elegant business cards with local photographers, caterers, and flower and bridal shops. These vendors service the wedding industry on a regular basis and will be important contacts for you when you're ready to plan your own wedding ceremonies and receptions. They can also refer valuable clients to you, if you promise to use their services in upcoming weddings. This is usually an unspoken agreement between vendors and wedding planners.

BECOMING A
FREELANCE WRITER

A career in writing is actually one of the most popular occupations among young people. Almost everyone we've talked to wants to crack the industry. And luckily, there are countless ways to make money plying the written word. There are magazine articles, press releases, greeting cards, corporate training manuals, brochures, catalog copy, book jackets, book writers, and television. The opportunities are vast, but the key to becoming successful is targeted marketing and, wouldn't you know it, writing ability. Of course, if you're weak in any of these departments, you can always improve your skills by taking courses and reading books.

While a writing career can provide some very handsome rewards, it is also fraught with many difficulties. Tight deadlines, writer's block, securing new accounts, rejections, constant networking, and late payments are just some of the occupational hazards. But there are plenty of rewards that can offset these potential problems. Setting your own schedule and finding your creative outlet rank highly on this list. What's more, if you're a hard worker, determined to succeed, you've already won half the battle.

RAKING IN THE DOUGH

Copywriters can make anywhere from $35,000 their first year out, to $175,000 after several years in the industry. The biggest names in the copywriting industry boast incomes topping the $200,000 mark.

If you're planning to write strictly for magazines, plan to make $15,000 in your first year, and up to $60,000 as a regular contributor for mid- to large-sized magazines.

For book authors, the numbers can fluctuate dramatically from year to year. If you sell two books per year, and receive a standard advance/royalty agreement, you can expect to make at least $20,000. That number can rise dramatically if any of your books turn out to be big sellers.

START-UP COSTS

Most writing businesses are started right out of the home. That means you can start your business for as low as $3,000. You will need some basic equipment to conduct an extensive marketing campaign. But all in all, this business can be started on virtually nothing down.

HELP IS ON THE WAY

Help for writers is always available. The following associations and publications will help you hone your craft, attract the right customer or publisher, and exchange ideas with other professionals.

Associations:

- American Marketing Association: 312/648-0536
  Chicago, Illinois

- Community Writers Association: 401/751-9300
  Providence, Rhode Island

- Direct Marketing Association: 212/768-7277
  New York, New York

Trade Publications:

- *Freelance Writer's Report*: 603/284-6367
  North Sandwich, New Hampshire

- *Poet and Writer*: Fax: 212/226-3963
  New York, New York

- *Writer's Digest Magazine*: 513/531-2222
  Cincinnati, Ohio

Read All About It:

- *How to Make $50,000 a Year or More as a Freelance Business Writer* by Paul D. Davis. Prima Publishing, 1992.

- *The Writer's Market*. R. R. Bowker.

- *The Writer's Market*. Writer's Digest Books: Cincinnati, Ohio.

- *Writing for Money* by Loriann Hoff Oberlin. Writer's Digest Books, 1995.

EQUIP YOURSELF

You'll need more than a Mont Blanc pen to make this business work. Some basic equipment will help you use your skills to their full advantage:

- computer with at least 1.2-GB hard drive and CD-ROM

- printer and/or copier machine

- fax machine or fax software

- business phone and extra line

- promotional materials: business cards, previously published writing samples

- office furniture

GETTING THE WORD OUT

For business-to-business scribes, the best method of advertising is always contacting the communications department of each company and dropping off some of your best writing samples. You can also network at trade shows and industry associations that you're planning to write for.

Copywriters interested in generating new leads should also offer their services directly to the corporations. Determine the type of promotional literature each company produces, and then set up a meeting to discuss how you can improve on their current concepts. You can also work as a freelance catalog copywriter and produce marketing material for publishing houses.

If you're trying to break into the magazine and book market, you will first have to generate some marketable ideas, then write a killer query letter and an outline for your article or book. After scouring the publishers' listings in *The Literary Market Place* and *The Writer's Market*, send your packages to every magazine and publisher that would be a good match with your topic of choice. Then cross your fingers and wait for the replies to start pouring in.

Part Three

THINK BIG:
IT TAKES MONEY TO MAKE
MONEY

OPERATING YOUR OWN
900-NUMBER SERVICE

There are so many options for entrepreneurs wishing to get into the 900-number business. You can start your own party line, astrology corner, restaurant finder, or traffic information line right out of your home. Every time a new customer calls in, they are automatically charged a set fee per minute. You don't have to do anything, except provide updated information for your callers and advertise your service.

The popularity of 900-numbers is growing every day. In the mid-1990's, pay-per-call lines produced a total of $2 billion in annual sales. People love the convenience of just picking up the phone and getting their ears on some vital or entertaining information. All you have to do is figure out what kind of service your number will be providing, set up the necessary technology, and wait for the phone to start ringing off the hook.

RAKING IN THE DOUGH

The size of your initial investment will determine the amount of your profits. The average 900 number operator makes around $60,000 per year, while the larger organizations sometimes make over $3 million in pretax income.

START-UP COSTS

A large portion of your start-up funds will be allocated to paying off the phone companies. Not only will you have to pay the company for the use of their phone line, but you'll also need to provide a security deposit of about $20,000.

Other initial expenses will go toward the purchase of telecommunications equipment, and a blitzkrieg of a marketing campaign. In sum, your start-up costs will amount to no less than $70,000.

HELP IS ON THE WAY

Volumes of valuable information will be at your fingertips if you look up these reliable sources.

Trade Publications:
- *Infotext*: 714/493-2434
  Capistrano Beach, California

Read All About It:
- *900 Know-How: How to Succeed with Your Own 900 Number Business* by Robert Mastin. Aegis Publishing Company, 1993.

- *Operating a "900" Number for Profit*. Irvine, 1991.

- *Opportunity is Calling: How to Start Your Own Successful 900 Number* by Robert Bentz. ATS Publishing, 1993.

MARKET RESEARCH AND LOCATION

Most 900-numbers are started right out of the owner's home. Because the start-up costs are so high, most entrepreneurs operating this service opt to cut overhead by working in a small home-based office.

The type of information you provide can be determined by the gap in a market, your interest, or a spin-off of another successful 900-number service. One actor living in Los Angeles had a hard time getting audition information, and decided to start a 900-number service listing every audition in the Los Angeles area. An antique dealer wanted up-to-date information about antique shows throughout the country. When he couldn't find the information he needed, he decided to start his own pay-per-call service announcing antique shows.

GETTING THE WORD OUT

A 900-number operator's main source of income is through his/her marketing strategy. Unless your customers know about your service, they cannot possibly call your number. You will have to spend at least 30 percent of your total revenue in advertising your phone number. There are many ways to effectively accomplish this task.

- direct mail

- special interest publications

- newspapers

- television

- radio

You should always test the effectiveness of an advertisement by tracking its results. Using the technique called spot advertising, you will be able track the number of calls you receive to a particular advertisement. It's a great way to keep your marketing strategy on track.

YOUR OWN
ALTERNATIVE VIDEO STORE

You know the drill; it happens every time you enter one of those heavy-duty video stores. You'll wander the aisles in vain search of that new Australian indie. Then, when you're just about ready to give up, you'll see a uniform-clad salesclerk, anxiously waiting to give you killer customer service. You'll ask about your precious film . . . but alas! your only reply will be a quizzical look, a chipper database search, and a distressingly upbeat "Sorry, sir/ma'am, that film is not in our records."

But you won't be dismissed. Oh, no! It takes more than that to dissuade you from your goal. To make a long story short, you get arrested for disturbing the peace, and have to cajole a reluctant parent into bailing you out. When you finally come home, you find that the three hours at the video store/ holding cell would have been far better spent watching the Superstation's presentation of *Tuff Turf*. You cry and vow never to set foot in that store again. But like Sisyphus and his rock, you're back at the gates of Video Hell come Monday. It's a vicious cycle.

This end need not befall all you film buffs on the fringes of Hollywood's bell-shaped curve. If you're the type who gets on-line and heads straight for a "Movie Madness" chat room to extol the virtues of Roger Corman and Ed Wood, then being a video store proprietor may just be in your stars. Whether you're stocking hard-to-find B-movies, cult classics, foreign films, independent works, or all of the above, you're cornering a niche overlooked by Block-buster—and in the dog-eat-dog world of video rental, that's no small consideration.

RAKING IN THE DOUGH

Pick the right location, and there's no telling how far your earnings can go. Your pretax net will probably hover someplace around $50,000, but who knows? A little cagey marketing, and you may be looking at a figure twice that size.

START-UP COSTS

So what if the movies you stock were made on a shoestring? This certainly doesn't go double for your business. You'll have to come up with an airtight business plan, and invest a minimum of $70,000 in this venture if you don't want it to end up on the cutting-room floor.

HELP IS ON THE WAY

Keeping up with industry standards is much easier if you're in the loop. It doesn't take much to become an insider—check out these sources for a head start.

Associations:
- American Video Association: 800/421-2300
  Chandler, Arizona

- Video Software Dealers Association: 800/257-5259
  Marlton, New Jersey

Trade Publications:
- *Film Culture*: 212/979-5663
  New York, New York

- *Twice*: 212/477-2200
  Twice Publishing Corp., New York, New York

- *Video Extra*: 215/629-1588
  Home Viewer Publications, Inc., Philadelphia, Pennsylvania

- *Video Store*: 714/250-8060
  Santa Ana, California

Read All About It:
- 1998 *Video Movie Guide* by Mick Martin, Marsha Porter. Ballantine, 1997.

MARKET RESEARCH AND LOCATION

You'll find demographics aplenty in the trade periodicals listed above. Match those numbers to the ones you get from the good old U.S. Census Bureau and then let your common sense go to work.

Consider the types of people who enjoy less box-office-y films . . . not your average fraternity brothers. As your wares can only be categorized as "outside the mainstream," the same will go for your audience. Look around the area for artsy movie houses and cheap-end art galleries; these will signal a plethora of Bohemian denizens. If you find that the burg is short one alternative video rental store, then plop down your deposit, baby, you're home!

LICENSE AND INSURANCE

Our hunch is that red tape wasn't exactly what you had in mind when you decided to go into the video-rental business. But unless you hire a lawyer and accountant to take care of the vital paperwork, such as membership contracts, tax laws, zoning ordinances, business licenses, and articles of incorporation, you'll have to get through miles of this red-tape stuff yourself before you see any of the videotape variety.

EQUIP YOURSELF

- a broad range of titles, numbering at least 900

- enough shelves to display your entire selection

- a counter with at least two cash registers

- a computer to keep track of inventory and accounts

- plenty of movie posters (a.k.a. one-sheets) to line the walls with

CAST AND CREW

An astute staff can only help matters, so be on the lookout for sharp minds and quick wits. Your customers will appreciate it. Also, encourage your employees to watch any stocked films that they may have missed out on. Then give them the go-ahead to recommend their picks.

With the mega-chains breathing down your neck, you're in no position to alienate anyone, so stress the importance of customer service. And we're not talking the bubble-gum variety either. Insipidly cheerful people will do more harm than good, so screen applicants carefully to find that golden medium. Once you've got your staff, make sure to provide fair compensation, wage increases, and regular pizza parties, and they'll be loyal to the end.

GETTING THE WORD OUT

Besides advertising in the film section of your city's newspaper, it may also be wise to look into less obvious forms of self-promotion. Many grocery stores now offer coupons on the back of receipts. This is a great way to attract new customers.

Keep them coming back for more by offering something in the way of incentives, like a punch card that entitles the bearer to a free movie after 14 rentals, free popcorn, or a special $0.99 film rack.

And while we're on the subject of spreading the news, let's not leave out that an alternative video store is just the thing for you media hounds. If you've always wanted to be in the papers, here's your big break. Because small, independent films are all the rage nowadays, go ahead and alert the local rags to your entrepreneurial premiere. It's as simple as drawing up a press release and sending it to all the Arts & Entertainment editors in the city. Follow up with friendly phone calls, and you're bound to get a mention. Now that's advertising money can't buy!

OPERATING YOUR OWN
AMUSEMENT ARCADE

Aaaaah, video games . . . the words alone are enough to plunge us deep into Kaboom! reveries and Centipede dreams. Ever since video killed the radio star, Ms. Pac Man has been wiping the floor with Barbie, and the Mario Brothers have been kicking those Parker Brothers where it hurts. Video games just about made our childhoods; now it's time to pass the torch. Making money purveying joy and hand-eye coordination to thousands of hapless youths, what can be nobler?

If you decide to venture into this particular genre of diversion, be prepared to keep up with an ever-changing market. You know all about kids and their new toys, so get ready to keep an eye perma-peeled for the latest in adolescent recreation.

RAKING IN THE DOUGH

Amusement is a high profit business. Your earnings may well top the $130,000 mark. The average amusement arcade income in the $70,000 to $130,000 range. So, even on the low end of the spectrum, you'll be making out like a bandit.

START-UP COSTS

You just knew there had to be a catch somewhere, right? Well, whoop here it is . . . $90,000 worth of tokens is required to get into this game. And even this number can fall short if you plan to include premier games such as virtual reality and laser tag.

HELP IS ON THE WAY

Reading the arcade news and mixing with other thrill vendors is crucial if you want to stay on top of your game.

Associations:

- American Amusement Machine Association: 847/290-9088
  Elk Grove Village, Illinois

- Amusement and Music Operators Association (AMOA): 800/937-2662
  Chicago, Illinois

Trade Publications:

- *The Location*: Amusement and Music Operators Association (AMOA)
  401 N. Michigan Ave., Chicago, Illinois

- *Play Meter Magazine*: Skybird Publishing Company, Inc.;
  504/488-7003
  New Orleans, Louisiana

- RePlay Magazine: 818/347-3820
  Woodland Hills, California

Read All About It:

- *Arcade One: Illustrated Historical Guide to Arcade Machines* by Richard
  Bueschel. Coin Slot Books, 1993.

MARKET RESEARCH AND LOCATION

Like it or not, your bread will be buttered mostly by the teen and preteen demographic. Righto! Mallrats! And what better place to find them than at a mall? You get what you pay for, so expect to fork over a higher rent for your higher profit margin.

If a shopping center location just doesn't jibe with your game plan, check out the library and the Chamber of Commerce for some stats on where the kids are. They're out there; all you have to do is find them.

LICENSE AND INSURANCE

A word of advice: You're dealing with youngsters who have discretionary income. That means only one thing—their parents can afford to sue the joystick off you. So play it safe by racking up the insurance policies.

CAST AND CREW

You can hire two full-time employees, or a bunch of part-timers. The latter option will save you some cash come benefits time. One of the best features of arcade ownership is that you never even have to show your face. The nature of the business is such that one employee can mind the joint, while you're off sipping Margaritas.

GETTING THE WORD OUT

When it comes to wooing your customers, nothing beats a good coupon. Offer discounts for groups of ten or more, or provide one free game to all first-time players.

The quality of your arcade will not go unnoticed. In teenybopper circles word of mouth travels faster than Mario Andretti on the Autobahn. So stock up on the newest and most sophisticated in gaming technology and watch the tokens come rolling in.

OPEN YOUR OWN
ANTIQUE SHOP

Today, antiques are a growing business in America. One can say that tastes have improved—after all, it wasn't so long ago that everyone wanted the most modern in Scandinavian or minimalist design. Blame it on the black lacquer dinette sets, but people have finally come back to the classics. Antique shops and malls are just teeming with shoppers, looking for that diamond in the rough. If you've always had a knack for discerning the treasure from the trash, then the antique business is for you.

RAKING IN THE DOUGH

The first years of business are best kept on the small side, so don't expect your profits to break the three-digit barrier. The most cost-efficient start-up locale is in an antiques mall (a space housing several antique shops), where you won't have to part with an arm and a leg to get yourself a foothold. Antique dealers working out of a mall can expect to see their profits fall somewhere in the $25,000-to-$80,000 range. Of course, the longer you remain in business, and the more you expand your enterprise, the higher your profits can go.

START-UP COSTS

Opening a small space in an antiques mall shouldn't be too pricey. The cashier services, insurance, utilities, and advertising will all be taken care of by the owners of the mall, so the only costs you'll have to worry about are rent and inventory—$15,000 to $50,000 should do the trick.

HELP IS ON THE WAY

Even if you've mastered the art of weekend-afternoons antiquing, you'll have to see how the purveying half lives before venturing into business.

Associations:
- Antique Appraisal Association of America: 714/530-7090
  Garden Grove, California

- Art and Antique Dealers League of America: 212/879-7558
  New York, New York

- World Antique Dealers Association: 419/756-4374
  Mansfield, Ohio

Trade Magazines:
- *Antique Review*: 614/885-9757
  Ohio Antique Review, Inc., Worthington, Ohio

- *Antiques and Collectibles News Magazine*: 619/593-2925
  El Cajon, California

- *Antiques Magazine*: 212/941-2800
  New York, New York

- *Antique Week*: 800/876-5133
  Knightstown, Indiana

- *Collectors News*: 800/352-8039
  Grundy Center, Iowa

Read All About It:
- *Buying and Selling Antiques: A Dealer Shows How to Get into the Business* by Sara Pitzer and Don Cline. Storey Books, 1986.

- *How to Start a Home-Based Antique Business* by Jacquelyn Peake. Globe Pequot Press, 1997.

- *The Upstart Guide to Owning and Managing an Antiques Business* by Lisa Angowski Rogal. Upstart Publishing Company, 1994.

MARKET RESEARCH AND LOCATION

The best way to learn about the antique market is to visit the trade shows and engage in heart-to-hearts with a variety of established dealers. They'll tell you about the best flea markets to visit, how to get the insider information on estate sales, and how to sniff out the best auctions. This will take care of your inventory, but what about the location?

If you're going in for an antique mall, check into a variety of locations, and give each one a thorough scoping out. Study the other dealers' pricing and negotiating policies. Ask them about the type of customers that frequent the joint, and pay special attention to their wares. If you think you've found a fit, then it's time to wrangle up a lease.

EQUIP YOURSELF

- a wide selection of objects d'art—even if you specialize in bric-a-brac, you should still ensure that there's something for every taste

- display cases and shelves

- business cards

- the most current edition of *Schroeder's Antiques Price Guide*, published by collector books in Paducah, Kentucky, or *Sotheby's International Price Guide: Antiques And Collectibles*, published by Rizzoli International Publications, Inc., in New York, New York

FINDING YOUR OWN
APARTMENT LOCATOR SERVICE

If you've ever moved to a new city, heck, if you've so much as moved to a new block, you know how to tough it is to find the right digs. People can spend months searching, without once coming across the optimal place to hang their proverbial hats. Imagine what happens to the poor cats who have to sign a lease pronto or it's (gulp!) streets-ville. Or what about those who have to look for a place from afar? Shudder at the thought, do you?

You don't have to sit idly by as your fellow human beings suffer in vain. Lend a helping hand, and you may find yourself moving to a swanky new address in no time.

RAKING IN THE DOUGH

Because the country's business sector is expanding into previously uncharted territories, you stand to make big bucks at any number of Boom Towns USA, which are drawing new residents by the thousands. The average income for an apartment finding service can run from $35,000 to $90,000 per year, depending on location.

START-UP COSTS

$40,000 should cover the entire works—office space, advertising, and computers with real estate software.

HELP IS ON THE WAY

If the competition is less than friendly when it comes to showing you the ropes, the following business associations can step in to answer even your toughest questions:

- National Association of Real Estate Brokers (NARB): 202/785-4477 Washington, D.C.

- National Association of Realtors (NAR): 312/329-8200
  Chicago, Illinois

- Real Estate Brokerage Managers Council: 312/670-3780
  Chicago, Illinois

MARKET RESEARCH AND LOCATION:

Keep your eye on the target, which in this case is a young, single professional, a recent college grad or a transfer from another city. Pore over statistics compiled on various neighborhoods in your proximity, and decide which zones will offer you the largest possible clientele.

Once you have your "hot list" in hand, check out the Yellow Pages. If you find quite a few such businesses, chances are you'll need to get out of the house to compete. Herewith, a list of location necessities:

- easily accessible by foot or car

- highly visible

- the closest competitor is nowhere in sight

DON'T SELL YOURSELF SHORT

The services of a leasing agent/apartment broker are free to the consumer. The people who pay your rent are the property management firms who hire you. The prices vary, but usually the fee assessed is something akin to half of one month's rent. Just to be on the safe side, telephone several leasing agents' offices, and inquire about their policies — no doubt some will be evasive, but you're bound to run across at least a few who are willing to help.

EQUIP YOURSELF

- one computer per employee

- appropriate software

- office furniture: desks, chairs, lighting fixtures

- multi-line telephones

- fax machine

- photocopier

- company stationery and business cards

- promotional material: brochures, fliers

GETTING THE WORD OUT

Since by choosing to be an apartment locator you have chosen to become a middle man, you are now saddled with two sets of clients—the suppliers and the consumers. In order to get the business of the former, you will have to:

- advertise in real estate and building management trade magazines
- go the direct-mail route, by sending fliers to building management companies
- network at real estate trade shows and conventions
- cold-call, otherwise known as telephoning potential clients in order to pitch your services

Just because your services are free doesn't mean that consumers will come flocking to your desk. You'll have to:

- put out ads in the local papers
- advertise in apartment hunters' guides
- participate in real-estate-related community events
- be nice to the clients and rely on word-of-mouth referrals

CAST AND CREW

You'll need a broker's license and nerves of steel to run your own show, but what about your employees? Make no mistake about it. With the heavy emphasis on customer service, you'll need plenty of help carting the clientele about from one flat to the next. Don't worry about paying your staff; the salaries for leasing agents are 100 percent commission. But when it comes to employee efficiency, a state real estate license isn't exactly "all she wrote." Look for these other qualities in your applicants:

- cheerful and outgoing personality
- salesmanship
- pragmatism
- dedication to career
- transportation decent enough to chauffeur around the clientele

OPEN YOUR OWN
ART GALLERY

Okay, admit it, many of you savored a shot of Shadenfreude when those art gallery snooties took that nosedive right around recession time. Served them right for staging all those ever-so-hip openings without inviting you! But hey, it looks like the industry is coming back to life! That's right, gallery openings, cocktail parties, those little black dresses and delectable crudités, they're all back! And look who's still waiting for an invite.

Before you follow your instincts, be forewarned . . . holding your breath ranks low on the list of attention-getting devices. Waiting for a miracle will also do very little to further your cause. If you truly love the field of art, what better way to land in the thicket than to start up a snazzy gallery of your very own? True, if parties are your only reason for crashing the biz, both you and your clientele may end up sorely disappointed. Yet, if your art acumen is unsurpassed by your Saturday night fever, and your friends agree that you are none other than Art Maven, opening a gallery is the venture for you.

Unfortunately, there's more to the business than art savvy. As a newcomer to the action, your gallery's fate will rely entirely on your charisma, cunning, and manipulations. Sound a little harsh, does it? Just wait until you realize the scope of your mission—to win over as many art dealers, art buyers, art collectors, and gallery browsers as possible. You see? If you don't simply relish the concept of schmooze, your gallery will probably attract more creditors than customers.

RAKING IN THE DOUGH

First things first. The art world is a risky business. Profits can vary dramatically from one gallery to the next. Not to rain on your parade, but the grand-opening/close-out-clearance ratio for art galleries is nearly 1 to 1. Nevertheless, if you do succeed in braving the storms of start-up, you can eventually expect an income that's anywhere between $30,000 and $1 million per year.

Much of your profits will depend on the type of art you are selling, For example, if you are dealing with contemporary artists, you'll get most of your work on a consignment basis. Your take of the sale will be approximately 50 percent, give or take 10 percent. If, on the other hand, you're dealing with a secondary market (this is "used" art, most often created by the dearly departed artistes), you can score up to 80 percent of a work's sale price, depending on what you can negotiate with the previous owner.

START-UP COSTS

Just because you can get your merchandise with no money down doesn't mean you can go into the business without liquid assets. That's right, you'll need capital with a capital C. Expecting the best is all well and good, but every successful art dealership prepares to run on empty for at least the first six months. If you can put together a bankroll sufficient to finance your rent, phones, electricity, marketing, and sales support—from $35,000 to $100,000 depending on location—until you're out of the red, you just may make it after all.

HELP IS ON THE WAY

Okay, so you don't really know the heads from the tails of art gallery proprietorship. If you've got ethics questions on the mind, or just want to get the real scoop from some old hands, contact:

Associations:
- Art and Antique Dealers League of America: 212/879-7558
  New York, New York

- Art Dealers Association of America: 212/940-8590
  New York, New York

Trade Magazines:
- *New Art Examiner:* 312/649-9900
  Chicago, Illinois

MARKET RESEARCH AND LOCATION

Location is mucho importanté in the gallery biz. You probably have the perfecto spot already in mind. But do look again . . . if a Gap has recently sprung up in your vicinity, head for the hills. It's not really all that difficult to pick a location. In fact, if you know the type of art you'll be selling, the location almost picks itself. For example, local (read cheap) talent can be displayed in lower-rent areas, which are fraught with starving artists and thriving galleries New York's Greenwich village used to be just such a locale. If you look around your ville, chances are you'll find a Greenwich to call your own.

But, there's more to owning an art gallery than discovering the next Herring or Basquiat; you may just want to capitalize on some well-established reps. If such is your plan, expect astronomical rents and even bigger amounts of schmoozing. You'll need a prime location to attract the moneyed collector folk. What's more, you'll need to have charm and chutzpah in spades if you're going to get the art stars aligned in your favor.

LICENSE AND INSURANCE

Before you deck your walls with art aplenty, you're going to have to go straight to the insurance man. You must obtain all the insurance necessary to cover each and every masterpiece housed by your gallery. This is your livelihood we're talking about.

In fine-printese, the art gallery is just like another retail store. Translation: You don't need any special "purveyor of fine art" license. All that's required is the basic package, no more and certainly no less than a Federal Tax ID number, a business license, and a sales tax number. You can check with an accountant to make sure all's right with your paperwork.

STOCKING UP

You'll have to tack up some artwork before you open for business. There's a variety of resources to choose from in every area. Check out your neighborhood Artists' Coalition. You'll find slides depicting a wide array of contemporary artworks. There are also various art fairs and exhibitions, which can put you on the right track.

Don't worry too much about the footwork; you'll have no shortage of artists petitioning for a shot at your display area once your tent has been pitched. Soon enough, your toughest task will lie in turning away those well-meaning applicants whose work is bound to die a slow and lingering death. And make no mistake about it, turn them away you must.

The key to a successful art gallery is sellable work. You'll have to keep a sharp eye out for work with broad appeal. Once you're more secure in your business, you can begin to take chances on experimental pieces. But in the meantime, remember you are a retailer, not a curator.

THE PRICE IS RIGHT

Most artists will know how much their masterpieces are worth. If you agree to the price, there's no problem. If you don't, the bookstores are stocked with negotiation tapes you can look into, or you can simply look to a different artist.

Should the artwork not sell like Beanie Babies, you may decide to lower the price. Don't forget to obtain the artist's approval if you're planning on a markdown. If you're still staring at the eyesore four markdowns later, cut your losses and start looking for a fresh canvas.

CAST AND CREW

You'll need to fund at least one other person's bed and breakfast if you're going to do this art gallery thing right. This assistant should be someone with an extensive art history background. That's right, if they can't play with the lingo of chiaroscuro, you'll be giving them the old don't-call-us-we'll-call-you number.

Also consider notifying your employee about a probationary period. This is crucial, because closing ability can't be judged at an interview—and a closer is exactly what you need.

GETTING THE WORD OUT

With art lovers as your target audience, you won't be needing the services of a hired gun to figure out where to stick your ads. Any popular art magazine should do the trick. You can also up your name recognition with the tourists by advertising on closed-circuit TV that is zoomed directly into hotel rooms, as well as special magazines such as *Where*, which outline your city's attractions to visitors. Another nifty venue for ad space, guaranteed to target your audience and bring in droves of serious browsers, is art gallery guides. Most art galleries will have an entire array at their entrance.

And finally, to get to the heart of this issue, no art gallery's marketing scheme is complete without a solid party. Send out a mailer whenever you feature a new artist. Invite everyone with whom you'd like to rub elbows, and then some. Don't forget to mention the free food and drink, and your gallery will be hopping come sundown.

LEARN TO EARN: TEST YOUR ART Q

Entrepreneurial spirit alone won't make your gallery a success. You have to be versed in the history of art to thrive in this business. If you're not acquainted with the following terms, check yourself into an art history program before investing your life's savings.

baroque

art nouveau

contrapposto

collage

casting

fresco

pointillism

genre painting

Rococo

iconography

mannerism

fauvism

silk-screen

op art

mural

dada

surrealism

happenings

classicism

expressionism

abstract expressionism

field painting

minimalist

art brute

SET UP YOUR OWN
BED-AND-BREAKFAST

This is a very picturesque business idea. You can even look at it as a permanent vacation. Just don't forget that the people who thrive in this trade work for a living; it's not all about clean air and foliage. Of course, you will get atmosphere in spades if you decide to chuck the rat race.

B&B's have become very popular with American travelers looking for a quiet retreat. At last count, there were 20,000 such inns in the U.S., and that's up from 3,000 in 1980. But the industry's recent growth should not hinder your chances for success. People are always on the lookout for a great place to visit—but only lucky you will get to live there.

RAKING IN THE DOUGH

This is a business with lots of potential. Unfortunately, "potential" is about all you're going to get in the first year or two of operation. You'll need a solid reserve of funds to tide you over until the real liquid starts pouring in—which it eventually will, as B&B owners report incomes ranging from $15,000 (for small-time operations) to approximately $170,000 (for the big-time, 21+ unit variety).

START-UP COSTS

The lack of money is the root of all evil. At least that's the tune you'll be singing if you're dead set on a B&B, but don't have a stitch of collateral when time comes to apply for a loan. There's no sugarcoating the fact that—depending on the size and location of your establishment—it will take 50 to 450 grand to make your enterprising dream a reality.

HELP IS ON THE WAY

A mint on every pillow isn't the be-all and end-all to a bed-and-breakfast. Here's where you'll find the rest of the nitty-gritty.

Associations:

- American Bed and Breakfast Association: 800/769-2468
  Richmond, Virginia

- Bed and Breakfast Reservation Services World Wide: 800/364-7242
  Baton Rouge, Louisiana

- National Bed-and-Breakfast Association: 203/847-6196
  Norwalk, Connecticut

Trade Magazines:

- *Bed and Breakfast: The Business of Innkeeping*: 602/990-1101
  Scottsdale, Arizona

Read All About It:

- *Bed and Breakfast Inn Business Guide*. Entrepreneur, Inc., Irvine, California.

- *Bed and Breakfast: Your Step-by-Step Business Plan* by Monica Taylor and Richard Taylor. Self-Counsel Press, 1996.

- *How to Open and Operate a Bed and Breakfast* by Jan Stankys. Globe Pequot Press, 1997.

- *How to Start and Operate Your Own Bed & Breakfast: Down-to-Earth Advice from an Award-Winning Bed & Breakfast Owner* by Martha Murphy. Henry Holt & Co., Inc., 1994.

MARKET RESEARCH AND LOCATION

Since the start-up costs and the income of B&B's vary so greatly, it is a wise entrepreneur who checks into the geographical considerations of this undertaking. Some parts of the country, for example the Western and Northeastern states, attract more B&B customers than others. Which isn't to say that the states less popular with the bed-and-breakfast set don't have their own advantages. One boon that comes with running a B&B in the Midwest, for example, is that it is much cheaper to get off the ground.

Thorough research will also enlighten you about reasonable rates. Going overboard on pricing will not win you any converts. As you'll find after doing your homework, much of a B&B's business relies on repeat visitors. But you won't see any repeat business if your exorbitant prices scare off prospective clients.

EQUIP YOURSELF

- a property with at least one spare room

- computer system with the necessary software

- business cards, brochures, stationery

- travel magazines that will keep you abreast of the trends in the tourism and hospitality industry

- a full spectrum of homeowner's insurance, from fire to theft to employee/guest liability

GETTING THE WORD OUT

Every year a variety of travel magazines highlight the best and brightest bed-and-breakfast inns. This can spell G-O-L-D for your business if yours happens to be one of the featured inns. Do whatever necessary to get your B&B the attention it to so richly deserves. Send pictures to a variety of magazines, pitch the benefits of your location, call and pester the magazines if you have to, just get your name where tourists will see it.

Scores of travel guides are also published every year. You can get their names through the various associations listed above. Put out a listing in as many travel guides as possible, and listen to those calls start coming in.

LAUNCH YOUR OWN
BODY-CARE SHOP

Whether you plan on selling environmentally safe, cruelty-free body-care products, or just want to feature top-of-the-line body lotions—scrubs, bath oils, etc.—you can make your body-shop boutique a huge success. Add a double shot of ambition, and your venture may one day give Anita Roddick's Body Shop empire a run for its money.

A fascination with the human body and cosmetics can be an asset. But you don't have to be a slave to your looks to make it big in the body-care industry. Since the inception of The Body Shop in 1976, the body-care market has been booming. The business grew to become a $19 billion industry by the mid-1990's. The emphasis most body-care entrepreneurs place on ecologically sound products may have something to do with it. Most consumers are becoming more and more aware of environmental concerns.

Any way you look at it, body-care boutiques are a refreshing alternative to the stuffy department store cosmetics counters. Customers welcome the pleasant environment and enjoy browsing through the aisles in search of that elusive kiwi/almond-blend exfoliant.

RAKING IN THE DOUGH

The profit you can earn from owning a body-care shop can be considerable. On average, body-care entrepreneurs can earn from $90,000 to $200,000 per year.

START-UP COSTS

Here's the rub: Body-care boutiques can clean out your savings. Most stores can be opened with a start-up investment of $30,000 to $90,000. Inventory, marketing costs, a space large enough to allow for comfortable browsing, and retail store equipment can add up. But the good news is that most body-care boutiques break even after their first year in business.

HELP IS ON THE WAY

Your expertise and knowledge about beauty products can help you make the wisest choices when purchasing inventory and selling to your customers. These associations and publications can make you a fit decision-maker in no time.

Associations:

- Cosmetic Industry Buyers and Suppliers: 516/775-0220
  New Hyde Park, New York

- Cosmetic, Toiletry, and Fragrance Association: 202/331-1770
  Washington, D.C.

- National Retail Merchants Association: 202/783-7971
  Washington, D.C.

Trade Publications:

- *Cosmetic and Drug Marketing*: 212/695-0704
  New York, New York

- *The Rose Street*: 301/657-9830
  Chevy Chase, Maryland

Read All About It:

- *Body and Soul: Profits with Principles: The Amazing Success Story of Anita Roddick and The Body Shop* by Russell Miller. Crown Publishers, 1991.

- *Mind, Body and Soul: The Body Shop Books of Well-Being* by The Body Shop. Little, Brown & Company, 1998.

IMAGE MATTERS

No body-care boutique is complete without soothing music, pleasant lights, and a bevy of tropical plants. The most successful shop owners know that the key to getting customers through their doors is the proper ambiance. You should make your store as inviting as possible; sounds of waterfalls and music and sweet smells should greet each customer at the door.

The layout should be simple and include space for your personal office and a storage area. The space in your store should amount to no less than 1,000 square feet. An interesting way to keep customers in your store is to set up a reading area where they can sit in a plush couch or chairs and read magazines and/or beautifully illustrated books about the environment.

EQUIP YOURSELF

Leasing equipment or buying used items can save you considerable funds. But whatever you do, keep in mind that the opening your body-care store will require that you purchase the following equipment:

- lighting

- a variety of body-care products and cosmetics

- several cash registers

- display items

- office equipment

GETTING THE WORD OUT

It's simple, just situate yourself in a highly trafficked area like a large shopping center or strip mall and watch the buyers flock to your store. Since most body-care patrons purchase on impulse, you will have to situate your store in a busy retail area.

Other ways to get the word out include:

- Display ads in local woman's magazines and newspapers

- Fliers with special discount offers

- Direct-mail promotions with a complimentary, trial-size product inside

OPEN YOUR OWN
USED BOOKSTORE

Forget about the publishers' panic. The printed word is not going out of style—no matter what those techies at the information superhighway will have you believe. The publishing industry may be scurrying to compete with the Internet, but as a bookseller you'll have more pressing concerns to worry about; namely, the super-bookstores.

A used bookstore is the perfect antidote to the competition created by the large bookstore chains. Not only are their books expensive, but their selection is limited. If you provide contemporary, classic, and out-of-print texts at rock-bottom prices, you'll have a readership in no time.

RAKING IN THE DOUGH

In literary circles, profits can vary dramatically. You can make as much as a $100,000 or as little as $10,000. It all depends on the efficiency of your market research, hard work, and ingenuity.

START-UP COSTS

With used books, start-up costs are literally a-dime-a-dozen. You can use your own books, put out a call via classified ads to people with books to spare, or scout the rummage sales. Used bookstores can be opened on a $5,000-to-$25,000 budget.

HELP IS ON THE WAY

Put yourself in touch with your chosen industry by investigating the following:

Associations:
- American Booksellers Association: 800/637-0037
  Tarrytown, New York

- Antiquarian Booksellers Associations of America: 212/757-9395
  New York, New York

Trade Publications:
- *American Bookseller*: 800/637-0037
  American Booksellers Association; Tarrytown, New York

- *Book Quote: The Book Trade Bi-Weekly for Buyers and Sellers of Out-of-Print, Used and Rare Books*
  The Spoon River Press; Peoria, Illinois

- *Independent Bookselling Today*: 615/298-2303
  Nashville, Tennessee

Read All About It:
- *Antique, Specialty, and Used Book Sellers: A Subject Guide and Directory* by James Ethridge and Karen Ethridge, Omnigraphics, Inc., 1998.

- *Book Dealers Used and Rare Directory*: 402/593-4600; American Business Directories, Inc., Omaha, Nebraska.

- *Book Finds: How to Find, Buy, and Sell Used and Rare Books* by Ian Ellis. Perigee, 1996.

- *Books: Identification and Price Guide*: Avon Books, New York, New York.

MARKET RESEARCH AND LOCATION

Book collectors and avid readers of all ages are the best sources of income for used-book peddlers. With such a wide range of potential consumers, it may be difficult to find a home for your shop based on target clientele alone. Other factors to consider when searching for a location are visibility, volume of foot traffic, proximity to universities.

EQUIP YOURSELF
- book stack shelves

- at least 5,000 titles

- computer to keep track of inventory, perform bookkeeping, and keep a database of customer names

- telephone

- cash register and sales counter

- price guide
- shopping bags, stationery, business cards

IMAGE MATTERS

When dealing with anything secondhand, the idea is to make the atmosphere cozy. You're going for that "grandmother's house" ambiance. Go for the trunk-style coffee table and flank it with overstuffed armchairs. Doilies have never looked silly at Grandma's house, and neither have candy dishes, so stock up on these staples. Let loose your imagination; just don't forget that the desired effect is decidedly warm.

GETTING THE WORD OUT

One way to get pedestrians to stop and take notice is to put out a table loaded with colorful, eye-catching books. No one can resist such a temptation, especially once they get a load of your pricing. Call this impulse-buyer trap number one.

Advertising in local papers is also sure to send some browsers through your aisles. Readings by authors, book discussion groups, and other creative means of drawing attention to your business should all serve to procure you an audience.

OPENING A
BREAD SHOP

There's something about the smell of freshly baked bread that reminds us of the good old days, when people baked their own rolls or purchased their daily loaf from the corner baker.

But wait! Looks like happy days are here again! Specialty bread stores are once again gaining in popularity. Maybe it's our nation's desire to get back to good old family values; maybe it's the new emphasis on healthy eating. Whatever it is, bread shops are back in vogue and are fast on their way to transforming the way bread is bought and sold in America.

Sure, you can walk into a grocery store and pick yourself up a baguette or two, but there's something special about purchasing it from a small bread shop, where you can talk to the owner, and sample various breads before selecting one to take home.

If you're into baking up some serious profits, while providing the down-home feeling your customers will expect, then get ready to learn anything and everything about owning your own bread shop.

RAKING IN THE DOUGH

Net profits for bread shop owners can be very high. These range anywhere from $60,000 to $170,000. Because ingredients are very inexpensive, you can charge much more than the actual costs of production. That makes for a great profit margin and a great investment portfolio.

START-UP COSTS

The cost of equipment and space rental can be very high. You can, however, purchase used equipment, thereby saving heaps of money. You will also need a solid marketing plan, which can add up to a significant investment. Look to spend in the area of $30,000 to $60,000 to open your shop.

HELP IS ON THE WAY

Where there are questions, there are solutions. Joining an association and/ or subscribing to trade magazines will keep you informed and your financial future stable.

Associations:
- Retailer's Bakery Association; 301/725-2149
  Laurel, Maryland

Trade Publications:
- *American Deli-Bakery News*: 415-512-7229
  San Francisco, California

- *Baking and Snack*: 816-756-1000
  Kansas City, Missouri

Read All About It:
- *America's Bread Book: 300 Authentic Recipes for Americas Favorite Home-made Bread* by Mary Gubser. Quill, 1992.

Franchise:
- Great Harvest Bread; 406-683-6842
  Dillon, Montana

MARKET RESEARCH AND LOCATION

A busy strip or indoor mall will obviously generate the most business. But if the rent costs are too high, you may have to forsake size for location. A bread shop near a supermarket will also be successful, since customers can pop into your store after making their grocery purchases. If you do settle on this location, make sure your prices are competitive and your service superior.

Whatever teeming shopping district you decide to call home, it had better be an affluent one. If your customers have to ask why they should pay you $2.50 per loaf (the approximate going rate) when Wonder Bread is only $.89, you're in the wrong ville, buddy.

EQUIP YOURSELF

The following items are necessary to proper operation. If you plan to purchase used equipment, make sure you check the items thoroughly for any damage.

- industrial oven

- industrial refrigerator

- freezer

- chairs and tables

- coffeemaker (cappuccino machine optional)

- office furniture

- computer system

- baking supplies

IMAGE MATTERS

A 1,000-square-foot store can accommodate your needs. The layout should include an area for ordering, a small dining area for customers, a storage area for supplies, and a room for your office. If you have a hard time fitting everything into one space, consult a professional interior designer. You'd be surprise at what they can do with a small space.

Your shop should have a comfy, rustic look that puts people in the mood to buy. Emphasize the old-fashioned feel of your shop by including wood counters and floors and hanging up black and white prints of families and restaurants.

GETTING THE WORD OUT

To market your bread shop effectively you will have to advertise in local newspapers. To cut down on costs, try writing a fun article about your business and the health benefits of bread. You may just get editorial coverage free-of-charge.

You should also distribute menus listing the varieties and prices of your bread. Make sure to include a special offer like: buy one, get one free, or get 50 percent off your first loaf. Distribute these brochures to residences throughout your area.

A TOAST TO YOUR OWN
BREWPUB

Doubtless some of you are stumped. What is a brewpub? A perfectly valid query, as there are only about 1,200 brewpubs in the states today. A brewpub is simply an American take on the English ale house. That's right, a neighborhood restaurant that serves freshly made microbrews (a beer produced in quantities lower than 20,000 barrels per year) instead of your usual Coors, Miller, et al.. Now, why, you may be asking, would anyone open a brewpub instead of, say, a bar? No, this is not one of those why-ask-why moments. There's a great reason behind the recent success of microbreweries.

With the turn of the century just a stone's throw away, Americans have been exhibiting some very strange behaviors. We vilify Joe Camel and the Marlboro Man, yet we sell our souls for Castro's cigars. We yearn for rusticity, yet we're constantly trying to improve technology. Can it be that the whole world has suddenly gone mad? Not at all. We want good health. We want nature. But we also want what we want. In other words, we're exhibiting man's timeless drive to have that cake and eat it too.

By opening a brewpub, you'd be joining some of today's greatest business minds, who are cleaning up in the "gourmet" vices racket. Check out Ben & Jerry, Starbucks, Outback Steakhouses, and American Spirit cigarettes. No matter what the FDA or the Surgeon General says, caffeine, cholesterol, and nicotine will turn a profit faster than a Good Humor man in the Sahara—if served up with the "freshest ingredients," that is.

Purity and freshness. These buzzwords are the reason that microbrewskis are gaining an ever-growing portion of the U.S. beer market. Since our nation's taste buds have only just begun to blossom, the time is ripe for you beer-loving entrepreneurs to take your passion and make it happen.

RAKING IN THE DOUGH

If you play your locale, decor, and advertising cards right, count on garnering anywhere from $500,000 to a cool million in profits each year. At this rate you could retire a millionaire by the time you're thirty.

START-UP COSTS

This here's the kicker. Starting up a brewpub takes some serious bank. Equipment, real estate, kitchen, and seating space don't come cheap. So, before you reap any profits, you're going to have to come up with a whopping $780,000 (on average).

You can ask your friendly neighborhood banker for a loan, or you can pitch your business plan to some ritzy acquaintances. If you're ready to part with a megachunk of business ownership, a venture capitalist may also come to your rescue.

If all else fails, there is always the U.S. Small Business Administration. Call 1-800-U ASK SBA for more information.

HELP IS ON THE WAY

Reading the trades may not sound like an evening at the Apollo right now, but just wait until you're at the helm of your very own enterprise. You'll find all the brewpub news that's fit to print in the pages of these mags.

Associations:
- Association of Brewers: 303/447-0816
  Boulder, Colorado

Trade Publications:
- *The American Brewer*: 800/646-2701
  Owens Publications, Hayward, California

- *Brewer's Digest*: 773/463-3400
  Siebel Publishing Co., Chicago, Illinois

- *Modern Brewery Age*: 203/853-6015
  Business Journals Inc., Norwalk, Connecticut

- *The New Brewer*: 303/447-0816
  Association of Brewers, Boulder, Colorado

Read All About It:
- *Brewery Planner: A Guide to Opening and Running Your Own Small Brewery* edited by Theresa Duggan, Kim Adams, and Elizabeth Gold. Brewers Publications, 1997.

- *Designing Great Beers: The Ultimate Guide to Brewing Classic Beer Styles* by Ray Daniels. Brewers Publications, 1996.

LICENSE AND INSURANCE

The business of alcohol is no laughing matter. Thou shalt cover your assets is the first commandment of liquor sales. If you don't want to lose your lock, stock, and barrels, hook up with an insurance salesman ASAP.

You'll also need a bevy of licenses if you plan to go legit: one for beer & wine sales, another for hard liquor sales, a local business license, and the required tax permits. Every restaurant in the country is also responsible for obtaining a county health permit.

You're playing with the big boys now; that's right, the ATF (Bureau of Alcohol, Tobacco, and Firearms). This is one gang you don't want to cross, so fill out the brewer's notice and the brewer's bond, and stay on their good side.

MARKET RESEARCH AND LOCATION

Use your Internet savvy to check out brewing industry statistics. There's quite a few sites out there just waiting to be tapped into. The bulk of your profits will come from alcohol sales, so price wisely. Here's a tip. A $2.00 mug of brew only costs you $0.07 to produce. Quite a markup!

Use your Internet savvy to check out brewing industry statistics on the web. These will give you a good idea of where to plant your business. In general, a community of over 50,000 will provide you with a solid customer base. Consider the more affluent areas and shopping districts, as true beer aficionados are still relegated to the higher income brackets. Brewpubs have been known to become quite the popular haunts in college towns such as Boulder, Colorado. Yet there are plenty of nice universities out there just waiting to be tapped into.

Before staking your claim to any one locale, investigate the competition. Check around area liquor stores, microbreweries, and brewpubs. If you find that you're the new kid on an already crowded block, wise up and scope out other zones.

GETTING THE WORD OUT

Witness the publicity hound's three steps: press release, grand opening, and free beer. The press release should announce this concept restaurant to the area's residents by way of a newspaper. You could also hit up some radio stations for air time. Maybe consider doing a promotion that would benefit both your brewpub and the radio station. The grand opening should be staged as an affair to remember. Provide music, party favors with your logo, tours of the brewing facility, and even beer samples. Free beer, well, that speaks for itself. Plant coupons in the Yellow Pages and the papers—"free microbrew with this coupon" is one slogan that's bound to get noticed.

CAST AND CREW

Contrary to popular belief, good help is not that hard to find. You'll need a restaurant manager, a few cooks, as well as scads of support personnel (waiters, bartenders, hosts, busboys).

Of course, you're not serving anything without the headliner of your pay-roll—the master brewer. Search long and hard for the best one money can buy. Remember, the quality of your product rests almost entirely upon this employee's shoulders, so be prepared to pay a lofty sum for the master's services.

OPENING YOUR OWN
CAR WASH

On average, Americans scrub their cars at least twice a month. Now consider that the average American family owns two cars, and you may find this business idea even more appealing. In the early 1990's, the car wash industry brought in an estimated $2.8 billion. With the fast pace of today's world, most of us just don't have the time to hose down our own cars. And that's where you come in.

While the car washing industry is fairly saturated with small operations, there's no reason why you can't join their ranks. If you offer competitive rates, a pleasant waiting area, and quality service, you're bound to make a splash in the car washing biz.

RAKING IN THE DOUGH

This small business has greater profit potential than most. During the first year car washes reap an average net profit of $90,000. But you can soon expect the cash to start flowing, since most established car wash enterprises report a gross revenue of $270,000 to $380,000.

START-UP COSTS AND EQUIPMENT

The total amount of your start-up investment will be determined by the type of car wash you choose to open. You have four main options: self-service, exterior-rollover washes, exterior only, and full-service.

Self-service is the cheapest car wash alternative, and will require the least equipment. While the popularity of such car washes has actually decreased slightly through the years, you can start this car wash with an investment of around $120,000.

Exterior-rollover car washes feature moderately priced equipment. These auto laundromats require the driver to guide the car through the maze of washing equipment. Once the car has been cleaned, attendants are on hand to dry and wax the vehicle.

Exterior and full-service care washes feature advanced and often expensive machinery that propel the car through a washing course. Full-service car washes offer full cleaning of the exterior as well as the interior. The driver usually waits outside while the car is being serviced. These car wash facilities should total around 3,000 square feet. The cost of equipment and space will, on average, total around $300,000.

HELP IS ON THE WAY
Working at the car wash is not as easy as it sounds. To get the kinks out of your business, you'll need a lot more than a little elbow grease.

Associations:
- Car Wash Owners and Suppliers Association: 414/639-4393
  Racine, Wisconsin

- International Carwash Association: 312/321-5199
  Chicago, Illinois

MARKET RESEARCH AND LOCATION
Many car wash owners conduct full-scale, computerized evaluations of various areas before deciding on a location. When you consider the high-costs of setting up, this option is a wise one to pursue. A good rule of thumb when scouting locations is to head for areas with heavy traffic flow. Busy intersections and areas near highway exits will bring in a steady stream of customers.

You should also screen the competition carefully. More than one car wash in a five-mile radius can work for you, provided you offer competitive prices and special services, like detailing and wheel treatments.

FRANCHISE OPPORTUNITIES
- Classic Car Wash: 408/371-2414
  Campbell, California

- Express Wash: 800/268-6792
  Tonawanda, New York

- Mermaid Car Wash: 608/833-9274
  Madison, Wisconsin

CAST AND CREW
You'll definitely require additional assistance in the car wash business. You'll need someone to work the register, and a crew of nimble car dryers

and polishers. To save on costs associated with a large staff, consider hiring part-time workers and students. Schedule each week ahead of time and tack it up where everyone can see.

GETTING THE WORD OUT

A large, prominent sign with a clever slogan can catch the eye of drivers everywhere. When you're ready for your grand opening, offer a special rate to celebrate your arrival. Another popular method being utilized by many car washes is to offer customers a punch card. Here's how it works: One wash equals one punch. Get 10 punches, and receive a free car wash.

KICK OFF YOUR OWN
CHARTER BOAT SERVICE

So you want to retire a millionaire and sail around the world by the time you're 35? Well, don't twiddle your thumbs waiting a second longer. At least not if you have the wherewithal to start your own charter boat business. If the sea keeps calling your name, answer its call and turn a profit—all in one fell sloop.

Whether you grew up sailing or just dreaming about it, this business will satisfy the seafarer in you. As the captain of your own ship, you'll meet many interesting people and embark on many an adventurous voyage. There will be parties, family outings, sporting adventures, and romantic getaways. And you can preside over it all.

Should the thought of parting with solid ground send you scurrying for the Mylanta, never fear, for a reliable crew is always near. If you're of the keep-your-sea-legs-to-yourself ilk, you can always hire a crew to handle the vessel. But remember—it pays to know about your business. And if you can't tell so much as a yacht from a lifeboat, our advice is that you partner with someone who has the boating background that is so desirable in this business.

RAKING IN THE DOUGH

Location and size of fleet often determine profits in the boating industry. So depending on the location and scope of your of operation, pretax profits can run anywhere from $20,000 to over $200,000 per year.

START-UP COSTS

Boats, even used ones, don't come cheap. A seaworthy, secondhand vessel costs at least $40,000, at least a quarter of which will have to be produced up front. After you factor in employees' salaries, docking costs, advertising, and a variety of other start-up essentials, you're looking at a start-up capital of at least $40,000.

HELP IS ON THE WAY

Everything from business financing options to marketing tips can be at your disposal if you look into the following.

Associations:
- Boat Owners Association of the United States: 703/823-9550
  Alexandria, Virginia

- National Association of Charterboat Operators: 800/745-6094
  Washington, D.C.

- National Party Boat Owners Alliance: 860/535-2066
  Groton, Connecticut

Publications:
- *Boating Business*: 416/695-0311
  Outdoor Canada Publishing Ltd., Toronto, Ontario, Canada

- *Charter Industry Magazine*: 407/288-1066
  Stuart, Florida

- *Marine Business Journal*: 305/538-0700
  Miami Beach, Florida

Read All About It:
- *Boat Handling Under Power* by John Mellor. Sheridan House, 1993.

- *Chapman's Nautical Guides: Boating Etiquette*. Hearst Books, 1990.

LICENSE AND INSURANCE

And they say Hollywood isn't education! If you missed Shelley Winters in *The Poseidon Adventure*, you probably saw Sandra Bullock in *Speed 2* and Leonardo DiCaprio in *Titanic*. If you learned anything from these movies, it's that insurance is a must-have in the mariner's business. You'll need liability insurance as well as hull and machinery insurance if you want to keep from going down with the ship should something go wrong.

Before you can say "Anchors away," the U.S. Coast Guard will insist that your boat pass inspections and that you get a captain's license. You may also need to obtain a liquor license if you plan on serving spirits. There is also the matter of registering your boat and documenting it. The U.S. Coast Guard Marine Safety Office has a list of regulations that must be followed.

You're dealing with the Feds now, so don't be surprised if you need a lawyer to get through all the paperwork.

MARKET RESEARCH AND LOCATION

When first starting out, you can base your office in a spare bedroom or even in the alcove of your studio apartment. The most important location will be that of your boat. The port you choose to dock in can make or break your business, so we suggest you look hither and yon to find just the right one.

Ideally, you're looking for easy-to navigate waterways, beautiful scenery, little competition, good climate, reasonable docking fees, and tourist attractions to draw attention to your business. If you can't find a port without several charter boat businesses already in operation, you should look for ways to differentiate yourself from these other businesses. Call their offices to find out what services they offer, where they take their passengers, and how much they charge. If you can find a niche (such as corporate events, wedding showers, etc.) and price your services competitively, you're in business.

GETTING THE WORD OUT

Well-targeted advertising can pay off in a big way. Travel sections of local newspapers, city tourist guides, and roadside billboards can all be great sources of revenue. You can also print some brochures, and pay people to circulate these in your area's airports and train stations.

Another way to generate business is to hook up with a charter broker. Charter brokers have elevated matching boats with customers to an art form. And if advertising and marketing has never been your cup of tea, listing with a broker could save you a great deal of time and money.

OPENING YOUR OWN
COFFEE SHOP

Mmmmm! A steaming mug of coffee, you can already smell its aroma and feel the velvety richness tingling your taste buds. Go ahead, admit it, your pulse quickens at the mere thought of that glorious concoction. Java gourmands have been coming out of the closet in droves since the early 1990's, and gourmet coffee sales have risen a sharp 33 percent. According to the National Coffee Association, Americans consume over 400 million cups of coffee on a daily basis.

What we have here is a national caffeine-swilling frenzy. And entrepreneurs are capitalizing on the American Joe Jones big-time. You've now got your coffee ice cream, coffee candy, coffee specialty stores, coffee newsletters, coffee-of-the-month clubs, coffee conventions, coffee books, and conventions about coffee books. Is it any wonder that a cafe is coming to every street corner near you?

Pretty soon, schools nationwide will be sounding a new anthem, something to the effect of "home of the coffee and the land of the crave." If you ever considered opening your own Java emporium, seize the day, because success has never smelled so much like coffee.

RAKING IN THE DOUGH
The income potential, on average, can amount to $500,000 gross sales annually, with an initial investment of $250,000. Sales may vary depending on location, shop size, and number of customers.

START-UP COSTS
- $80,000 to $250,000 for sit-down coffeeshop

- $200,000 for franchise

- $15,000 for pushcart

HELP IS ON THE WAY

The following industry associations are a valuable source of information. Joining an association entitles you to special offers and you'll be the first to receive ground-breaking industry news—membership does have its privileges.

Associations:
- National Coffee Association of USA: 212/344-5596
  New York, New York

- Specialty Coffee Association of America: 310/983-8090
  Long Beach, California

Trade Magazines:
- *Fresh Cup Magazine*: 503/236-2587
  Portland, Oregon

- *Tea and Coffee Trade Journal*: 212/391-2060
  New York, New York

Read All About It:
- *Coffee Shop: Start Your Own Coffee and Tea Store* by Joanne Padgett. Prentice Hall Trade, 1996.

- *Espresso: Starting and Running Your Own Specialty Coffee Business* by Joe Monaghan and Julia Huffaker. John Wiley and Sons, 1995.

MARKET RESEARCH AND LOCATION

Location can make or break a coffeeshop, so choose wisely. You'll need to set up shop in a high-foot-traffic zone to get a broad customer base. The customers you'll be targeting are generally between 23 and 45 years of age in the middle-to-upper-income brackets. Keep in mind that women make up a large percentage of coffee consumers.

Accessing the proper clientele will require that you acquire some demographics on your target area. These vital stats should include population density, purchasing power, eating and spending habits, as well as median income. The U.S. Census Bureau and your local Chamber of Commerce will be your best friends when scouting such info. But never underestimate the value of field research.

After narrowing your options to a few select locales, explore the areas to get better acquainted with the general populace. Talk to nearby store owners to learn more about the neighborhood patrons. Do they meet your criteria?

Highly populated commercial zones will amount to higher rent, but if you factor in the open-handed spending practices of the average resident, it may all balance out in the end.

LICENSE AND INSURANCE

Before opening up your cafe, you will have to acquire a business license, check out city zoning ordinances, and get a clean bill of health from the health department. Insurance is also a must. Protect your business by purchasing standard business insurance and liability coverage, which will protect your establishment in case of food poisoning. And don't neglect to check if your cafe complies with the federal Occupation Safety and Health Act (OSHA), the American Disabilities Act, and the Immigration Reform and Control Act. Let your fingers do the walking towards the "U.S. Government" category in your phone book. One phone call will tell you if you meet the standard requirements.

EQUIP YOURSELF

Essential equipment includes:

- espresso/cappuccino machine
- commercial scales and coffee mills
- display jars, cases, and shelves
- ceramic mugs, glasses, and paper cups

If food figures into your menu, acquire:

- an industrial fridge
- eating utensils
- dishwear

STOCKING UP

The name of the game is coffee, and the better the quality, the greater the sales. Variety is the key when ordering coffee. Flavored, blends, decaffeinated, and dark roast are staples of any cafe. When purchasing from a supplier, ask about their best-sellers. And never stockpile the inventory for fear of a shortage. Coffee loses flavor very quickly, so keep your order between 500 and 750 pounds of coffee.

IMAGE MATTERS

Thirst is important, but let's face it, in the coffee game, image is everything. Today's gourmet coffeehouses are a refuge from the daily grind and the littered streets. The cafe's ambiance can attract a slew of customers and will have them begging for seconds. Keep the atmosphere trendy but cozy. Couches, old books, and funky wall colors will enhance the aesthetics of your shop. Salvage old tables and chairs by painting directly over the wood. Or hire an artist to transform dilapidated furniture into today's hottest look — shabby chic.

CAST AND CREW

A small staff of two or three employees can be all it takes to satisfy your customers' thirst for the brew. Neither is it uncommon to find a shop owner manning the counter and giving regular customers the old "hi-dee-ho." Hire only a few employees until you get a better sense of the traffic flow generated by your shop. You can always bring more helping hands on board at a later time.

Your staff should become very familiar with your shop's coffee selection, so make sure they consume mass quantities. Customers want the inside scoop on the latest varieties, and will look to your staff to recommend their favorites. Encouraging your employees to sample the wares will not only give them the energy to work diligently, but will also provide an invaluable referral service to your customers.

GETTING THE WORD OUT

Flyers, word of mouth, and special offers (buy one drink, get one free) can get your shop the attention it deserves and won't cost you an arm and a leg. Sometimes patrons will order one drink and take up a table for hours at a time. Don't look down your nose. You can't buy this kind of advertising! Passersby will notice that your cafe is filled to the max, and will assume your shop is the best around.

Use the local talent to stage shows from art to music to poetry. Once you've got the act, the news release will be printed in the local paper free of charge (ask about the Calendar of Events section).

Stock up on extra chairs and tables. You'll need them.

OPENING YOUR OWN
NEW AND USED COMPACT DISK STORE

The CD industry has been growing steadily since the early 1990's. The compact disc has revolutionized the music industry, and has surpassed the popularity of audiocassettes. So much so, in fact, that many retailers no longer even stock the archaic cassette. Owning your own CD store can pay off big-time, provided you offer the latest releases and an interesting setting.

When the CD innovation debuted on the scene, we were told the $15 price tag would soon be slashed. But alas! Due to the great popularity of this product, such a markdown was not to be forthcoming. As a result, certain entrepreneurs began to sell used CD's for low prices. To stir thing up a bit, you can offer both options. This alternative to traditional CD emporiums can secure a snug niche in the CD industry and a large share of its profits.

RAKING IN THE DOUGH

Depending your store's square footage, inventory, and location, you can make anywhere from $50,000 to $130,000. Many CD entrepreneurs opt to branch out and open stores in multiple locations to increase profits.

START-UP COSTS

To open an average-sized store with extensive inventory, you'll need around $60,000. But costs can skyrocket well above $100,000 if your store is situated in a busy commercial setting and is over 4,000 square feet.

INVENTORY

Inventory costs will make up the bulk of your start-up costs, around $30,000 to $60,000. When planning your inventory, you should decide how much inventory you wish to purchase for each music category. There's rock, pop, country, jazz, blues, and many others. A good way to determine how much inventory you'll need is to order a small amount at first, and then gauge your customers' requests. If rap is high on their list, then make sure you have plenty of rap CD's to go around. To get your hands on reasonably priced CD's, you will have to contact distributors and manufacturers directly.

If you're planning to offer used CD's, you can either pay your customers directly or give them the option to exchange their used CD's for others. Many people respond favorably to this equitable exchange, and actually seek out CD stores where they can experience the barter system at its best.

HELP IS ON THE WAY

If you're planning to open a CD store, joining an industry association can save you both time and money. These associations can put you in touch with reliable CD suppliers and the right financing outlets to get your operation of the ground.

Associations:

- National Association of Recording Merchandisers: 609/596-2221
  Marlton, New Jersey

- National Retail Merchants Association: 202/783-7971
  Washington, D.C.

- Recording Industry Association of America: 202/775-0101
  Washington, D.C.

Trade Magazines:

- *Billboard*: 800/745-8922
  New York, New York

- *CMJ New Music Monthly*: 800/745-8922
  Boulder, Colorado

- *Spin*: 212/633-8200
  New York, New York

IMAGE MATTERS

CD stores have to have a bright, colorful, and clean interior. It is the owner's job to create an environment that will keep customers browsing for hours and coming back for years.

The layout of your stores should be clearly determined before you begin setting up. You should incorporate two checkout areas at two ends of the store for faster service. Each music category should be clearly marked with a sign and be housed in a section of its own. You should also make sure to allow for plenty of space between the aisles. And remember to house the new and used CD's in separate areas.

EQUIP YOURSELF

To cut costs, scope out stores going out of business, and offer to buy their equipment. You will need:

- special CD shelving
- several cash registers
- display cases
- several phones dispersed throughout the store
- office equipment
- several computers for record-keeping

GETTING THE WORD OUT

Advertising your store in alternative newspapers can be a sound marketing move. Young and old people alike will be drawn by your used-CD option and the special-offer announcements.

Another way to boost sales is to hold live artist performances at your store. Bands will appreciate the exposure, and you can clean up like a bandit. Make sure to post fliers and maybe even send out a few press releases to local papers before the big event.

OUTFITTING YOUR OWN
COSTUME/NOVELTY SHOP

While Michael Meyers doesn't hold a candle to the killing most costume shops make come Halloween, this type of business can be a year-round success as well. Some funny novelty items, wacky greeting cards, and funky wigs should provide your store with paying customers on a daily basis.

A wide variety of costumes will make your store a fun place for people of all ages to visit. You can also offer party planning services for masquerade balls and other off-beat theme parties. Just think how the kids at malls across America would react to a Santa sans beard, or even elves sans culottes for that matter. And while we're on the subject, where would society balls be without the notion of masquerade? In black tie, of course.

RAKING IN THE DOUGH

Costume shop owners, with a large inventory and shop, can expect to make from $60,000 to $170,000 per year. If you're planning a quickie, in-and-out Halloween venture, you may see as much as $20,000 come your way in as little as three months.

START-UP COSTS

Inventory, space rental, and marketing will probably contribute the most to exhausting your start-up resources. You will need a start-up fund of at least $30,000 to $50,000 in cold hard capital.

HELP IS ON THE WAY

Costume shop owners will benefit from distributor and wholesaler information. You will have to keep your stores stocked with the latest cartoon characters and action heroes. Joining an association and reading up on the art of costume design will give you the insight needed to make this business a huge success.

Associations:
- Costume Society of America: 410/275-2329
  Earleville, Maryland

- National Costumers Association: 419/334-4098
  Fremont, Ohio

Read All About It:
- *Easy to Make Costumes* by Kathryn Harrison and Valerie Kohn. Sterling Publishing, 1993.

- *Historical Encyclopedia of Costumes* by Auguste Racinet and Albert Racinet. Facts on File, 1995.

MARKET RESEARCH AND LOCATION

Your customers will be as varied as your selection of costumes. Everyone from little kids to senior citizens wants to get in on the fun of dressing the part. The best way to attract a steady stream of buyers is to open your shop in a large city. You may want to choose an indoor- or strip-mall setting to maximize your store's visibility.

IMAGE MATTERS

Your store should consist of the main area for customer browsing, a dressing area for fittings, a storage area for surplus inventory, and a small office where you can keep track of sales and rest your feet after a weary day. You will need at least 3,000 square feet to house these elements.

When designing your store, keep in mind that your customers don't always have to buy; it's enough that they want to come in and just browse at first. To encourage this practice, make sure to keep plenty of novelty items around for the customers to play with. You can also set up a mirror next to the wigs and encourage people to try them on. The key is to create a carnival-like experience that will keep your customers coming back time and time again.

EQUIP YOURSELF

Costume shop owners should secure the following items before opening their doors to the public:

- cash register
- commercial lighting
- phone system

- computer for tracking inventory and invoices
- beams for hanging costumes
- display cases and shelves

GETTING THE WORD OUT

The best time to open your store is a few months prior to Halloween. You can schedule a grand opening party and really go all out to make this celebration as profitable as possible. Advertise your party in local newspapers and on the radio. Create a spooky haunted-house feel and watch your customers squirm in anticipation. By doing this, you will have attracted a loyal customer base from the get-go.

You should also advertise your services to school theater departments and regular theaters around town. Passing out fliers at the concerts of shock rockers such as Marilyn Manson may be a great source of new clientele. These potential customers have a year-round need for costumes and can bring you steady business in the years to come.

OPENING YOUR OWN
DANCE STUDIO

Ballet, ballroom, hip-hop, jazz, salsa, square, and swing classes have kept Americans in shape for years. And unlike traditional exercise, dance is an uplifting means of self-expression that has kept many a satisfied customer on their toes and in tip-top condition.

Opening a dance studio is an exciting venture for anyone who loves to dance and wants to help others perfect their moves. You don't have to be a Fred Astaire or Ginger Rogers to make this enterprise a profitable venture. All you'll need is a couple of experienced instructors. So, if you think you have what it takes, put on your dancing shoes and get ready to make some serious money.

RAKING IN THE DOUGH

The average-sized dance school with a small staff will bring in at least $40,000 per year. Larger dance schools, with a variety of studios and instructors, can bring that number up to a whopping $90,000+. Not bad for dancing your nights and days away.

START-UP COSTS

Even a smaller school will require an investment of at least $20,000. That total should cover the cost of leasing a space, installing a sound system, mirrors, railing, office supplies, a computer, and a marketing campaign.

Some of you may want to go all out, and secure a large space with several dance studios. If that is the case, expect to invest at least $45,000.

HELP IS ON THE WAY

Knowing what's going on in the dance world is vital to your studio's survival. Make sure you're up on the latest in techniques and educational methods by consulting with these valuable sources.

Associations:

- American Dance Guild: 212/627-3790
  New York, New York

- Professional Dance Teacher's Association: 201/769-2069
  Waldwick, New Jersey

Trade Publications:

- *American Dance*: 212/627-3790
  New York, New York

- *Dance Magazine*: 212/956-6487
  New York, New York

- *Dance Teacher Now*: Fax: 919/872-6888
  Raleigh, North Carolina

Read All About It:

- *The Dance Studio: Business Managing for Aerobics, Dance and Gymnastics Teachers* by Marie Zima. McFarland and Company, 1987.

- *How to Operate a Successful Dance Studio* by C. Farell. Gordon Press Publications, 1986.

MARKET RESEARCH AND LOCATION

Your customers will mostly consist of girls ages five through eleven. You'll find that both parents and children are most keen on dancing lessons in these formative years, before there is a marked indication of talent and ability.

While you'll have fewer students of junior high and high school age, you will still be able to fill your classes due to the serious nature of those students who decide to continue their dance education.

For physical fitness reasons, adults are also big fans of the dance class. If you tailor certain classes to appeal to the fitness enthusiasts in your neighborhood, you're sure to find a following.

Take a good look at your neighborhood before you roll out this business venture. Make sure that parents have the time, the money, and the inclination to chauffeur their kids around from school to dance lessons. Check to see how well the health clubs are doing, as well as how much memberships go for. Whether you're in the city or the suburbs, most middle- and upper-middle class areas should fit this description.

CAST AND CREW

This is one business employees can easily make or break. Hiring professional and experienced dancers is a priority for would-be dance school owners. Your clients will want to feel secure in their instructors' dance abilities. Make sure to only hire dance instructors with professional dance experience. Depending on the background and training of the instructor, you can expect to pay your employees anywhere from $30 to $60 per hour. But don't worry about this expense. If there's one thing that's guaranteed to keep your customers dancing in your aisles, it's the quality of your dance staff.

GETTING THE WORD OUT

To attract new clients and keep them coming back for more, you may start by advertising in local papers. Emphasize the fitness benefits and celebrate your grand opening with a complimentary class.

You should also target mothers with young children by posting your ads at day care centers and nearby schools.

Another great way to bring in new customers is to send out press-releases highlighting your dance instructors' experience. Give the story a human-interest bent and you may just be allotted valuable editorial space in the local paper.

To maintain your steady stream of clients, most studio owners offer cost-effective enrollment plans, where the student signs up for a set amount of time and pays in advance. But be sure to make a "pay per class" option available to your more cautious students.

OPENING YOUR OWN
DELICATESSEN

Americans are gobbling up deli sandwiches and submarines by the foot. For years now, submarine-sandwich-makers have been cutting into the profits of burger-flippers by positioning their product as a healthy alternative. According to the U.S Department of Commerce, there was a 36 percent increase in sandwich shop sales between 1988 and 1990. Fresh ingredients and fresh-baked bread can be all it takes to lure a platoon of salivating throngs to your shop's doorstep.

Everyone from college students to baby boomers loves the do-it-yourself format of delicatessens. The ability to customize your order and watch its preparation is very important to today's consumers. People want to know what they're getting, and increasing numbers are looking to sandwich shops to satisfy this desire.

RAKING IN THE DOUGH

Most sandwich shops can expect to bring in at least $70,000 per year. Large operations, with indoor seating and a variety of food selections, can garner over $120,000 in profits each year.

START-UP COSTS

The price of starting your own deli can be high. The average-sized shop will require at least $60,000 in start-up costs. That includes inventory, design, space, office supplies, staff, and marketing costs. If you have a larger enterprise on the mind, don't ring that dinner bell until you have at least $80,000 on hand.

MARKET RESEARCH AND LOCATION

Where you situate your sandwich shop is crucial to your continued success. College towns are havens for the deli-minded entrepreneur. With little money to burn and a growing concern for their health, college students will greet your business with open arms. If you do plan to open a shop on a college campus, make sure it is close to where most students congregate in between classes.

You should also consider situating your sandwich shop in busy commercial areas. Patrons from nearby businesses will account for a large portion of your customers, so make sure there are plenty around before settling on a location.

Don't forget to check out the competition. If there are well-known delis in your area of choice, try to find a nearby area that isn't already saturated with sub shops.

FRANCHISES

The great thing about opening your own sub shop is that sub shops have already proved to be successful, money-making operations. Investing your capital in a popular sub chain can be an easy way to gain credibility, training, financing, and a steady stream of customers. The following is a sample of the biggest names in the sandwich biz:

- Blimpie: 800/447-6256
  Atlanta, Georgia

- Scholtzsky's Deli: 512/480-9871
  Austin, Texas

- Subway Sandwiches and Salads: 800/888-4848
  Milford, Connecticut

IMAGE MATTERS

The look and layout of your sub shop should be comfy, unique, and inviting. Unless you're buying a brand-name franchise, you will have to determine the design of your shop, its layout, and which equipment to purchase. Design-wise, your shop should have a clean, spacious feel. Plants, wooden counters, wicker baskets, and interesting tables and chairs will give your shop its own special identity.

Depending on your plans to open a strictly take-out or dining-in operation, the space you decide to purchase should have enough room to fit your clientele. If you're omitting the dining room factor, make sure to have enough space and a comfy sitting area for customers. A storage area is also essential, so make sure your layout plans include this necessary component.

EQUIP YOURSELF

- industrial refrigerator and freezer
- commercial oven, range, grill, and hood
- microwave
- dishwasher
- three-bin sink
- beverage dispensers
- baking sheets
- Tupperware
- cooking utensils
- dining tables and chairs
- cash register
- paper cups, plates, carry-out bags, napkins, straws, etc.
- computer with a variety of restaurant-related software
- desk and chair
- phone and fax

GETTING THE WORD OUT

An eye-catching menu with a variety of offerings is a good way to entice customers. Offer a variety of menu items, including sandwiches, salads, chips, and dessert. To set your shop above the rest, consider offering a variety of coffees and desserts. You can even bring in a gourmet coffee cart to save on room and emphasize this special amenity.

Local businesses will generate a steady stream of walk-ins, so why not send out a press release for a discounted catered lunch. Once your wares have been sampled, you may be on your way to landing important corporate lunch accounts.

Special offers can also boost your business's profit margin. Take out coupon ads in local newspapers. Buy one, get one free, 20 percent off your total order, complimentary beverage or cookie—all these giveaways will give you more than customers than you've ever imagined.

OPENING YOUR OWN
DRESS SHOP

How many times have you wandered through the aisles of some upscale boutique, only to exclaim, "Alas! Clothes, clothes everywhere, but not a thing to wear!" Okay, maybe you didn't use those exact words, but you get the picture — many apparel stores are not meeting consumer demands. If you feel that you've got your finger on the pulse of today's fashion-conscious customers, then opening up your own store can be more than a pipe dream.

RAKING IN THE DOUGH

Unless you really know your togs, and expand your business along the lines of a "Limited" or a "Contempo," it's not likely that a dress shop will make your get-rich-quick dreams become reality. Instead, your annual profits will hover around the $75,000 figure. But with first dibs on all the latest fashions, at least you'll always look like a million bucks.

START-UP COSTS

Even if you pinch those pennies until they turn blue, you're still going to need at least $40,000 to get into business. And that's the really low end. Equipment, electricity, rental payments, advertising, and a stash to see you through the initial months of operation will all total up to an average start-up cost of $80,000.

HELP IS ON THE WAY

The following sources can teach you the tricks of the trade like nobody's business.

Associations:
- American Apparel Manufacturers Association: 703/524-1864
  Arlington, Virginia

- National Retail Federation: 202/783-7971
  Marlton, New Jersey

Trade Publications:
- *Apparel Industry Magazine*: 404/252-8831
  Atlanta, Georgia

- *Women's Wear Daily*: 212/630-4000
  Fairchild Publications, Inc., New York, New York

MARKET RESEARCH AND LOCATION

Ask yourself this question: What kind of person will shop at your store? Will your racks boast anything and everything for the big and tall man, the average Joe, the plus-sized Sally, the teenybopper, or the urban sophisticate? The possible markets are endless, and once you decide which ones you want to lure, the best place to cast your bait won't be hard to find.

Checking out demographics via magazine subscriptions is a stroke of genius. If you decide to go for the teen market, check out those areas with the highest concentration of subscribers to the magazines targeting your demographic. If the up-and-comers are who you want to dress, investigate which part of your city receives the most copies of *Details*, *Mademoiselle*, and such.

It may go without saying, but here we go again: high volumes of foot traffic are an absolute imperative, so tailor your site search to malls and busy shopping districts.

EQUIP YOURSELF
- computerized cash register

- glass-encased counter

- wall racks

- mannequins

- shelves

- hangers

- personalized shopping bags

- price/security tags

- mirrors galore

STOCKING UP

If you want to keep up with the trends, you'll have to do more than stay glued to MTV's *House of Style*. The fashion business is where you get to write off travel expenses to New York, San Francisco, and Los Angeles. No one's knocking homegrown designers and clothing manufacturers, but you're going to have to go out of your way to find the kind of styles and labels that will have your customers singing a happy tune.

GETTING THE WORD OUT

In the garment district, a smart window display and a clever sign can take you places. But don't limit yourself to passersby with a penchant for fashion; make sure people go out of their way to get their hands on your goodies with well-placed advertising. The free city papers and magazines get wide circulation, so look into their advertising rates. Tourists are also good for a buck, so call up your city's tour guide publishers and ask for a mention.

OPENING YOUR OWN
ENVIRONMENTAL STORE

Environmentally safe products, from makeup to pens, have been teaching retailers a new lesson in ecological economics. Since the early 1990's, when many natural, global disasters were televised, America's environmental awareness has been on a steep incline. All you have to do is go outdoors to see proof in the form of recycling bins on every corner. The environment is a hot button for most consumers, and that concern is here to stay.

If you've ever thought about joining Greenpeace or just have a keen interest in preserving the wonders of Mother Nature, opening an environmental store is a great way to make a positive contribution, while making a very swift profit.

RAKING IN THE DOUGH

The *New York Times* projected environmental store sales to reach $95 million in 1997. That figure grew at an astounding rate of 65 percent in 1994. These figures alone indicate a dramatic profit margin for environmental entrepreneurs.

Depending on the size of your store and the type of products you plan on selling, your store can bring in anywhere from $40,000 its first year to over $160,000 after expansion.

START-UP COSTS

Plan to invest at least $35,000 in a small retail shop, and over $70,000 into a larger operation. This will cover inventory, decor, cashiers, display shelves, and marketing costs. To lower this start-up figure, you may want to search for the most affordable distributors and skimp on design costs with a do-it-yourself strategy.

HELP IS ON THE WAY

Getting the latest on new products and industry events is important to your image as an environmentally conscious business owner. Your customers will consider you an expert in the field, so make sure you don't disappoint them by looking into these helpful resources:

Association:

- Co-Op American Business Network: 202/872-5307
  Washington, D.C.

Trade Publications:

- *Environment*: 202/362-6445
  Washington, D.C.

- *The Green Consumer*: 212/645-4500
  New York, New York

- *In Business: The Magazine for Environmental Entrepreneuring*: 215/967-4135
  Emmaus, Pennsylvania

Read All About It:

- *Ecopreneuring: The Complete Guide to Small Business Opportunities from the Environmental Revolution* by Steven J. Bennett. John Wiley and Sons, 1997.

MARKET RESEARCH AND LOCATION

Environmental stores are generally more favored by the middle- and upper-class consumers because of the higher costs. So it is crucial that you study the local demographic breakdown before laying down your business roots.

Certain cities like San Francisco, Berkeley, California, Boulder, Colorado, and Madison, Wisconsin, have long been fertile ground for environmental shops, but stores are already cropping up all over the country. This is truly a nationwide phenomenon.

When picking a city or region, you should also find out which areas boast large numbers of environmental groups. Many smaller cities are known for their ecologically conscious dwellers. The introduction of your unique enterprise may very well spawn great interest in large and small cities alike.

EQUIP YOURSELF

- computer with necessary software, fax/modem
- fax machine

- photocopier

- office furniture (filing cabinets, desk, chair, etc.)

- store supplies (credit card machine, sales slips, etc.)

- display fixtures

- cash registers

- extensive stock of inventory

- promotional materials (business cards, brochure, etc.)

INVENTORY CHECKLIST

The goods you choose to sell may practically sell themselves provided you choose properly. There are a whole slew of products that will sell like hot-cakes, and others whose sales may be as flat as old soda. Choosing popular product ideas will place your store in the forefront, and boost your profits considerably. Some popular items among the environmentally concerned set include:

1. recycled napkins, paper plates, and stationery
2. cruelty-free and environmentally safe beauty products
3. energy-efficient appliances
4. organic cotton clothing
5. environmentally safe toys

GETTING THE WORD OUT

When it comes to marketing your environmental store, getting people involved is the name of the game. The majority of people who fail to appreciate the value of environmentally safe products may just be unaware of their benefits. Provide the community a service and yourself with more customers by:

- offering classes and presentations after hours

- posting your notice at local community colleges and around town

Once you educate others about the state of our environment, they will be anxious to pitch in and lend a hand . . . and maybe even a dollar.

OPENING YOUR OWN
FLOWER SHOP

Owning a flower shop can give a whole new meaning to the term "flower power." Flower shop owners everywhere attest to the satisfaction of working with flowers for a living, and spreading that joy to everyone who enters their shop. Whether it's a wedding, an anniversary, or an apology, flowers have a way of bringing people together. Today, the U.S. boasts around 30,000 flower shops, and over 10 billion dollars in annual flower sales.

If you're a budding entrepreneur with a green thumb to boot, then a flower shop can bring you years of prosperity and happiness.

RAKING IN THE DOUGH

On average, flower shops can bring in about $80,000 to $150,000 in annual revenues. But these figures can soar even higher if you offer gift items and delivery, or franchise your operation.

START-UP COSTS

Your initial investment can total anywhere from $30,000 to $90,000 depending on the size of your staff, the size of your store, and overhead.

HELP IS ON THE WAY

If you've never worked at a flower shop before, but simply like the idea of stopping to smell the flowers every day of your life, then associations are definitely the place for you. After all, how else will you know when orchids are as vied after as Uma Thurman's phone number, or when poinsettias are as de rigueur as mistletoe?

Associations:

- Florist's Transworld Delivery Association: 810/355-9300
  Southfield, Michigan

- Society of American Florists: 703/836-8700
  Alexandria, Virginia

Trade Publications:
- *Floral Management*: 800/336-4743
  Alexandria, Virginia

Read All About It:
- *Creative Floral Arranging*. Cowles Creative Publishing, 1998

- *Festive Flowers* by Paula Pryke. Rizzoli, 1997.

- *Fresh Cuts: Arrangements with Flowers, Leaves, Buds, and Branches*, by Edwina Gal and John Hall. Artisan, 1997.

MARKET RESEARCH AND LOCATION

Your potential customers will include middle- to upper-class individuals. Some florists swear by a commercial location in large cities, claiming that the bulk of their sales come from white-collar workers on their way home from work. But a small suburban shop catering primarily to women can also reap big rewards. Weddings, baby showers, and graduations can bring steady business to your shop over many years.

IMAGE MATTERS

The great thing about flower shops is that they already contain everything you'll need to decorate your store. Flowers have to be the most decorative elements around. That is why you have to bring attention to your arrangements by situating them attractively in windows and display cases throughout your store.

If selling gift items figures into your plans, then display these attractively near the counter. Shoppers tend to make impulse decisions, and you should encourage their impulsiveness by displaying merchandise near the register.

STOCKING UP

A well-stocked flower store includes (obviously) a variety of flowers, plants, and gift items. Wholesalers can provide you with the inventory you'll need to keep your customers satisfied and yourself in the green. As a flower shop owner, you'll have to reconcile yourself to wilting flowers. Many floral entrepreneurs either donate their flowers to hospitals and social organizations, or dry their flowers to sell at a later time.

Some gift items you'll want to stock up on include: stuffed animals, gardening books, mugs, and cards.

EQUIP YOURSELF

Flower shops will require plenty of display cases to exhibit your beautiful arrangements. You will also require a glass cooler that will keep your arrangements fresh and ready to be sold. Other equipment will include a cash register, storage area, and office equipment.

GETTING THE WORD OUT

Besides traditional advertising outlets—like local radio stations and newspapers—you should offer your flower arrangement expertise for weddings, graduations, and other parties. Once you become established, a major event just won't be the same without your beautiful flowers to brighten it up.

RESTORED FURNITURE STORE

The past ten years have seen painted and restored furniture come to the forefront of "what's hot" in home decor. Often referred to as shabby chic, this style has every homemaker trading in their new, polished bedroom sets for much, much older models.

But don't start kicking the living mothballs out of your armoire just yet. Beautifully restored and professionally painted furniture is what these new decorators require. In other words, business owners who have a handle on restoration techniques and have a talent for painting can make a significant income making the old and weather-beaten look fresh and appealing. In the early 1990's, the furniture restoration industry experienced a significant slump, due to the wide-range availability of moderately priced new furniture.

But business has been looking up ever since. You'd be surprised to find how much stores are charging for custom-painted furniture—almost twice as much as if the item was new and previously unused. And boy, are the customers ever biting. So, if you are lacking in formal art training, consider taking a few courses to brush up on your technique. Your business will thank you.

RAKING IN THE DOUGH

Because of the rock-bottom prices at garage and moving sales, there's no limit to how high your profit margin may go. Expect to make anywhere from $40,000 to $80,000 selling restored furniture.

START-UP COSTS

Leasing a store space in a highly trafficked area will be your highest start-up expense. You will also have to put aside at least $3,000 for marketing expenses. On average, your start-up costs will total anywhere from $20,000 to $40,000.

HELP IS ON THE WAY

The following sources will provide you with the basics of furniture care and repair. They will also fill you in on the new furniture fashions, as well as the tricks of the merchandising trade.

Trade Publications:

- *Furniture Retailer*: 910/378-6065
  Greensboro, North Carolina

- *Furniture World Magazine*: 914/738-6744
  Pelham, New York

Read All About It:

- *Furniture Restoration* by Kevin Jan Bonner. Sterling Publications, 1996.

- *How to Recognize and Refinish Antiques for Pleasure and Profit*, by Jacquelyn Peake. Globe Pequot Press, 1997.

- *Pocket Guide to Wood Finishes* by Nigel Lofthouse. Betterway Books, 1992.

- *Wood Furniture: Finishing, Refinishing, Repairing* by James E. Brumbaugh, Macmillan Publishing, 1992.

MARKET RESEARCH AND LOCATION

Your primary demographic will be people in their thirties and forties with an household income over $50,000. Because you will be marking up your original creations dramatically, you will have to target those customers who can afford these artistic pieces of furniture.

Choose an area with several upscale furniture shops. Make sure there aren't too many stores around that are selling your type of ware. Once you're settled in, your shop will be the only one to offer a new take on the same old bedroom set.

EQUIP YOURSELF

In order to create elaborate furniture designs, you will have to obtain the following tools of the trade:

- drills and electric saw

- sanding machine

- wood-carving tools

- paint brushes
- wood finishes and stains
- vehicle for scouting and transporting furniture

GETTING THE WORD OUT

The window display is your most powerful marketing tool. Make sure to showcase your most attractive pieces of furniture in this spotlight. You should also simulate a country-charm feel by adding drapes and other home accessories to your display. Passersby will have no choice but to come and browse through your shop.

Display advertisements in the local newspapers can also bring some business your way. Make sure to take out bigger ads and schedule sales during the holidays.

Some other marketing strategies include:

- listing the business in the Yellow Pages
- direct-mail campaign

LAUNCHING A
HAIR SALON

If you think opening your own salon sounds like a hairy proposition, think again. Hair salons have been doing quite well, even in hard economic times. During the 1980's, hair salons experienced rapid expansion. And while profits declined in the 1990's, people are now going back to enjoy the therapeutic benefits of grooming. Everyone wants to look well-groomed, and will go the extra mile for that special treatment your salon will offer.

We all love the feeling of sitting high on those swivel chairs, feeling like kings and queens as an expert stylist shapes our mops into dazzling hair creations. While many people don't allow themselves the luxury of facials, waxing treatments, and massages, they will gladly fork over the money for a haircut. Face it, hair stylists perform a vital task that is sure to never go out of style.

If you are a licensed hair stylist or just have an overwhelming desire to capitalize on people's vanity, then read on to find out how you can own a hair salon of your very own.

RAKING IN THE DOUGH

If you're planning on starting a small business out of your house, you can expect to bring in about $30,000 per year. Large salons with numerous hair stylists can reap profits of $100,000+ per year depending on location, marketing, and customer satisfaction.

START-UP COSTS

For a home-based operation, costs will be very low. You can start this business for as little as $1,000. But that price tag increases dramatically if a full-service salon is what you're after. A space of approximately 1,000 to 3,0000 square feet will be needed, and when you consider the high cost of advertising, you're looking at an investment of $30,000 to $90,000.

HELP IS ON THE WAY

Standards of beauty are changing daily—especially when it comes to hair. The "it" hairstyle can go from the Julia Roberts toussle to the Jennifer Aniston layers in one week flat. Keep up with the times by checking with the following experts.

Associations:
- National Beauty Culturists League: 202/332-2695
  Washington, D.C.

- National Cosmetology Association: 800/527-1683
  St. Louis, Missouri

- World International Nail and Beauty Association: 714/779-9883
  Anaheim, California

Trade Publications:
- *American Salon*: 212/951-6600
  New York, New York

- *Salon News*: 212/630-4607
  New York, New York

Read All About It:
- *Hair Color and Styles* by Ellen Bolz and Anthea Bain. Foulshan and Company, 1996.

- *How to Start and Manage a Hair Styling Business*. Lewis and Renn Associates, 1992.

FRANCHISES
- Cost Cutters: 612/331-8500
  Minneapolis, Minnesotta

- Fantastic Sam's: 901/363-8624
  Memphis, Tennessee

- Super Cuts: 800/999-2887
  San Rafael, California

MARKET RESEARCH AND LOCATION

Upscale hair salons tend to attract a wealthier clientele, so if you plan on offering special beauty treatments, you may want to check out the location's demographics. If your salon targets an offbeat, younger crowd, you'll want to set up your store in an area replete with a "bohemian mix" of characters. But no matter what your targeted clientele, when it comes to picking a location, areas with a high volume of traffic are always preferable.

IMAGE MATTERS

A special ambiance can boost your profits considerably. Shops with a unique decor and an interesting layout will attract attention. Since clients will end up spending hours sitting in your salon, you should pay special attention to layout and design.

The front of your shop should have a waiting area with plenty of magazines to keep your customers patient. The salon should have a main room, with a station set up for each stylist. And don't forget to include a storage area for products and equipment in your layout schemes.

Depending on the type of clientele you wish to attract, certain shops opt for a funky and offbeat decor, while others try to create a posh environment for their older and more sedate clients. To create a fun look, consider installing a metal-tiled ceiling, some funky chandeliers, and interesting prints. Some salons tailored for the younger set install pinball machines and pool tables. If you're targeting an older, more established crowd, then a sophisticated design—wooden floors, elegant couches, chairs—will be more apropos.

EQUIP YOURSELF

Some equipment you'll be required to purchase includes:

- mirrors
- barber chairs
- hair dryers
- portable hair-styling equipment (hair dryers, curling irons, brushes, scissors, hair clips, shampoos, conditioners, etc.)
- specialized sinks
- display area
- office equipment

CAST AND CREW

Your salon's reputation is in the hands of your stylists. You should seek out hair stylists with licenses from prestigious beauty schools and with impeccable chair-side manners. As customers have a tendency to bond with their hair-dressers; it will be up to you to provide your valuable clients with plenty of bonding-worthy stylists.

When determining wages, the best option for a salon owner is to provide a set salary for your stylists. This will keep your valuable stylists from going to other shops, and taking your customers with them.

GETTING THE WORD OUT

Advertising in local papers is a smart move. When you're planning your ad, don't forget to include a special offer for first-time customers. If you've managed to hire camera-friendly and skilled hair stylists, include their pictures and bios to personalize your salon and distinguish it from the others.

Word of mouth can spread like wildfire in the salon business, so always make sure to keep your customers satisfied and follow their instructions as carefully as possible. You should also encourage your stylists to bring in their own clients.

MANAGE YOUR OWN
HEALTH CLUB

Ever since the 1980's Pied Piper, in the form of a spandex-clad Olivia Newton John, sashayed her narrow hips to the tune of "Let's Get Physical," people have been doing just that. In cities all across America, citizens have taken to the treadmill en masse. Everybody's doing it. "To work out, or not to work out" is all but rhetorical. "Where" on the other hand—now, that is the question.

While some choose to exercise at home or take it to the street, most people still need the extra adrenaline kick that comes of the knowledge that you've spent a whole lotta nickel on a health club membership. It's the all-you-can-eat-buffet mentality all over again; you'll get your money's worth even if it kills you.

This is where you come in. People are loyal to their health clubs, that's for sure. But every new exercise craze draws neophyte iron-pumpers by the hundreds of thousands (witness Step Aerobics, Spinning, and Pilates). Grab one such health fad while its hot, and establish a loyal following of your very own.

RAKING IN THE DOUGH

While a larger establishment will bring in more profits in the long term, you'll make out like a bandit no matter what size a facility you operate. There are more start-up expenses involved in running one of those 5,000-square-feet numbers, but the extra members and higher rates will tally up to profits in the lower six digits. If a small club is more your speed, you can still expect an annual take-home of 40 to 80 large.

START-UP COSTS

Unless you've had a serious run of good fortune with your investment portfolio, or have parents and friends in high places, you will most likely have to seek a bank loan to start this business. This goes double if you've got your mind on an warehouse-sized space in a central location. Plan on making an initial investment of no less than $50,000 (for a small storefront or loft-space health club) to well over $100,000 (for a grand, pool-privileged, sauna-equipped, hot tub–boasting facility).

HELP IS ON THE WAY

Think of these sources as your business "spotters." Whether it's insurance, employee certification, or financing woes, these guys have got you covered.

Associations:

- IDEA: The Association for Fitness Professionals: 800/535-8979
  San Diego, California

- International Health, Racquet and Sportsclub Association: 800/228-4772
  Boston, Massachusetts

- International Physical Fitness Association: 810/239-2166
  Flint, Michigan

- National Health Club Association: 800/765-6422
  Denver, Colorado

MARKET RESEARCH AND LOCATION

Fitness business success, thy name is location. That's right, a choice address is of paramount importance. To zero in on this elusive hot spot, you'll have to hit the library and the U.S. Census Bureau for neighborhood demographics. Your object: people with money that needs spending. Per capita income and real estate rates are good measures of an area's discretionary dollars.

You'll also have to hit the H (for Health Club) section of the phone book. Your object: to be the only fitness club within at least a five-mile radius. The competition is starch-stiff, so avoid it at all costs.

Since people are only too eager to travel an extra mile or so for an unrivaled rate, pricing is another heavyweight issue. Extensive cost analyses — calculating and projecting your expenditures vs. your income — will be required. But if you can settle on a rate that will put the competition to shame and keep your business healthy in one tell bicep curl, you're ready for round one, the grand opening.

EQUIP YOURSELF

Besides the usual doodads that will make up your office equipment (computer with software, filing cabinets, phone, fax, desk, chair), you'll also need mass quantities of exercise equipment. This is no time to get chintzy. A solitary Soloflex won't impress. Health fanatics are out for state-of-the-art fitness gear, so just forget about cutting costs via Thigh Master. To find out which suppliers have got the right stuff, survey the most happening health clubs to see what they've got going—and follow suit.

GETTING THE WORD OUT

Remember all that "this is not a popularity contest" stuff your teachers used to feed you back in Traumaville Junior High? Well, that advice will net you precious little in the real world. Make like you're running for class president and promote the bejeesus out of your new venture. That means fliers everywhere: car windshields, condominium lobbies, grocery store bulletin boards . . . you get the picture.

You may have to employ some more costly forms of advertising. Local newspapers will provide you with the ideal audience. Direct mailings of free trial memberships will also make an impact on your membership headcount.

Since there's nothing so humbling as watching one's nearest and dearest shrink to a shadow of one's own self, word of mouth is a major player in the exercise game. Once you've got a solid number of health nuts in your database, make sure they get the royal treatment. If you score power points in the customer satisfaction department, your clients' friends will soon be waiting on line for your Stairmasters.

OPENING YOUR OWN
HEALTH FOOD STORE

A healthy lifestyle is not something most people take for granted. More and more emphasis is being placed on preservative-free, organic foods. And it's not only the vegan set making all the fuss about healthy eating. Everyone wants a piece of the arugula pie. Surveys in the early 1990's showed that 90 percent of consumers preferred to buy healthy grocery items. That's right, Americans are trying hard to maintain a nutritionally balanced diet, and are turning to health food stores for assistance. Today, there are around 12,000 health food stores in the country.

You don't have to be a nutritionist to know a healthy deal when you see one. Anyone with an interest in helping others improve their health can take advantage of the lucrative health food market.

RAKING IN THE DOUGH
Because the majority of health food stores charge higher rates for their healthy produce, profits can be very high, with an average pretax net income of $110,000 per year. Smaller stores in less densely populated cities will most likely see incomes in the $40,000 to $70,000 range.

START-UP COSTS
The overhead of this business can make a significant dent in your pocketbook. Inventory and leasing or renting a space will account for the majority of your start-up investment. This amount will probably total anywhere from $30,000 to $80,000.

HELP IS ON THE WAY
Healthy habits have a way of popping up and disappearing overnight. Oat bran and melatonin, for example, were hardly the stuff billion-dollar enterprises were made of. So keep up with the rapid succession of industry changes by joining up with the people in the know.

Industry Associations:

- National Nutritional Foods Association: 714/966-6632
  Costa Mesa, California

- Natural Food Associates: 800/594-2136
  Atlanta, Texas

Trade Publications:
- *Fresh Cut Magazine*: 509/248-2452
  Yakima, Washington

- *Health and Natural Foods Market*: 800/346-3787
  New York, New York

- *Health Foods Business*: 201/487-7800
  Hackensack, New Jersey

MARKET RESEARCH AND LOCATION
When selecting a location, make sure to check out the area's demographic breakdown in terms of age and income. Those consumers who fall in the middle- to upper-class income brackets will account for a large portion of your customers. Towns inhabited with a significant number of twentysomethings may also offer you plenty of reliable and loyal followers.

EQUIP YOURSELF
- shelves for displaying your wares

- cash registers

- scanning equipment for quick checkout

- signs denoting various food categories to guide customers

- a storage area to house surplus inventory

- several freezers

- an office for tracking inventory and accounting purposes

CAST AND CREW
Your staff should be a veritable wellspring of reliable information about the products offered in your store. Make sure there are several sales employees scattered throughout the store, ready to help out any novice health food shop-

pers. Train them carefully to be able to recognize and describe every piece of inventory

Invest in T-shirts with your store logo and encourage every employee to wear one. It will make it that much easier for customers to recognize them and ask for help.

GETTING THE WORD OUT

Many conventional grocery stores advertise weekly food specials in the local papers' food sections. You will do well to secure a display ad nearby. You should also organize a grand opening with announcements on the radio and in the events section of your local paper. Arrange for your new employees to serve samples of the store's food, and watch the hungry throngs flock to your doorstep.

STARTING YOUR OWN
HYPNOTHERAPY BUSINESS

In the past, hypnotherapists were either considered quacks or villains à la Simon Bar Sinister. These days hypnotherapy has been cited as a legitimate medical practice that can cure everything from diabetes to obesity, and even help people to quit smoking. Even if you're not a believer, one thing is certain: Hypnotherapists are making a good living by helping people battle health problems and improve their lives.

But a hypnotherapist is not born overnight. You'll have to get a license to hypnotize and practice for at least a year before you can go out on your own. But once you're trained in the art of suggestion there is no limit to how much you can contribute to your customers and your bank account.

RAKING IN THE DOUGH

Hypnotherapists regularly charge $100 per hour. And with prices like these, you can't go wrong. The key to making a steady income is finding loyal customers who appreciate the benefits of the practice. Expect to make around $30,000 your first year, and $70,000+ after you've established yourself as a true miracle worker.

START-UP COSTS

The bulk of your investment will likely go towards marketing and education, which will cost you anywhere from $3,000 to $10,000. If you decide to eschew the home office route and lease an office space, depending on the location and size of your office, start-up costs can shoot up to the $15,000 to $30,000 range.

HELP IS ON THE WAY

You will have to network with other hypnotherapists in order to learn the ins and outs of this business. And if you're looking to improve your skills, the following aids can get you started:

Associations:

- American Council of Hypnotist Examiners: 818/242-1159
  Glendale, California

- International Society for Medical and Psychological Hypnosis: 212/874-5290
  New York, New York

- National Guild of Hypnotists: 603/429-9438
  Merrimack, New Hampshire

Read All About It:

- *The Art of Hypnotherapy* by C. Roy Hunter. Kendall Hunt Publications, 1997.

- *Handbook of Hypnosis for Professionals* by Roy Udolf. Jason Aronson, Inc., 1995.

- *Hypnosis* by Ursula Marham. Charles E. Tuttle Co., Inc., Boston, Massachusetts

MARKET RESEARCH AND LOCATION

The majority of people into hypnotherapy are thirtysomething women in the lower- to middle-income brackets, but that's not to say you won't see men crossing your threshold either. Suburban areas brimming with such demographics are a good bet for your business location. The same is true of major cities, which usually boast large populations with client bases to match.

IMAGE MATTERS

Whether you're working out of your home or from a commercial office space, you will have to isolate a private room for hypnotherapy sessions. When designing this office, think comfort and relaxation. Bright colors should be avoided. Instead, hang up prints of natural settings and invest in a plush couch where patients can relax during sessions.

GETTING THE WORD OUT

If you don't advertise your Svenghali-ness, asset liquidation won't be long in the coming. A sound marketing strategy should include the following:

- listing in the Yellow Pages
- display ads in local newspapers and women's publications
- direct-mail offers
- word of mouth
- special workshops and classes for new customers

ROLLING OUT YOUR OWN
LIMOUSINE SERVICE

Who wouldn't love being chauffeured around town in a fully stocked limousine? Most people don't object to this kind of luxury service, and welcome the opportunity to lay their weary travelers' bones in a plush stretch limo. The limo business made a killing in the 1980's, but sales slumped in the early 1990's. But all is well, because it looks like people are once again enjoying this indulgence. Besides being quite popular with the jet set, limousines are also accessible to people from all backgrounds. Proms, funerals, weddings, romantic nights, or any special occasion can make people anxious to ride the limo train.

Owning your limousine service can be a very lucrative business. A few limos, a few drivers, virtually no overhead. Sounds tempting? Well, read on to discover the joys of starting up your own limousine service.

RAKING IN THE DOUGH

Limousine service proprietors, who one two to three limos, can expect to bring in anywhere from $70,000 to $160,000. If you're planning on going solo, and taking care of your customers' needs yourself, you can still make a sizable pretax income of $25,000 to $40,000 per year.

START-UP COSTS AND EQUIPMENT

To start your business you'll need a small office, in your home or elsewhere, from which you will take orders, market, and dispatch your drivers. You will need a computer system for record-keeping and other office equipment like a fax, desk, and several telephone lines.

To cut down on your initial investment, you can choose to either rent or lease a limo, or even buy used limos in good condition, thereby risking very little of your money. Once you secure however many limos you see fit, you can begin marketing your business like there's no tomorrow. Total start-up costs can range from $10,000 to $40,000.

HELP IS ON THE WAY

Whether it's limousine maintenance, special new amenities, or driver etiquette, these industry mags can save you a whole lot of guesswork.

Associations:
- National Limousine Association: 202/682-1426
  Washington, D.C.

Trade Publications
- *Limousine and Chauffeur*: 310/376-8788
  Redondo Beach, California

- *The Limousine Journal*: 602/483-0014
  Scottsdale, Arizona

- *National Limousine Exchange*: 512/345-5316
  Austin, Texas

Read All About It:
- *How to Start and Operate a Limousine Service* by Randell Nybory. Universe Publishing House, 1988

MARKET RESEARCH AND LOCATION

The majority of your clients will be corporations and major hotels. Opening shop in the most well-to-do part of town can help your business experience steady growth. On-the-go executives often require the services of limousine drivers, and tourists staying in large, prestigious hotels are often accustomed to traveling limo-style.

If a smaller, suburban setting is your ideal location, you will still have many opportunities to make a good profit. Wedding, prom, and funeral attendants also make up a large portion of limousine service customers. So if you're living in a smaller city and don't want to relocate, you can still make it big in the limousine scene.

CAST AND CREW

For every limo, you'll need at least one driver to be on call 24/7. Polite, well-groomed chauffeurs with a good driving record and a driver's license will qualify to work for you. Make sure to screen all applicants carefully, as their mannerisms and rapport with others will determine whether or not your customers will welcome a repeat performance. When determining wages, you can either pay a base salary or an hourly rate plus tips.

GETTING THE WORD OUT

Limousine services can thrive very well provided they secure a solid clientele. The loyalty of local corporations can help your business significantly. To market your services to other companies, you should start a campaign that includes fliers, special offers, and group rates.

Another solid source of revenue will be hotels and resorts. Make sure to leave your card with the concierge and ask for referrals. You should also find out which services each hotel usually uses, and then try to lower your prices to get a competitive edge.

STARTING YOUR OWN
MAGAZINE

A fast-paced lifestyle goes hand in hand with this business. Working with writers, photographers, artists, and being invited to the coolest places in town are just some of the perks this business has to offer. But starting a magazine from scratch is a project that's downright riddled with "challenges." You'll have to choose your subject matter, invest a lot of capital, and make sure you can secure enough advertisements to offset the costs of printing and staffing.

Yet as most successful magazine publishers will tell you, there's still nothing quite like running your own magazine. Especially if you believe in the premise and mission of your publication.

RAKING IN THE DOUGH

Because the majority of your money will come from advertisers, you will have to wait to get the big bucks until your circulation numbers increase. Since many magazines are free, or sold at newsstands, subscription numbers are not often valid indicators of readership. The higher your circulation, the more willing advertisers will be to pay higher rates.

Large magazines with a planned circulation of 250,000 their first year can expect to bring in around $500,000 in this time—and much more once they're fully established. For magazines with lower circulation figures, expect to make anywhere from $50,000 to $120,000 your first year.

START-UP COSTS

Hatching a teeny-weenie zine may not take a lot of money, but it won't give you a dime. As you will see, putting out a magazine may cost you a king's ransom, but in the publishing industry—being as dependent on marketing as it is—it's all about nothing ventured, nothing gained. You will need between $50,000 and $1 million in start-up capital to cover the following expenses:

- leasing an office space

- several computers with database and desktop publishing software, such as Pagemaker, Illustrator, QuarkXpress, and Photoshop

- staffing (sales manager, circulation manager, and managing editor)

- printing costs

- marketing costs

HELP IS ON THE WAY

Why reinvent the wheel, when just one look at the newsstand will tell you that no magazine is an island? That's right, you've got plenty of predecessors and contemporaries who know what it takes to put an issue plan together and get that reading material out by deadline. Find them at:

Associations:
- American Society of Magazine Editors: 212/872-3700
  New York, New York

- Association of American Publishers: 212/255-0200
  New York, New York

- Magazine Publishers of America: 212/872-3700
  New York, New York

Trade Publications:
- *Folio*: 203/358-9900
  Cowles Business Media; Stamford, Connecticut

- *Magazine & Bookseller*: 212/620-7330
  New York, New York

- *Masthead*: 301/984-3015
  Rockville, Maryland

Read All About It:
- *The Magazine Publishing Industry* by Charles P. Daly, et. al. Ally and Bacon, 1996.

- *Starting a Successful Newsletter or Magazine* by Cheryl Woodard. Nolo Press, 1997.

MARKET RESEARCH AND LOCATION

If you're interested in starting a local magazine, you will have to conduct an extensive demographic analysis. Lifestyles magazines are a dime a dozen, so make sure you check out the competition in your area before launching a magazine devoted to reporting local events and goings-on about town.

You should also decide on the subject matter of your zine, and make sure you have a unifying theme. The theme is very important to a magazine's success. Unless your name is John Kennedy, Jr., you should aim for an original theme with high widespread appeal. To research the magazine market, head to your local bookstore or newsstand.

CAST AND CREW

Four key players hold the future of your journal in their hands: the circulation manager, the sales manager, the art director, and the managing editor. If you don't have much money to work with, search around for competent friends or acquaintances willing to risk their livelihoods on your venture. Since many people are falling all over themselves for such an opportunity, you needn't worry—you will have some takers.

Of course, if money is no object, then place a classified ad and only hire those with talent and ample work experience.

GETTING THE WORD OUT

Your marketing campaign will be divided into two phases: targeting advertisers and the subscribers. To market your magazine to advertisers, you will have to create or purchase a mailing list of companies who market to your target audience. For example, if you plan on covering the music scene, you will have to contact record companies and stores. For a women's lifestyles magazine, you will have to spread the word to companies specializing in cosmetics, clothes, and women's accessories. To target these advertisers effectively, you will have to forward a sample of your magazine, projected circulation figures, and special introductory rate schedule.

Marketing to your target readers requires an onslaught of publicity. Your mission: to dominate the airwaves. Send a press release to every media outlet announcing the launching of your publication. Host a gala in honor of your venture, and send invitations to all your print reporters. Try to arrange television and radio interviews while you're at it.

Other means of magazine marketing include traditional advertising and setting up a Web version of your publication. The latter will allow you to reach a wider audience and accept subscription orders through e-mail.

ESTABLISHING YOUR OWN
MODELING SCHOOL

Doubtless you've heard about the heartless rip-off artists who prey on the hopes and dreams of teens nationwide. Usually these ne'er-do-wells come in the form of disreputable modeling schools. These "entrepreneurs" are the black sheep of the modeling industry, and we are not recommending you join their flock.

Countless professional models do, in fact, voice their gratitude to the schools that gave them the confidence to start their careers. By opening a facility that's on the up and up, you'll be casting your vote against the ill-conceived con artists that cheat their young charges out of their life's baby-sitting savings. And don't worry, a sizable income will also prove not long in the making.

So if you enjoy working with the teen population, have an eye for talent, and know what it takes to make it in the world of modeling, then get ready to make a million or just look like one.

RAKING IN THE DOUGH

Fact is, there's lots of competition in this business. A student could just as soon take his/her business elsewhere. This is where your salesmanship comes into play. Depending on how many people you can convince to choose your school, you're looking at $30,000 to over $100,000 in annual profits.

START-UP COSTS

You won't discover the next Kate Moss by relying on a model-thin start-up budget. If you're serious about a career in fashion modeling, then you already know that appearances are everything. Because of the high glam outfit you'll need to pull together, your initial investment will be in the $30,000 to $60,000 range.

HELP IS ON THE WAY

If it's expertise that you're selling, make sure you're an expert by reading up on what's in and out in the business. Publications will tell you about the crucial models conventions, the latest big-ticket looks, and the available contracts. You'll also be more likely to impress prospective paying customers if you're hip to the lingo.

Trade Publications:

- *Club Models*: 802/767-9341
  Aquino International; Rochester, Vermont

- *Model Call*: 213/969-9990
  Los Angeles, California

- *Model Women*: 312/263-3513
  Chicago, Illinois

- *Tearsheet Magazine*: 305/673-5327
  Miami, Florida

Read All About It:

- *The Professional Model's Handbook* by Linda A. Balhorn. Milady Publishing, 1991

MARKET RESEARCH AND LOCATION

Major cities are where the real action is. But you can start a school even if you live in a town of 100,000 people. It's what you do with your model-wannabes that matters. Teaching guys and dolls how to dress, walk, and do their hair can all be done on the home front—as long as you take your students to modeling meccas when the time is right.

You'll have to learn about all the modeling conventions, where the major agency scouts look for new recruits. Then arrange to take your top students for their chance at stardom.

You need also to make connections with the reputable agencies in nearby cities, where you can take your students to meet with the booking agents and learn about the business side of glamour.

As far as pricing goes, you'll have to determine a fee based upon the hours you and your staff put in, the average household income of your target market, and, of course, the desired profit margin. Charging a fee of $1,000 per course is not at all uncommon in the bigger cities, but you should check out what's feasible in your neighborhood before making any such demands.

LICENSE AND INSURANCE

In all likelihood you'll find that many of your clients are minors. For this reason, it is best to form a corporation so you will be personally protected from all liabilities. Doing this would require that you either read one of the heavy volumes on do-it-yourself incorporation, or seek the services of a seasoned attorney.

Insurance is also vital. If anyone is injured in your runway class, your school can be held accountable, so stock up on as much insurance as is necessary to give you peace of mind.

EQUIP YOURSELF

- multi-suite office space with special movement room à la dance studio, offices for account executives, reception lobby, and classroom

- computers with database and accounting software

- cameras and videotaping equipment

- office and lobby furniture

- professional makeup and styling tools

- promotional brochures, business cards, stationery

- office supplies

GETTING THE WORD OUT

If you play the location card right, you shouldn't have any difficulty finding suitable candidates. Nonetheless, a few dollars for advertising should prove money well spent, so consider the following:

- a display ad in the Yellow Pages

- an open call for models in the help-wanted section of the newspaper

- signs on bulletin boards

- fashion shows in the local malls

- direct mail of promotional materials

CAST AND CREW

A first-class operation requires a staff of top-of-the-line professionals to see it through. You'll need at least one account executive aside from yourself.

Sales ability, good communication skills, and an outgoing personality are what you should look for.

You can't run a school without a teacher. Find a former model or two to instruct your slew of students on everything from makeup tips to proper "go-see" etiquette.

Finally, to present a resplendent front, you should hire a receptionist that represents the image you wish to convey. Look for someone who's patient, friendly, and has a sweet-as-pie phoneside manner.

OPENING YOUR OWN
MOVIE BAR

Used to be people went to the movie theater to relax. They would smoke, imbibe, and maybe even shout at the screen. But what would today's moviegoers know about any of that? Plenty, now that movie bars have made a comeback.

Movie bars, those gone-but-not-forgotten bastions of entertainment, are cropping up all over the nation to thunderous applause. "The perfect alternative to the swap-meat atmosphere of traditional nightclubs," raves one reviewer.

Celluloid bars are taking the pressure off singles everywhere. "Finally, a fun place to kick back, take in a flick, and get sauced," says a Big Ten university student, "without coming off like a total letch." "A social environment with a higher purpose," is how one Chicagoan describes her favorite ale/film house.

Yes, the results are in and it's official — well-managed movie bars are a box office hit. This business is great for anyone wishing to combine their head for business, love for nightlife, and appreciation for cinema. If that sounds like you, read on.

RAKING IN THE DOUGH

You can make a considerable profit with this business venture. The film offerings will allow you to assess a higher cover charge. Add in the cost of drinks, and you've got big budget profits — somewhere in the neighborhood of $70,000 to $150,000 per year.

START-UP COSTS

While the income potential is high, so are the start-up costs. Since the liquor license alone may run you as high as $50,000 (see "License and Insurance" under nightclub profile on page 333), you will have to invest at least $70,000 to start this exciting and rewarding business.

HELP IS ON THE WAY

These resources will keep you abreast on what's going on in film and how you can stay on the cutting edge of the industry. Your movie selections will have to come from a wide selection of genres to please your equally diverse audience.

Associations:

- American Bartenders' Association: 800/935-3232
  Plant City, Florida

- American Video Association: 800/421-2300
  Chandler, Arizona

- Video Software Dealers Association: 800/257-5259
  Marlton, New Jersey

Trade Publications:

- *Beverage Media*: 212/620-0100
  New York, New York

- *BIN* (*Beverage Industry News*): 415/986-2360
  Industry Publications, Inc., San Francisco, California

- *Top Shelf: Barkeeping at Its Best*: 203/926-8996
  Shelton, Connecticut

- *Twice*: 212/477-2200
  Twice Publishing Corp., New York, New York

- *Video Extra*: 215/629-1588
  Home Viewer Publications, Inc., Philadelphia, Pennsylvania

MARKET RESEARCH AND LOCATION

Since your bar will be targeting young people in their twenties, you will have to do a demographic study on your chosen area. Another way to scout the area is to check out the nearest bars in terms of popularity.

You may want to situate your celluloid bar in a busy area with plenty of drinking establishments. Don't worry about the competition, since the nature of your bar will help it stand out from even the liveliest of joints.

You'll also be faced with a tough decision: whether to show second-run pictures (movies that are not yet available on video, but are no longer shown at big movie theaters, are usually kept alive at second-run movie theaters at a fraction of the original cost to the ticket buyer) or those already out on video. The second-run films will cost more to acquire, but you may also find that these draw a larger audience. Video releases will cost you relatively little, but you'll have to decide whether your audience is the type that will pay to see *The Graduate, Swingers,* or *Pulp Fiction*.

IMAGE MATTERS

The best way to lay out this unique bar/theater is to have two separate areas. One for theatergoers, and the other for die-hard partyers. Make sure to include a small bar in the screening room, so patrons won't have to leave the room to refill their goblets and quench their thirst.

Use your imagination when it comes to decor. You can adorn the bar with posters of old Hollywood stars or new blockbusters. You should also strive to create a comfy and welcoming environment in the screening room, using couches and velvet drapes.

EQUIP YOURSELF

Remember: This enterprise will involve purchasing equipment for a bar as well as a theater. So prepare to make a serious investment. For bar equipment, see nightclub profile on page 331.

Screening Room:

- theater chairs

- high-quality projector

- sound system

- a wide selection of cult-movie favorites

- large screen

GETTING THE WORD OUT

You will have to list your movie show times in the newspaper. Submit your information to the editor in charge of listing local events. Most of the time such advertising comes free of charge. You should also institute a special plan that offers free tickets to frequent moviegoers.

Display ads in local papers are also a must. Once everyone is familiar with your establishment, every weekend will be a full house. To get people in on weekdays, you'll have to try a little harder. Launch special theme nights, offer discounts on movie passes, do whatever it takes to get customers through your doors.

RUNNING A
NEW AGE STORE

You've heard the rumors—everyday miracles, eerily accurate tarot card readings, UFO sightings, apparitions of Mary and Baby Jesus, conjuring up the dead. If those phenomena seem like a bunch of hoopla to you, you're a skeptic and this business is not for you. If you can swear on the power of your ancient healing crystal that spiritual enlightenment is as much your concern as is making a swift profit, then read on, for you've come to the right place.

There are many individuals who faithfully believe in the power of holistic healing and other forms of spiritual rejuvenation. Actually, our country is becoming more and more spiritual by the minute. Just look at the many bestsellers lining the bookstore shelves. There's *Celestine Prophecies, Conversations with God,* and *The Corporate Mystic.* Surveys also said that in the 1990's, 5 to 10 percent of the population participated in the New Age industry. Many people, from administrative assistants on up to CEOs, are anxious to fulfill their spiritual potential, and you can help them by providing services and products that will awaken their inner enlightened being.

RAKING IN THE DOUGH

New Age entrepreneurs have a variety of business options to choose from. You can either sell New Age merchandise, become an educator, or both. New Age shops offering a variety of merchandise, astrological readings, and courses can stand to make up to $60,000 per year in a busy commercial area.

START-UP COSTS

Opening up a New Age service out of your home is the cheapest alternative to this business. You can hold meetings, offer courses, and even sell certain merchandise that is key to your educational program. You can start operating out of your home for $3,000 or less.

If you plan on running a full-service retail shop, you will be required to shell out much more cash up front. Expect to invest no less than $30,000 for a small shop in an easy to access location.

HELP IS ON THE WAY

You will need to establish a good relationship with wholesalers and members of the New Age industry. The following resources can put you on the right track to networking with like-minded professionals.

Associations:
- New Age Publishing and Retailing Alliance: 360/376-2702
  Eastsound, Washington

Read All About It:
- *Channelers: A New Age Directory*: 800/631-8571
  Putnam Publishing Group

- *The New Age Catalog: Access to Information and Sources*: 212/765-6500
  Doubleday and Company

MARKET RESEARCH AND LOCATION

The majority of your customers will be women and men in their forties; people who have achieved a certain amount of financial success and are now looking to accelerate their spiritual development. Check the U.S. Census Bureau for areas conducive to this demographic.

When choosing a retail location, you should consider that the majority of your business will come from walk-ins. Situate your store in a busy commercial area or in a strip mall.

STOCKING UP

Whether you choose to sell New Age merchandise directly out of your home through mail order or out of your retail shop, the following products are sure to be popular with your customers.

- books on astrology
- tarot cards
- crystals
- wishing candles
- music for meditation

GETTING THE WORD OUT

Marketing your New Age services and/or products can be easy, provided you exhaust every available option.

- Yellow Pages
- display ads in specialty publications
- special direct-mail offer to local residents
- posting brochures and fliers around your area
- distributing press releases describing your shop and services to local newspapers
- mail-order catalogs

ESTABLISHING YOUR OWN
NIGHTCLUB

You're young, you're single, and you're ready to mingle. But you know the drill: Golly, gee whiz—in yours, the city of a million and one bars, lounges, and dance clubs—there's absolutely nothing to do! That's right, after a few months of being there and doing that, what's left but the same old, same old.

Bank on this ennui and the returns won't disappoint. In this age of frenetic change, what better way to access the pocketbooks of the fun-starved throngs than by providing a wee bit of entertainment? Today's nightlife is a testament to the "anything goes" motto—anything new, that is. Our advice: Put together a think tank and brainstorm away until you hit upon a boîte concept to make your VIP card a hot commodity.

RAKING IN THE DOUGH

The nightclub business is ripe with profit potential. If you play your cards right, you could be looking at a cool mill. Depending on the scope of your operation, annual pretax income can range from $70,000 to over a million dollars.

START-UP COSTS

When you really want the big bucks, a penny ante just won't do. You'll have to sink a heavy dose of liquid—anywhere from $60,000 to $600,000—into this project if you want high-disco dividends.

HELP IS ON THE WAY

Keeping up with industry standards is much easier if you're in the loop. It doesn't take much to become an insider—check out the Nightclub and Bar and Restaurant Expo convention by calling 800/247-3881. Also, getting in touch with these sources is a good start:

Associations:
- American Bartenders' Association: 800/935-3232
  Plant City, Florida

- National Licensed Beverage Association: 703/578-4200
  Alexandria, Virginia

- National United Licensees Beverage Association: 412/241-9344
  Pittsburgh, Pennsylvania

Trade Publications:
- *Beverage Media*: 212/620-0100
  New York, New York

- *BIN* (*Beverage Industry News*): 415/986-2360
  Industry Publications, Inc., San Francisco, California

- *Cheers*: 212/274-7000
  Jobson Publishing Corporation, New York, New York

- *Top Shelf: Barkeeping at Its Best*: 203/926-8996
  Shelton, Connecticut

Read All About It:
- *How to Manage a Successful Bar* by Christopher Egerton-Thomas. John Wiley & Sons, Inc., 1994.

- *Night Club Promotions Manual and Source List* by K. S. Jones. The Hughes Company, 1997.

MARKET RESEARCH AND LOCATION

Market research plays a large part in your choice of location. But what's more, it may also factor prominently in your club's theme. The best way to get a feel for a region's public is to mix among them. There's nothing wrong with laying aside as much as an entire year for the development of a sixth sense, a gut feeling, or an instinct for what the nightcrawlers want.

By asking club and bar owners about their businesses, you can make well-informed decisions regarding the format of your nightclub. For example, are you angling for a "House of Style" or a "Beverly Hillbillies" motif? This shouldn't be based on personal taste alone, because after all, while the former may be more appealing, the latter may just hit the bull's-eye where your checkbook is concerned.

LICENSE AND INSURANCE

Since you have dared to wander smack dab into the center of the booze business, a.k.a. Red Tape Central, you will have to pay. Be forewarned, a liquor license is not only de rigueur, but it is also expensive. Buying one may run you anywhere from 5 to 50 G's. What's more, you will most likely have to wait several months for the privilege. You'll also have to make sure that your chosen locale is zoned for serving alcoholic beverages.

And if the licensing doesn't derail your hopes, then get ready for the insurance. Check your state for "dram shop" laws. These make servers of alcohol, namely you, responsible for any injuries their overzealous employees may have caused by "over-serving." The only way to stave off sleepless nights is to load up on insurance.

IMAGE MATTERS

The design of your lounge should play up your concept or theme. If you're going for a sleek, futuristic atmosphere, you'll have to look into a lot of minimalist and Star Trek/Jetsons-inspired props. If you think retro is the bee's knees, look into some plush, Art Deco pieces. Phony bronze sculptures and frames make a strong statement, as do velvet curtains with ornate tassels. In short, when it comes to designing your club, go crazy. This is one place where more is more.

Lighting is another deciding factor. We suggest you err on the side of caution, so save yourself the electric bills and dim those bulbs! Present company excepted, people look much better in the dark. Customers will appreciate both your discretion and the "attractive" patronage. Watch them come back every chance they get.

EQUIP YOURSELF

- bar—this centerpiece should be of appropriate stature, sturdy and well-crafted; make sure its design creates the desired effect

- bar stools—comfort is key

- bar tables, chairs, couches or booths, and coffee tables

- glassware, serving trays, and bartenders' accouterments

- cash register

- a top-drawer sound system

GETTING THE WORD OUT

If you want to be a proud hotspot owner, then get ready to pull some smooth promotional moves. The name and logo deserve some serious deliberation. If you have many club-hopping contacts, you may choose to overlook advertising traditional advertising altogether. Hire graphic designers to create fliers and calling cards that you can pass around to your extensive network.

Take this private-party routine one step further by hand-delivering invites to all the happening businesses in your area. This may cost you, but we recommend you hire a team of top-notch models (male and female) and set them up with a hit list of carefully chosen locales. Get them to chat up the invitees, and make as if they'll be present for the grand opening. Now who'd pass up an invitation like that?

Of course, in spite of all this, you may still decide to broadcast your club's debut from sea to shining sea. Nothing wrong with that. We recommend you cash in on all the free advertising with the city paper's "goings on about town" section (nearly every ville has one), announce the opening on the radio, take out ads, do a veritable blitzkrieg of advertising. If you hype it, they will come.

OPEN YOUR OWN
PARTY SUPPLY STORE

If you think life is just one big party, you may not be entirely in the wrong. Party supply stores have been experiencing steady growth since the early 1980's. With an average sales increase of 15 percent during the 1990's, it's easy to see why so many entrepreneurs are being lured by this business idea.

The tremendous success of these shops has a lot to do with people's busy lifestyles and inability to run from store to store in search of the perfect streamer. And with the increase of party supply emporiums, planning a bash has never been easier.

The popularity enjoyed by these retailers can also mean high revenues for you. Provided you offer a wide selection of party goods and practice the art of superior customer service, there's no reason why your store can't give everyone something to celebrate.

RAKING IN THE DOUGH

Party supply store owners can expect to break even after the first year. On average, a 3,000-square-foot store in a bustling commercial zone can make up to $110,000 a year. That amount can increase if your store is larger and can house a more extensive inventory.

START-UP COSTS

Party supply stores will require anywhere from $40,000 to $120,000 to get off the ground. Leasing a space will make up the bulk of this start-up figure, and inventory comes in a close second, totaling anywhere from $20,000 to $50,000.

FRANCHISES

If you choose the franchise route, you may have a greater chance of succeeding. Not only are you buying an established name in the party biz, you can also get help from these pros in terms of inventory, location, equipment, and training. Here's just a few to get you started:

- Party City: 800/883-2100
  Parsippany, New Jersey

- Party Land: 215/364-9500
  South Hampton, Pennsylvania

- Party World: 818/762-7717
  North Hollywood, California

HELP IS ON THE WAY

Don't let the party start without you. Check into the following publications and get all you need to get going.

Trade Publications:
- *Party & Paper Retailer*: 203/845-8020
  Norwalk, Connecticut

- *Party Supplies Directory*: 402/331-5481
  Omaha, Nebraska

MARKET RESEARCH AND LOCATION

Since you'll be looking to purchase the largest store for the smallest price, your best bets for a location is a strip mall. Space in indoor malls usually runs higher, but if you can be satisfied with a smaller space, indoor malls generate a heavy volume of foot traffic.

For those of you wishing to open a party super-store, consider the strip mall alternative. Your store will be that much more visible to passersby.

As always, keep in mind that cheaper isn't always better. While depressed areas may boast low rents, you'll be hard pressed to find any revelers spending their hard-earned dollars on your products.

CAST AND CREW

The size of your store will determine how many employees you'll need to hire. The most important ingredient to a successful party supply store is the skill and enthusiasm of your staff. If your store is vast and houses a variety of party products, your employees will be responsible for guiding your customers in the right direction.

Each section of your store should have an employee waiting to assist your customers. You should also make colorful uniforms mandatory for all employees, which will create a signature look for your store and will save your customers from wasting their time looking for in-store assistance.

You would also be wise to have a professional party coordinator on-site at all times. This service can an added charge to the customer. But you'll be surprised at just how many people have limited party-planning skills.

GETTING THE WORD OUT

Your grand opening will require a fair amount of hype. One clever store owner sent out invitations to prospective customers, billing his opening day as the "Biggest Party" of the year. He noted that the festivities would include refreshments, a local band, and special discounts on all merchandise.

More traditional forms of marketing include advertising in newspapers and on the radio. And fliers advertising your store should be secured in local flower shops, bakeries, and day care centers.

OPENING YOUR OWN
PET SHOP

The number of pet shops has been multiplying steadily. Today, there are an estimated 20,000 pet shops in the U.S. This could be the result of disregarding Bob Barker's warning to "help control the pet population by having our pets spayed or neutered," or it could be that the strong economy has propelled more people into "pet friendly" income-tax brackets—regardless of the reasons, people are spending more and more money on their pets.

Special treats, supplies, and even clothes have been popular items for people living with pets. Sales of premium pet food have tripled in the last decade, and show no signs of slowing down. If you want to help others spoil their pets or just match pets with new families, this business will suit you to a T.

Owning your own pet shop can be a rewarding experience for all animal lovers. You'll be around animals all day, and customers may even begin asking your advice about their pets' health and care instructions. Since you are a pet shop owner, your knowledge of domesticated animals can serve as a vital asset to the business. Of course, you could always hire someone with animal expertise to field the really tough questions, while you handle the business aspects. As a business owner, the choice is yours.

RAKING IN THE DOUGH

Depending on your store size, location, and inventory selection, pet shop entrepreneurs can make from $75,000 to $180,000 in annual net profits. Pet superstores can bring in figures in the high six digits—assuming the location is right.

START-UP COSTS

Here's the rub: The cost of opening a pet shop can be very high. Because you'll need a large space to house your pets and your supplies, you may need to secure some sort of financing to make ends meet. The range of start-up costs for pet shops is $30,000 for a smaller shop to $400,000 for a mega-superstore.

HELP IS ON THE WAY

As a pet shop owner you'll need to establish vital contacts with manufacturers, distributors, and wholesalers in the industry. These associations will also provide you with important licensing requirements and procedures:

Associations:
- Pet Industry Joint Advisory Council: 800/553-7387
  Washington, D.C.

- World Wide Pet Supply Association: 818/447-2222
  Arcadia, California

Trade Publications:
- *Pet Age*: 312/663-4040
  Chicago, Illinois

- *Pet Industry Distributors Association Bulletin*: 410/931-8100
  Baltimore, Maryland

SELECTING A LOCATION

Have you ever noticed the pervasiveness of pets in large cities. A pet shop in a large metropolitan area is bound to thrive, provided the competition is not too steep. Affluent suburban areas with many families can also provide you with a steady stream of four-footed traffic.

Extensive research should include checking with the library about such neighborhood features as median family income, cost of real estate, and yes, percentage of pet owners. Make sure you pick a winner by sniffing around for competitors. People are often loyal to their pet stores, so don't open up shop within easy walking distance of your competition.

EQUIP YOURSELF
- cages
- fish tanks
- window displays
- shelving for pet merchandise
- a reserve of food for pets

- cash registers

- computer system and office equipment

- lighting

CAST AND CREW

A helpful and organized staff is a vital asset to your business. When hiring, find out about employees' knowledge of animals. The more they know, the more qualified they will be to help customers make their selections.

GETTING THE WORD OUT

Local newspapers, Yellow Pages, and radio spots are the best way to advertise your store. Throw in some special offers and coupons to win over even more customers. And make sure you're in plain sight of impulse buyers by designing an eye-catching sign and logo.

OPEN UP YOUR OWN
PIZZERIA

Often dubbed the "perfect food," pizza has all the makings of a bankable business. Whereas taste and nutritional value have often been at loggerheads, this is one edible that manages to corner the market on both counts. What's more, you can tailor each and every slice to a customer's needs, no matter how idiosyncratic (witness the inspired pineapple/Canadian bacon combo). Because pizza never goes out of style, this is one enterprise which can set you up for life.

RAKING IN THE DOUGH
If the mere thought of pizza isn't enough to start those salivary glands working overtime, the profits sure are. Are you ready? As the proud proprietor of a pizza parlor, you stand to reap anywhere from 100,000 to 300,000 American dollars (gross profits) per year.

START-UP COSTS
The average investment for a small pizza parlor runs around $100,000. But if you really scrimp, you can cut that cost in half. Also, keep in mind that larger pizza joints may take as much as $200,000 to get going—never mind a franchise, which can run into the $500,000+ range. But as the saying goes, no pain, no gain.

HELP IS ON THE WAY
Think "network" if you want to get the goods on the best distributors, the top-grade product, and the newest trends. The following sources will help in all matters pizza.

Associations:
- National Association of Pizza Operators: 812/941-9711
  New Albany, Indiana

- National Pizza and Pasta Association: 800/844-5049
  Holland, Indiana

- National Restaurant Association: 800/424-5156
  Washington, D.C.

Trade Publications:
- *Pizza and Pasta*: 312/951-2236
  Talcott Communications Corp., Chicago, Illinois

- *Pizza Today*: 812/949-0909
  ProTech Publishing and Communications, New Albany, Indiana

MARKET RESEARCH AND LOCATION
Carefully screen the potential area for your restaurant. Look for a highly visible site in a busy area. Also consider setting up next to popular watering holes, because pizza cravings reach all-time highs after a night of carousing.

Because consumers tend to stick with the familiar, seek a spot that's suffering from major pizzeria deprivation. The surest road to success is a captive clientele—and don't you forget it.

EQUIP YOURSELF
- cash register

- 3–4 pizza ovens

- industrial refrigerator and freezer

- microwave

- sink and dishwasher

- cooking utensils

- high-quality counter

CAST AND CREW
The simple fact of not knowing the first thing about pizza shouldn't stop you from making a bundle in the racket. If throwing dough does not rank among your fortes, bringing in a reputable consultant—someone who's already made in the pizza biz—is a viable and popular option.

Unless you want to spend your life in the kitchen, you will need to hire employees. Find customer-service-oriented individuals who know their way around a restaurant kitchen. Seek out people with previous restaurant experience, and here's a tip: don't scrimp on the training.

GETTING THE WORD OUT

Even the best-established pizza places have to advertise. No one can afford to let the hype die down. Good marketing can make your pizza what it ought to be—a household word. Let freedom ring on opening day by dishing out free pizza in honor of yours truly. If your hot dishes are savory fare, the customers will come back bearing billfolds.

Hungry eyes make for full cash registers, so keep up the promotions year round by distributing fliers prior to dinnertime, and placing coupon ads in the restaurant section of the local rags.

OPENING YOUR OWN
POOL HALL

The game of billiards, once an exclusive gentleman's pastime, has gained in popularity at groundbreaking speed. No longer is one required to be a card-carrying lad/y of leisure to enjoy this test of skill. And it's a good thing too—few diversion are as addictive as the game of pool.

Because the likes of Paul Newman and Tom Cruise have got us convinced that it takes more than an ordinary yokel to really school at pool, experts and neophytes alike are congregating at billiard halls to either flaunt or practice their stuff. And neither do they show any signs of slowing down. The great thing about this business is that there's no fear of recession-induced bankruptcy, because when the going gets tough, people get going—to the pool halls.

RAKING IN THE DOUGH

The income potential ranges from $80,000 to $250,000 in annual profits. If you're a real billiards buff, you'll also save a bundle by making use of all that free playtime.

START-UP COSTS

In the game of pool, the more you put in, the more you'll get out. For this reason, you may want to start off with a sizable investment.

A bigger pool hall will be most advantageous where profits are concerned—no one wants to dodge cue sticks when they're paying 8 to10 bucks for an hour of play. But space also costs, so if you're going for a square-foot extravaganza in a densely populated area, don't expect it to come cheaply.

You may also decide to provide food and drink at your site, thereby upping your ante with kitchen expenses. In sum, your investment may run somewhere from $130,000 to well over $200,000.

HELP IS ON THE WAY

It never hurts to do more research. Improve your business game by remaining current with these sources:

Trade Publications:

- *Billiards Digest*: 312/341-1110
  Chicago, Illinois

- *Pool & Billiard Magazine*: 630/260-8500
  Glendale Heights, Illinois

MARKET RESEARCH AND LOCATION

Okay, let's get one thing straight, people who shoot pool tend to populate colder climes. There's something about those long winters that gets 'em hankering for a game of eight ball. The Billiard Congress of America, at (319)351-2112, in Iowa City, Iowa, will give you all the statistics you need to set up in the right place. They'll tell you who plays pool in which areas, and how much they are willing to pay. Your job is to pinpoint the spot the data describes.

Scouting sites is a serious business. You'll have to hit the streets and check things out for yourself. Note the surroundings:

- Is there parking?

- How about a college or a large business district?

- Is there a substantial number of pedestrians?

- Do people in the area generally enjoy playing the game?

- How large is the viewership of the Billiards Tournaments in the area?

LICENSE AND INSURANCE

If all you purvey is pool (which, by the way, is ill advised), you'll need:

- a business license

- standard business insurance and liability coverage

- compliance with zoning codes

If you're offering food & drink to boot (now that's more like it!), make sure to apply for:

- a health inspection

- a liquor license

- extra liability insurance because of new laws making servers of alcohol responsible for accidents resulting from over-serving.

IMAGE MATTERS

After you've honed in on your location and clientele, the fun part begins. You have to make your pool hall as inviting as a milk shake on a hot summer's day. Come up with a decorating theme, and work around it. If your clientele is young and happening, consider using music as a reference point. Disco, rock, blues, the sky's the limit. If professionals are the target consumers, go for the appeal of an antiquated "Gentleman's Club"—we're talking a fall color scheme and lots of oak.

GETTING THE WORD OUT

A highly publicized grand opening is where you want to start your promotion efforts. But don't stop there. Make sure to place an ad in the city paper every week. People are always on the lookout for "what to do," and your ad will answer that question. Special offers are another good idea, something to the effect of "free hour with every entree," or buy nine hours, get the tenth one free. And keep doing that public-relations schtick. Extensive media solicitation should get your name in the papers, and that's the type of advertising no money can buy.

GEARING UP YOUR OWN
RECORDING STUDIO

Ever wonder what it would be like to be one of those guys behind the plate-glass wall? No, we're not talking about a police lineup. What we have in mind is something a whole lot more interesting. Watching up-and-comers, or just wannabe-up-and-comers, jam out in your very own recording studio, and getting paid handsomely for the privilege, now that's the life. And to make the opportunity even more attractive, consider that you can gear up a studio right in your very own home.

No longer just about records, the recording industry has many specializations. Struggling bands, voice-over artists, and the burgeoning independent film industry are just a few of the many customers looking to buy some studio time. If your city is short on recording space, then you may be looking at a sound investment.

RAKING IN THE DOUGH

A home-based operation can pay off big. If you invest in state-of-the-art technology, and learn the fine art of recording studio management, you can easily bring home an average of 70,000 large each year.

START-UP COSTS

Even if you decide to skip the rental overhead, our guess is you'll still have a lot of renovations to do (most homes don't come equipped with soundproof studios and control rooms). The average start-up cost will most likely fall in the 60–90 thousand-dollar range. This is a sizable chunk of change, and the industry is fiercely competitive, so get your business strategy straight before going in.

HELP IS ON THE WAY

There's nothing like insider information when it comes down to learning how to man a control booth. Check out what the players have to say by looking into the following sources:

Associations:
- National Academy of Recording Arts & Sciences: 213/849-1313
  Burbank, California

- Recording Industry Association of America: 202/775-0101
  Washington, D.C.

- Society of Professional Audio Recording Services: 407/641-6648
  Lake Worth, Florida

Trade Publications:
- *The Absolute Sound*: 516/676-2830
  Pearson Publishing Empire, Ltd., Sea Cliff, New York

- *Home and Studio Recording*: 818/346-3404
  Music Maker Publications, Inc., Chatsworth, California

- *Pro Sound News*: 212/213-3444
  New York, New York

Read All About It:
- *How to Set Up a Home Recording Studio* by David Mellor. Cimino
  Publishing Group, 1996.

- *The Sound Studio* by Alec Nisbett. Focal Press, 1995.

MARKET RESEARCH AND LOCATION

If you decide that your home is capable of housing a recording studio, we highly recommend that you check out both the market and the competition. What kind of services are the competitors offering? Is the competition prospering? What percentage of recording studios has closed within a short period of time? Why? These are just some of the questions you'll need to answer if you want to be certain about your future success.

Pricing is another issue you'll have to address. Undercutting the competition may serve to establish your rep, but "value-added" service is where the industry is really at. Instead of selling yourself short, try to offer more services than your competitors for the same price.

EQUIP YOURSELF

Because of the fast pace of technology, and the importance of your equipment's compatibility with other systems, check out the latest recording industry product reports to get the goods on the most efficient equipment. To get your studio up and running, you'll need to purchase the following items:

- console/mixer
- analog multi-track tape machine
- power amplifiers
- an equalizer
- field monitors
- signal processors
- compressors
- microphones

But recording studios are not built in a day. Aside from the standard-variety office equipment and a hodgepodge of miscellaneous apparati, you'll also need to outfit your studio space with a well-endowed control room and a soundproofed studio that can boast killer acoustics.

GETTING THE WORD OUT

People are interested in all things entertainment. The music and recording industry are thereby human-interest material. Use this to your advantage by compiling some background material on the industry and, of course, your studio's unique role within it. Send these materials to all the local papers—pitch the story idea to small-business, music, and entertainment editors. If so much as one mentions your business (positively or even neutrally—you're not Susan Powter, negative publicity can only hurt your venture) in an article, chalk it up as a major endorsement.

Sending fliers out to area talent management companies will also boost business. You can walk into their waiting areas and make nice with the receptionists. Ask to leave some of your fliers and cards in the hallway, and you won't be disappointed.

RUN YOUR OWN
RESTAURANT

For many restaurateurs, the daily grind is a misnomer—daily party is much more like it. Just think. Receiving dinner guests, engaging in witty repartee with the regulars, and making sure that everything is running according to plan every night of the week, now that's entertainment. And provided you offer up a world-class establishment with greater-than-thou ambiance, all this can indeed be yours.

But be forewarned: This is one risky business. The failure rate makes for such a dismal picture that many banks won't so much as touch your loan application with a ten-foot pole. But to a Generation, Inc.-er, "fail" is a four-letter word. With a solid business plan in hand, you need not dwell too long on the negative. After all, if you weren't willing to lay it all on the line, you wouldn't bother to start a business in the first place.

RAKING IN THE DOUGH

With new restaurants popping up faster than a bag of Orville Redenbacher's microwave popcorn, it's a wonder that any proprietor can actually stay in business. But stay in business they do—to the tune of approximately $100,000 to $1 million in profits per year.

START-UP COSTS

Wonder why people are no longer encouraged to sing for their suppers? Because nowadays, you can't open so much as a diner—much less a full-scale restaurant—on a mere song. As a matter of fact, even the most cachet-less of locales will require an investment of at least $35,000. But don't expect to meet this budget limit if you're angling for a bustling business. Most restaurants are started on little less than $100,000, with many start-up investments running as high as $500,000.

HELP IS ON THE WAY

You wouldn't believe how many stars there are in the food service industry. We've all heard of Wolfgang Puck and Arnie Morton, but there's scores more where these come from. Joining an industry association and reading the trades will give you just what you're looking for—a clue to what is up and coming in food service.

Associations:
- The Educational Foundation of the National Restaurant Association: 800/765-2122
  Chicago, Illinois

- National Restaurant Association: 202/331-5900
  Washington, D.C.

Trade Publications:
- *Nation's Restaurant News*: 212/756-5000
  New York, New York

- *Restaurant Business*: 212/984-2436
  Bell Communications, Inc., New York, New York

Read All About It:
- *How to Open Your Own Restaurant: A Guide for Entrepreneurs* by Richard Ware and James Rudnick. Penguin USA, 1991

- *The Upstart Guide to Owning and Managing a Restaurant* by Roy S. Alonzo. Upstart Publishing Company, 1995

MARKET RESEARCH AND LOCATION

Aspects such as operating expenses, type of food, decor, restaurant size, and affordability are inextricably bound to an establishment's environs. A savvy would-be proprietor would decide what kind of an operation to run before trolling random streets for FOR SALE signage.

The search for a location should be your second order of business. Keep an eye out for an area that your target clientele is likely to call home. Also, keep in mind zoning ordinances and proximity to pedestrian traffic and parking space. Much of your business can come from a high-visibility, high-appeal facade.

Aside from location, there are only two roads that lead to success in the field of restaurant ownership; the quality of your fare, and/or the cleverness of your advertising/marketing/public relations campaign (read on for more on the latter).

LICENSE AND INSURANCE

What with mad-cow disease, e-coli, botulism, and salmonella outbreaks, food safety has been in the news quite a bit these past years. Expect to meet some serious health code regulations before opening for business.

Regulations are also levied upon alcohol-serving establishments. You'll no doubt need a liquor license if you want to boast an extensive wine list. What's more, you'll need to double up on liability insurance, because many states are now passing laws which make the server (that's you) responsible for anybody who gets sauced at his/her establishment.

Hire a competent attorney to see you through the fine print of start-up — this is not a business to go into blindly.

EQUIP YOURSELF

In the Kitchen:

- walk-in or industrial refrigerator and freezer
- commercial oven, range, grill, and hood
- microwave
- dishwasher
- three-bin sink
- coffee, espresso/cappuccino makers
- pots, pans, baking sheets
- Tupperware
- cooking utensils
- full range of kitchen appliances

In the Dining Room:

- walls decorated for desired atmosphere
- lighting fixtures with dimmers

- tables and chairs that complement your motif

- a comfortable and inviting bar with stools

- a stand for the host/maitre d'

- dessert carts

- flatware, glassware, and silverware

- cash register

In the Back Room:

- computer with a variety of restaurant-related software

- desk and chair

- filing system

- stationery and business cards

- phone and fax

CAST AND CREW

One of the biggest determinants of restaurant success is the quality of the food and service. In order to swing the popular vote in your favor, you'll need to hire a talented chef. Culinary schools are literally breeding grounds for chefs, so this is where you can start your search. If you decide to put an ad in a trade magazine, make sure to list the qualifications you desire. Because the chef is so crucial to your business, run complete work history and academic record checks on all applicants.

Great service can be had by hiring and training servers, bartenders, and bussers. Hire experienced personnel, and train all new hires thoroughly before setting them loose on the customers.

GETTING THE WORD OUT

Another direct route to success in the field of food service is a clever advertising/marketing/public-relations campaign. The first step is to orchestrate a grand opening celebration—with complimentary hors d'oeurves and a cocktail or champagne reception for all parties who RSVP. Send invitations to prestigious area businesses, such as newspapers, advertising agencies, photography studios, art galleries, and upscale boutiques. Design some high-quality fliers trumpeting your new arrival along with your menu, and post them on neighborhood bulletin boards.

Once you have the initial rush of satisfied customers, word will spread like wildfire. But that doesn't mean that you should transfer those advertising dollars to other areas. Besides placing a listing in the Yellow Pages and every restaurant guide you can round up, you should also find your way into the papers.

Call the newspapers and inform them of your existence. Chances are one of them will call your bluff and send a restaurant critic to your door right quick. If you can trump this bon vivant, it's going to be a full house every night.

OPEN YOUR OWN
SEX SHOP

Sex shops are no longer strictly for the "hey, little girlie, wanna see what I've got underneath this trench coat" consumer. Go into any such store, and you'll find everyone from housewives to business executives browsing in their enticingly stocked aisles. There are a myriad of sex shop connoisseurs who either want to improve their sex life or find an adequate substitute for the lack thereof.

Opening your own sex shop can be a fun and interesting experience for anyone who enjoys bringing pleasure to others. Whether it be risqué lingerie, sex toys, or multi-colored condoms and lewd greeting cards, if varied and displayed properly, your merchandise can bring in some serious profits.

Many of your customers will be window-shoppers interested in a little amusement. The great thing about most successful sex shops is that they don't take themselves too seriously, and they make their patrons comfortable. So store those whips and chains towards the back of your store, and only take them out for your more adventurous couples.

RAKING IN THE DOUGH

A sex shop that emphasizes racy lingerie usually brings in the most profits. Because your store windows will be adorned with beautiful underwear, the majority of your customers—primarily females and couples—will feel more secure entering your doors. Once they're in, they can feel free to explore anything on the shelves. Stores using this tactic and located in busy commercial areas usually bring in around $40,000 to $100,000 per year. What can we tell you? Sex sells.

START-UP COSTS

Besides the initial cash you'll be allocating to your unconventional inventory, a large number of start-up dollars will go towards leasing or renting: a space of no less than 1,000 square feet, display shelves, cash register, and store decor. Depending on the extent of your inventory and store space, these elements can add up to $35,000 to $80,000.

HELP IS ON THE WAY

Cole Porter sang it best. "In olden days a glimpse of stocking was looked on as something shocking." Now, as you know, no sooner does something get an X rating, then someone like Madonna comes along and changes it to PG. These sources can keep you from falling into a rut:

Associations:

- Intimate Apparel Council: 212/675-3534
  New York, New York

Trade Publications:

- *Intimate Fashion News*: 212/679-6677
  New York, New York

MARKET RESEARCH AND LOCATION

Sex shop customers are a motley crew. But the majority of your patrons will be professional women and young couples with a hefty disposable income. To determine the demographics of your chosen area, call the U.S. Census Bureau for more information.

Since most of your business will be generated by walk-ins, situate your store in a busy area with heavy foot traffic. College towns are also ideal areas for fun and novel sex shops.

STOCKING UP

The more diversified your merchandise will be, the more customers you can potentially attract. Some popular items in sex shops include:

- glow-in-the-dark prophylactics

- sexy lingerie

- adult board games

- adult greeting cards

- sexual devices

- sex instructional videos and reading material

- massage oils

IMAGE MATTERS

The layout of your store can make or break your customer's shopping experience. The ideal layout would include two main rooms, one in the front for lingerie, and the other in the back for sex devices and other more private merchandise. You should also have a cash register for each room. Make sure to leave space for at least two fitting rooms and a storage area for surplus inventory.

GETTING THE WORD OUT

If you play your marketing cards right, the news about your store can spread like wildfire. A listing in the Yellow Pages and advertisements in alternative newspapers are a good start.

A more creative way to get customers can be an in-store lingerie fashion show. Hey, if Victoria's Secret can get away with it, why can't you? Models strutting down the runway in alluring lingerie, what better way is there to attract a slew of anxious buyers? Send out frilly invitations to local area residents and serve refreshments to all guests.

JUMP START YOUR OWN
SOCIAL CLUB

The world can be a lonely place. All those nameless, faceless people struggling to make their way can lead many to think that we're all just out for number-one. But thinking so doesn't make it true. Just ask the many outgoing entrepreneurs who are making a bundle by bringing people together.

Social clubs operate on the premise that everyone wants to make merry. With cities growing more and more populated with every passing year, individuals are becoming increasingly alienated. Things such as making new friends, or even coordinating volleyball games, group vacations, and poker nights with your old pals seem fraught with difficulty.

This is where the social club directors step in. "Just show up, and leave the rest to us," they say, and people do show up—in droves. But taking care of the details is a full-time job. You'll be dealing with city officials when arranging to use the public grounds such as parks and beaches. You'll also be hammering out contracts with various clubs, vacation getaways, and watering holes. While many business owners and civil servants will be responsive to your needs, you will still have to spend a lot of time arranging every last festivity. Highly organized, energetic people with interpersonal and leadership skills to spare are the ideal social coordinators. If that's you, what are you waiting for? If your borough is lacking in the good-cheer department, take it upon yourself to add a party to this life, and extra digits to your bank balance.

RAKING IN THE DOUGH

A solid marketing strategy should see your earnings increase with each passing year. The first annum may see you struggling, bringing in about $20,000. But try to regard this time as a planting period. The seeds you sow today are likely to reap rewards tommorow—bringing you as much as $150,000 per year in profits.

START-UP COSTS

This type of unorthodox business must be started off on the right foot. You'll have to invest in a clubhouse (a.k.a. office space), as well as a painfully loud promotional campaign. All in all, your expenses should hover around $20,000.

MARKET RESEARCH AND LOCATION

An office in a fun shopping district is the ideal location. Since your clientele will consist mainly of young, affluent city dwellers, your club should be located in the hub of this demographic.

Research the operations of similar clubs in the area. Once you know all there is to know about what these organizations offer and to what sorts of people they appeal, you can work out a plan to differentiate your operation and pick up on the would-be joiners that your competition left in the cold.

EQUIP YOURSELF

- computer with fax modem and accounting and database software
- fax machine
- photocopier
- multi-line telephone system
- office furniture
- file cabinets
- office supplies
- letterhead, promotional literature

GETTING THE WORD OUT

A Web site is the ideal way to reach a young audience without squandering all your hard-earned start-up dollars. Direct-mail and flier-distribution campaigns will also help to propagate your cause. In addition to these marketing tricks, you can also zero in on those people recently relocated by advertising your organization in city guides and magazines, as well as in newspapers dealing exclusively in real estate and apartment rentals.

OPEN YOUR OWN
TANNING SALON

Now that heroin-chic is strictly démodé, people are once again scurrying to the tanning booths in record numbers for that ever-golden glow. Even in hot-weather climes, the convenience and cleanliness of a tanning salon is unrivaled by the beaches. The fact is that you're not the only one who must work for a living. And earning a livelihood from nine to five means saying adieu to prime tanning hours — thereby making tanning salons one of the hottest businesses going.

Factor in the safety aspect, and you end up with yet another reason for the primacy of the bulb. With the ozone layer at ground zero, the tanning bed has actually become a safe alternative to the real deal. And while no ultra-violet exposure is 100 percent risk-free, you'll be providing a valuable service by keeping these UV users off the beaches and the baby oil, where they're liable to acquire some serious sun damage.

RAKING IN THE DOUGH

Expect many a bright sunshine day when the profits start pouring in. After you pass through the dark cloud of business start-up, you'll be clearing from $40,000 to $70,000 per year. Now that's a rainbow many an entrepreneur is praying for.

START-UP COSTS

If you want this scorcher of a business, there's no two ways about it — it's going to cost you. Technological advances haven't made the tanning beds any cheaper, so expect to shell out upwards of $45,000 for a prime-time operation.

HELP IS ON THE WAY

These publications will keep you informed on important tanning regulations and industry news.

Trade Publications:
- *Tanning Trends*: 517/784-1772
  Jackson, Michigan

- *Today's Image*: 919/461-8484
  Weston, Massachusetts

MARKET RESEARCH AND LOCATION

As you research the library's wealth of information, keep your eyes peeled for areas ripe with single, young professionals. The stats on average household income should also serve your purposes, as you're looking for people who have discretionary income burning holes in their pockets.

After you're enlightened to the hot zones for your business, look through the directory and drive around the areas to see how many tanning salons are already in operation. Remember, people want convenience in their tanning booths. If your shop happens to be in a thriving neighborhood, you're bound to be closer to some die-hard tan hounds than the competition, which will give you a leg up. What's more, if you hit on a place with better access to parking, you're in business no matter how stiff the competition.

Just one word of caution, and that's price. Tanning salons provide a luxury service. By no means are you necessary to anyone's existence. So price yourself accordingly. Above all, be reasonable. Calculate your fees so that they're both competitive and business-sustaining.

LICENSE AND INSURANCE

Aside from the usual business license, you'll also need to comply with a long list of health regulations. Since you're dealing in potentially hazardous services, protect yourself against every contingency by hiring a lawyer to draw up contracts for your consumers and make sure you are in accordance with every last letter of the law.

EQUIP YOURSELF
- tanning beds

- facial tanning lamps

- sanitizing supplies

- fans

- protective eyewear

- radios

- computer with appropriate software

- chairs, couch, coffee table, and magazines for the waiting area

GETTING THE WORD OUT

Advertising gets top billing in this mega-competitive business. A display ad in the local directory and newspaper ads bearing coupons for first-time customers are two tried and true ways to get that client list under way.

Keep track of your customers to compile a mailing list. Then send word of all new offers or promotions to anyone who's ever tanned at your salon.

Don't forget that much of your business will come from passersby. To milk this walk-in cash cow for all its worth, make sure your sign and window display are hard to miss. Bright colors, vibrant graphics, and a scorching name should set your beds a-burning.

SETTING UP A
TATTOO STUDIO

At first sighting (circa 1991), the tattoo craze was all the rage. Once models, actors, musicians, and Cher bonded together to popularize the art formerly known as self-mutilation, no longer were tattoos relegated to the ranks of masochists and death-row inmates. But even so, no one expected the fad's heyday to last out the decade.

Yet to the naysayers' distress, the tattoo industry shows no signs of slowing down. Check this: The millennium is barely a stone's throw away, and people are still opting for ornamental body art. As much as some may hate to admit it, it looks as though the trend has become a classic.

RAKING IN THE DOUGH

If you plan to open a tattoo parlor, be prepared to russle up some quality tattoo artists. These are the folk who will be signing your checks. The tattoo salon's M.O. is much like that of a hair salon; your "employees" are actually tenants who rent space from you. Depending on the size and locale, your profits can make for quite a pretty picture, ranging anywhere from $65,000 to $270,000 per year.

START-UP COSTS

While you won't need to spiral into major debt to realize the bounteous profit potential of a tattoo salon, you will need to ante up approximately $10,000 for the tattooing and office equipment. You'll also have to put a down payment on a space, furnish, decorate, and advertise—all while maintaining a safe balance in the bank account. In sum, approximately $25,000 to $35,000 will be needed to give this business a fair chance.

HELP IS ON THE WAY

Even if you've never so much as scribbled graffiti on the bathroom wall, associations and trade periodicals can provide you with all that's key to the successful practice of tattoo art.

Associations:

- Alliance of Professional Tattooists, Inc. (APT): 410/768-1963
  Glen Burnie, Maryland

- National Tattoo Association: 215/433-7261
  Allentown, Pennsylvania

- Professional Tattoo Artists Guild: 914/668-2300
  Mount Vernon, New York

Trade Publications:

- *National Tattoo Association Newsletter*: 215/433-7261
  Allentown, Pennsylvania

- *Skin Art*: 212/564-0112
  Outlaw Biker Enterprises, Inc., New York, New York

- *Tattoo*: 818/889-8740
  Paisano Publications, Inc., Agoura Hills, California

Read All About It:

- *The New Tattoo* by Victoria Lautman and Vicki Berndt. Abbeville Press, 1996

MARKET RESEARCH AND LOCATION

Because you wouldn't want to open your tattoo studio in anything resembling a retirement community, it is wise to do a little research before settling in for the long haul. You're looking for a diverse and progressive population. Young people make the best customers, so check out the demographics provided by the U.S. Census Bureau.

Your location should also be in a densely populated area, amidst a thriving business district. Since you're the new kid on the block, make sure your business has a high visibility factor—while a studio of great repute could probably flourish in an alleyway, you've got a ways to go before you can boast the same.

A LICENSE TO DRAW

The regulations levied on tattoo artists vary from state to state, so contact your local health department to insure that you adhere to the letter of the law.

EQUIP YOURSELF

- 2–3 tattoo machines

- 5–8 sets of needlebars

- 1 autoclave sterilizer

- a variety of commercial permanent tattoo patterns

- temporary tattoo sheets

- chairs and tables for your customers

- mirrors to give the full view

CAST AND CREW

Whether or not you're a trained tattoo artist, make sure your employees are. If you faint at the sight of blood, and get dizzy just looking at a needle, let the pros take care of customer service while you take care of business.

If at all possible, hire tattoo artists with a good record and even better customer base. This tactic will net you a fast rep and a fast profit.

GETTING THE WORD OUT

In the first year of operation, you'll have to rely on advertising to bring people to your door. New converts don't always have the inside track on the "hip" place to go, so ads in the city paper will draw the uninitiated. But word does tend to get around, so after you've had a solid run, the advertising will take care of itself.

OPENING YOUR OWN
TOBACCO SHOP

Dominicans, Cubans, Jamaicans—people of the Caribbean? Maybe, but chances are that if you hear any of these nationalities bandied about in daily conversation, they're in reference to cigars. Now that cigars have gained so much ground, pipe smoking may very well be the next big thing.

Regardless of what Californians, with their neo-prohibitionist tactics, would have you believe, a large percentage of the population still enjoys a good cigarette now and again. The popularity of cigar magazines testifies to the fact that many people are still experimenting with recreational tobacco use. Okay, so maybe it's not the healthiest of habits, but we don't hear anyone making a huge row over how Beefeater staged the martini's comeback.

RAKING IN THE DOUGH

This is the time to rub your hands together and cackle over your impending riches. A smoke shop, featuring quality cigars, cigarettes, and the usual accessories, can bring you as much as $200,000 per year.

START-UP COSTS

A store rarely comes cheap—and a smoke shop is no exception. You'll need to put money down on the lease, install custom shelves and cases, and then stock your shelves with inventory. All this can be had at a price that's between $40,000 and $100,000.

HELP IS ON THE WAY

Even if you're a seasoned smoker, chances are there's much to the tobacco industry that you still don't know. No need to worry, that's what the following sources are for.

Associations:
- Cigar Association of America (CAA): 202/223-8204
  Washington, D.C.

Trade Publications:
- *Cigar Aficionado*: 212/684-4224
  New York, New York

- *Smokeshop*: 212/594-1120
  New York, New York

Read All About It:
- *Cigar Aficionado's Buying Guide: Rating and Prices for More than 1,200 Cigars.* Running Press, 1998.

MARKET RESEARCH AND LOCATION

You'll have to check your area to find out how many smokers you can expect to lure into your dragon's lair. You'll also want to understand your potential customer in terms of gender breakdown, age, and spending habits. The library and Census Bureau are full of information about residents of different areas. You can, for example, find out how much they are willing to pay for their cigarettes via their average household income. You can also find information through fieldwork—calling other tobacco peddlers in the area and inquiring about prices should give you a good indication of your markup.

EQUIP YOURSELF
- computer with accounting and database software

- fax machine

- phone system

- cash register

- shelves and glass cases

- inventory of cigarettes, cigars, loose tobacco, and smoking paraphernalia

- promotional items, such as matchboxes and matchbooks with the store logo

GETTING THE WORD OUT

Most successful smoke shops open for business in a locale with a high visibility rating. If your space is near a busy intersection, or in a popular strip mall, you won't have to worry about advertising.

Of course, a top notch location isn't as important if you plan to boast smokes on the cheap. In such a case, an ad in a well-circulated local newspaper, trumpeting your prices, will serve you just as well. Where cigarettes are concerned, consumers are extremely price-sensitive — few want to pay a lot for their emphysema. But, if you've got the deal, they've got the time.

BECOMING A
TOUR OPERATOR

Making travel plans can take a toll on any voyager. That's where tour operators come in. It's hard enough to plan where you will sleep, let alone the daily itineraries and special outings. Travelers who want an offbeat exploration, but would rather do without the hassles of planning it, can find warm refuge in a tour operator's office.

You will charge a percentage of every tour you book. You can either choose to specialize in one type of tour, or run the full gamut of travel alternatives. There are tours for food lovers, art lovers, gambling fiends, ancient-edifice lovers, safari lovers, and even sinister tours where you can visit the homes and burial grounds of the world's most notorious criminals. Remember: The more sensational and popular your tours are, the greater your success will be. So if one tour is bringing in more customers, you may want to expand and focus solely on that tour.

RAKING IN THE DOUGH

The popularity of your tours and their price tags will determine your success. Since your profits will come directly from the travelers, make sure you mark up the actual price of the tour by about 45 percent in order to stay in business. Keep in mind that your goal is to provide a tour expensive enough to bring you some profit, while still being affordable enough to entice budget-savvy travelers. Expect to make $30,000 to $150,000.

START-UP COSTS

You will have to spend most of your money on an office space where customers can consult with you about their plans, and a marketing strategy that will attract plenty of customers to your doorstep. You will need $20,000 to $40,000 to start operating your business.

HELP IS ON THE WAY

Besides updating your travel magazine subscriptions, your business will benefit to no end if you familiarize yourself with these valuable resources.

Associations:

- The Adventure Travel Society, Inc.: 303/649-9016
  Engelwood, Colorado

- National Tour Association: 606/226-4444
  Lexington, Kentucky

Read All About It:

- *Conducting Tours: A Practical Guide* by Marc Mancini. Delmar Publishers, 1995.

- *Marketing Tourism Destinations: A Strategic Planning Approach* by Ernie Heath. John Wiley & Sons, Inc., 1992.

- *Start and Run a Profitable Tour Guiding Business* by Barbara Braidwood, et al. Self-Counsel Press, 1996.

MARKET RESEARCH AND LOCATION

The type of tours you will offer will determine which customers you will need to target. Some tour operators target senior citizens, while others focus on the well-to-do baby boomers. Before you decide if your area fits the demographic of your tours, decide which kind of tours you will offer. Once you've honed your customer profile, you can do research on your area to see if there are enough potential clients living in your area.

In terms of location, you will have to situate your office in a highly trafficked area, A strip mall is the ideal location, since cost of space will not be as expensive as in an indoor mall.

DESIGN AND LAYOUT

Your store should highlight the theme of your tours. You can tease potential customers by creating a virtual tour environment where customers can sample the pleasure and fun of your expeditions. Hang up vivid posters and maybe commission a mural or two to create a vivid experience for everyone that walks through your door.

Your waiting area should come complete with plenty of color brochures, which your customers can read while waiting for your assistance. Make sure these pamphlets or books illustrate the type of tours you will be offering.

The entire facility should measure a minimum of 900 square feet, and should have a private office in the back where you can work without being disturbed.

EQUIP YOURSELF

- computer with fax/modem, internet hookup and necessary software

- office furniture (desk, chairs, file cabinets, etc.)

- fax machine

- dual-line phone system

- promotional material (both for the tours and for your business)

GETTING THE WORD OUT

To get people interested in your tours, you will have to leave your card with local travel agencies and advertise in the travel section of your local newspaper. You should also take out ads in specialty magazines. For instance, if you are planning a gourmet tour of France, you would want to advertise in food magazines. Gambling tours will be best highlighted in gambling magazines. It's really quite simple.

Setting up your own Web site can also be a boon to tour sales. If you market your Web site well, and hook it up to a variety of search engines, customers all over the U.S. will come knocking.

You can also offer specials through direct mail and decorate your storefront with bold signs that emphasize your reasonable rates and exciting destinations.

LAUNCHING YOUR OWN
TOY STORE

Think you know what kids like? Think you can recognize the kind of toys that will hold children's attention for hours on end? You may just have what it takes to run a successful toy store.

But be forewarned, the competition is stiff as it gets. What with certain toy stores growing larger by the second, you may find yourself overshadowed by these towering toy infernos. Many of these stores have been known to pull some sly stunts, like strong-arming manufacturers of popular toys into exclusivity agreements. And you know what that means—no Tickle Me Elmo for you come Christmastime. So if your plan is to build business on the basis of these "most wanted" toys, we see a Plan B headed straight in your direction.

You can transcend the bourgeois mass market by catering to those outside of the middle class. The lower and upper income groups have children too. And if you can tailor your inventory to their specific needs, you'll come out a winner in the game of toys.

RAKING IN THE DOUGH

In this toy story, size really does matter. Whereas a small toy store will probably net you profits of about $35,000 to $80,000 per year, a larger setup can bring in well over $100,000.

START-UP COSTS

Capital of $90,000 to $125,000 is the toy industry's start-up average. This figure may be much lower for a bastion of lower-end merchandise. You'll also be well on your way to slashing costs if you can find an existing toy store that's going out of business. Of course, buying out a previous store owner will cost you dearly if the location or size of the premises does not fit in with your business plan.

HELP IS ON THE WAY

Get in touch with the toy makers and other toy peddlers like yourself through:

Associations:

- American Specialty Toy Retailing Association: 515/282-8192
  Des Moines, Iowa

- Toy Manufacturers of America: 212/675-1141
  New York, New York

Manufacturer/Supplier/Distributor Directories:

- *American International Toy Fair Official Directory of Showrooms and Exhibits*: 212/675-1141
  Toy Manufacturers of America; New York, New York

- *"Juvenile Merchandising" Directory and Buyers Guide Issue*: 212/532-9290
  Columbia Communications, Inc.; New York, New York

MARKET RESEARCH AND LOCATION

Look to population profiles to find the proper fit for your store. If your store is stocked with cut-rate merchandise, a good location would be a blue-collar or immigrant neighborhood. These segments of Americana often have kids, but little money to spend on toys. When birthdays and holidays come around, chances are parents will head for your conveniently located and reasonably priced goods.

Of course, if your toy store wouldn't be caught dead stocking anything that's worth less than three figures, you're looking at a ritzy location. The kind where the most expensive car gets the right of way at a stop sign.

But whatever the real estate values boasted by your neighborhood, you'll need plenty of foot traffic to keep inventory circulating. Much depends on visibility—last-minute gifts, impulse buys, and such—so as they say in show business, out of sight, out of mind.

GETTING THE WORD OUT

Let's just get one thing straight. Without advertising, America would be a third-world country right now. Even if your store is in plain sight, a little strategic publicity never hurt anyone. You can be sure to profit by listing your ad in the paper. The more people that hear about your low, low prices or your rare and exotic goods, the more customers you're bound to have.

Whether your mission is to provide affordable toys to neighborhood children or educational games that the whole family can play, the local paper just might find your cause worth celebrating. The only way to make certain is to mail out press releases to neighborhood papers, and follow up with calls to see if there are any reporters willing to pen a piece about you.

OPENING YOUR OWN
TRAVEL BUREAU

If travel figures high on your list of priorities, opening your own travel bureau can be a very rewarding endeavor. During the early 1990's, the travel industry was worth $86 billion, and of the 32,000 agencies nationwide, more than 70 percent were owned by independent agents. Besides the obvious travel perks and discounts, you will act as a liaison between the customer and airline companies. Your job is simple: Find the best deal for the buck. If you can do this time and time again, your customer base will become a large and loyal constituency who wouldn't dream of booking their flight, hotel, and car rental reservations without your say-so.

Today's travel agency has to be concerned with providing the best customer service available. Web-based travel magnates are making it easier and easier for travelers to search for the lowest available fare, get the scoop on their destinations, and book their flights within minutes—and all without your help. Unless you're planning to open shop on the Web and construct an elaborate search engine, you'll have to compete by offering the kind of personalized services virtual travel agencies cannot.

RAKING IN THE DOUGH

The profit margin for a full-service travel agency can range from $70,000 to $120,000. Smaller, more specialized agencies with one or two employees can make anywhere from $40,000 to $60,000 per year.

START-UP COSTS

The majority of your start-up funds will go toward leasing a space and outfitting your new office with equipment, furniture, and able staff members. This start-up sum can total $10,000 to $40,000. Running a smaller agency out of your house or from an inexpensive office space can place your start-up costs on the lower end of this spectrum.

Becoming an accredited agency can also raise your start-up costs. Keep in mind: You don't have to receive accreditation, but since most agencies make their money from commissions from travel suppliers, you cannot qualify for these without receiving your stamp of approval from the Airlines Reporting Corporation.

You will also do well to secure the aid of a computerized airline reservation systems. These systems — the most popular of which is called Sabre (American Airlines) — will require a substantial monthly payment, but will help your agency provide the best service available.

HELP IS ON THE WAY

Anyone who is thinking about trying their luck with their own travel agency is strongly encouraged to join an agents' association. By joining your peers and subscribing to industry literature, you will receive the vital 411 on accreditation, financing, suppliers, and a myriad of other areas of the business.

Associations:

- American Society of Travel Agents: 703/739-2782
  Alexandria, Virginia

- Association of Retail Travel Agents: 800/969-6069
  Arlington, Virginia

- Independent Travel Agencies of America Association: 716/436-4700
  Rochester, New York

Trade Publications:

- *Travel Agent Magazine*: 212/370-5050
  New York, New York

Read All About It:

- *Home-Based Travel Agent: How to Cash in on the Exciting New World of Travel Marketing* by Kelly Monaghan. Intrepid Traveler, 1997.

- *Start and Run a Profitable Travel Agency* by Richard Cropp and Barbara Braidwood. Self-Counsel Press, 1993.

- *Travel Perspectives: A Guide to Becoming a Travel Agent* by Ginger Todd and Susan Rice. Delmar Publishers, 1996.

MARKET RESEARCH AND LOCATION

Your travel business can target a number of customers. You can start by offering package vacations to tropical destinations, specialize in corporate travel, or offer a more generalized service for a variety of customers.

Determining the allocation for your office can be tricky. If you're planning on handling corporate travel only, you can open a small office in your home or an inexpensive office building. Since you will be conducting most of your business by phone, you won't require a large space. If you're looking to make the travel moves on a wide range of travelers, a space in a strip mall or a busy commercial zone will encourage walk-ins. And that means better profit margins for you.

EQUIP YOURSELF

- computer system with Sabre and accounting software, internet and fax/modem

- fax machine

- photocopier

- telephone system

- travel brochures

- promotional materials (letterhead, business cards, calendars, etc.)

GETTING THE WORD OUT

If your agency provides the customers with competitive rates and friendly service, you may not have to worry about finding new customers. But you should still do a fair share of marketing to pull in your first stream of travelers.

If business accounts are what you're after, make cold calls to each company and ask who handles their travel services. Follow up each call by sending a brochure and special corporate rate card. Make sure all your brochures present a professional and reliable image of your agency.

To attract another type of customer, you should consider placing an ad in local papers, advertising your best deals. If you make an offer no one can resist, customers will be calling in by the dozen to cash in on their savings.

MANAGING YOUR OWN
WINERY

Ever since the days of Bacchus, wine has been inextricably linked with the pursuit of pleasure. Always at the hilt of fashion, wine is one luxury that becomes any budget. What's more, the popularity of wine has recently been bolstered by medical studies that indicate that a glass per day keeps the doctor away.

Before you begin interviewing migrant workers, be aware that the technical aspects of vineyard cultivation are numerous, and must be mastered if you are to succeed. Winery owners are responsible for wine production, distribution, and marketing. But nowhere does it say that you must venture forth alone. You can always hire, or form a partnership with, a seasoned wine cultivator.

There are many advantages to owning your own winery. Besides a lifetime supply of high-quality wine product, you will also get plenty of fresh air in your very own vineyards. And once you're successful, your name will be toasted by wine aficionados everywhere.

RAKING IN THE DOUGH

There are no limits to how much you can make as a winery owner. Depending on the size of their operations, some winery owners make as much as two million dollars per year. But such riches only come to those who serve no wine until it's time. You will have to spend enough time in this business to recognize a good vintage and set up widespread channels of wine distribution. While you're in this business-building process—which may take anywhere from one to three years—expect to slave away just to break even.

START-UP COSTS

If you own the right type of land, you can start your winery on a relatively small budget of $40,000 to $70,000. This figure will climb exponentially if you're not fortunate enough to have been born into the landed gentry. Land ripe for vineyards doesn't come cheap, so expect to invest a minimum of $700,000 for a plot suited to your purposes.

HELP IS ON THE WAY

No matter how ideal a vineyard you inherit, no one is born a great wine producer. The making of fine wine is nothing short of an art form, and every art must have its technique. The following sources can provide you with the information you'll need to know.

Associations:

- Association of Winery Suppliers: 415/924-2640
  Corte Madera, California

- Home Wine and Beer Trade Association: 813/685-4261
  Valrico, Florida

- Sommelier Society of America: 212/679-4190
  New York, New York

- Wine and Spirits Guild of America: 612/377-6459
  Minneapolis, Minnesota

Trade Publications:

- *Practical Winery & Vineyard*: 415/429-5819
  San Rafael, California

- *Vineyard & Winery Management*: 607/535-7133
  Watkins Glen, New York

- *Wines & Vines*: 415/453-2517
  San Rafael, California

Read All About It:

- *Wine for Dummies* by Ed McCarthy and Mary Ewing-Mulligan. IDG Books Worldwide, 1995

MARKET RESEARCH AND LOCATION

You will have to select a prime area in which to cultivate your vines. Since vines are very susceptible to extreme climates, you will have to study some weather patterns to determine the best region for wine production.

You should also perform certain cost analyses before going into business. Calculate how much your wine will cost to produce, as well as how much similar wines sell for. This will give you a good idea of your future budget, as well as your potential profit.

EQUIP YOURSELF

- pruning equipment

- a watering system

- large cases for collection purposes

- bottles and labels

- a van for transportation

- a computer system for inventory tracking and accounting

- cool storage area

CAST AND CREW

Depending on how much money you have to invest, hiring an expert wine grower can give your business an added boost. You can take care of the business details, while your savvy employee makes sure you produce a first-rate product. You can also hire part-time workers to collect the vines when they're ready to be harvested.

GETTING THE WORD OUT

Once your wines have aged considerably, you will be ready to market your product. You will have to obtain the services of a good distributor, as well as target fine dining establishments, liquor stores, and supermarkets to make the maximum profit. Consider advertising in restaurant and grocery-store trade magazines, or start up a public relations campaign to get your label noticed.

You can also take out display ads in cuisine, lifestyles, and wine magazines to give your fine spirits the ultimate exposure. And if you feel confident, as hopefully you will, enter your wine in taste contests. Should your entry prevail, great things will be sure to follow in the payoff department.

OPENING A
YOUTH HOSTEL

Youth hostels are affordable lodging alternatives for young adults on the go. There are thousands of youth hostels across America and throughout the world that offer low-cost accommodations to these worldly youngsters.

There are ample rewards to opening a youth hostel. You will meet new people from different countries and various backgrounds. You'll also provide an invaluable service for those free spirits who have little more than a zest for travel and a thirst for adventure to their name. Translation: You'll be helping out the thousands of idealistic vagabonds who have yet to squirrel away the funds for a regular hotel room.

In short, this business calls for those with the desire to contribute to the next generation. It calls for those who want to hang out with some of the wildest revelers this side of *Animal House*. Most of all, it calls for someone who wants to earn a decent living while having fun. Sound just right? Then maybe this business is calling for you.

RAKING IN THE DOUGH

Since these establishments operate solely on a not-for-profit basis, your main source of income will be generated by government-grant funding. You can also solicit funds from private organizations that aim to heighten global awareness and encourage international exchanges.

START-UP COSTS

Before you begin shelling out your own cash, you will have to apply for funding. Call Hostelling International-American Youth Hostels to figure out all of the application details. Warning: Mountains of paperwork are ahead.

HELP IS ON THE WAY

Whether you'd like to exchange notes with other hostel owners, obtain more specific information about licensing and zoning regulations, or figure out how to apply for a grant, these resources will point you in the right direction.

Associations:
- Hostelling International-American Youth Hostels: 202/783-6171 Washington, D.C.

Read All About It:
- *Hostels USA: The Comprehensive, Unofficial Opinionated Guide* by Paul Karr. Globe-Pequot Press, 1997.

CAST AND CREW
A youth hostel must come equipped with two or more employees. As the head honcho, you will act as the executive director. However, you can also take on any other responsibilities that you find appealing. For example, if you are a heavy-duty people person, manning the front desk should turn out to be interesting. On the other hand, if your head is made for business, you can concentrate on grant-writing and financial management.

Whatever responsibilities you take on, chances are you'll need at least one other full-time employee. Hostel operators often employ a live-in house attendant/housekeeper. This person is responsible for greeting the guests, and making them comfortable in their new home. When you're looking to fill this important post, your best bet is a polyglot with good people skills.

MARKET RESEARCH AND LOCATION
In order to keep on receiving that all-important grant money, you'll have to attract a substantial amount of visitors. Busy metropolitan areas are ideally suited for youth hostels. Hostels located in cities such as Los Angeles, New York, Miami, Boston, and New Orleans are sure to receive their fair share of wayfarers, whereas those in smaller, less tourist-centered towns may prove lonely lodgings.

When you're scouting for a home to call your own hostel, make sure there isn't a preponderance of other such operations in the same area. An excess of hostels in your borough may make your business look less federal-funding-worthy.

IMAGE MATTERS
After you have signed the lease on a building, you will have to make sure to design it with the utmost consideration. Use the space to its full potential; set up bunk beds to save space in the sleeping quarters. And don't forget to

make way for a rec room, complete with a television, a stereo system, and maybe even Ping-Pong.

GETTING THE WORD OUT

Once you're ready to accept your first set of boarders, you will have to list your hostel in directories and with travel agencies catering to young students. You will get plenty of business from these sources, so make sure you register your facility early.

You should also list your hostel in budget-conscious travel books. A quick browse through a bookstore's travel section will provide you with all the necessary contact information.

And never overlook the Yellow Pages — still the most popular directory in town.

Leah and **Elina Furman** are sisters who have written a wide variety of books together. They are also the writers of *Tripod*'s Small Business Brainstorms column. Their other books include *The Everything After College Book, Heart of Soul: The Lauryn Hill Story,* and *The Everything Dating Book.*